THE GOD THAT FAILED

THE GOD
THAT FAILED

Richard Crossman, Editor
with a New Foreword by David C. Engerman

COLUMBIA UNIVERSITY PRESS ☾ NEW YORK

Columbia University Press
Publishers Since 1893
New York   Chichester, West Sussex

Library of Congress Cataloging-in-Publication Data

The god that failed / Richard Crossman, editor ; with an introd. by
David C. Engerman.
p. cm.
Originally published: London : Hamilton, 1950.
ISBN 0-231-12395-7 (paperback : alk. paper)
1. Communism.   I. Crossman, R. H. S. (Richard Howard Stafford),
1907–1974.
HX72 .G62 2001
320.53'22'0922—dc21
2001032546

Casebound editions of Columbia University Press books are
printed on permanent and durable acid-free paper.
Printed in the United States of America
p 10 9 8 7 6 5 4 3 2 1

CONTENTS

Foreword to the 2001 Edition

David C. Engerman
Department of History
Brandeis University

The God That Failed is, in many ways, the collective auto-biography of a generation. The book also served as a political call-to-arms and an opening shot in the cultural Cold War. Lauded on its initial publication in early 1950, *The God That Failed* went on to sell more than 160,000 copies in English in its first four years, with editions produced in sixteen languages.[1] Even beyond this wide circulation, the book defined a new paradigm for Western intellectual life in the Cold War: American-centered, closely tied to political power, and staunchly anti-Soviet.

The God That Failed is effective because it does not assert this new paradigm directly, but instead provides compelling autobiographical sketches about prominent intellectuals' encounters with radical politics. The contributors include some of the most important figures in the world of arts and letters in the United States and western Europe. Essays by three "initiates"—novelists Arthur Koestler, Ignazio Silone, and Richard Wright—describe life within the German, Italian, and American Communist Parties respectively. Three other essays—by French novelist André Gide, American journalist Louis Fischer, and British poet Stephen Spender—appear under the rubric "worshippers from afar," indicating the authors' involvement in communist politics without formal Party membership.[2] The book was assembled and promoted by a young Member of Parliament in the "Keep Left" group of the British Labour Party, Richard H. S. Crossman.

The narrative power of the book's essays played a great

role in its initial success. The essays both dramatize and personalize the allures of radical politics, explaining how communism answered each author's economic, political, and social concerns. Taken together, the book's essays offer profound introspections about Western intellectuals' attractions to communism and the Soviet Union in the interwar period as well as thoughtful reflections on the loss of faith.

The political trajectory these authors describe, from interwar communism to Cold War anti-communism, was common in the United States and Western Europe—"familiar enough to be banal," in the words of one such apostate.[3] The shift was part of a top-to-bottom reconfiguration of Western politics that unfolded in each nation, separately, in the decade after World War II. These reconfigurations ultimately reshaped the relations between intellectual life and political institutions. *The God That Failed* and its authors did not merely reflect these dramatic changes, but in fact helped spur them. Starting with a description of the events that attracted these authors to radical causes, this introductory essay will describe the fate of radicalism through the dramatic events of the late 1930s and World War II. It will dwell also on the crucial half-decade after the end of the war, including both the rise to power of left-wing parties across Europe and the simultaneous onset of the Cold War. A final section will consider the book's contemporary relevance.

The Soviet Union and the Western Left, 1917–1945

To become disillusioned with communism, as these authors did, presupposes a prior "illusionment." The six essayists in *The God That Failed* joined the communist cause for a variety of reasons. All six saw the Soviet Union as a crucial actor in remaking human society, resolving the problems of inequality and disorganization that seemed inherent in capitalism. While the essays here are deeply personal, they also represent the close intertwining of private lives with national and international politics. Recounting the "illusionment" and disillusionment of these six intellectuals, then, is to recount the tempestuous political and intellectual history of Europe and the United States between the wars—a history defined in large part by rapidly changing events in Russia.

During the confusion and violence of World War I, the newly formed Bolshevik regime found itself with many friends but even more enemies. Few intellectuals remained neutral about its threats to established economic and political systems, or about its promises of "a new world in birth" (in the words of the revolutionary anthem, the Internationale). Vladimir Lenin masterminded what the Bolsheviks later called the Great October Socialist Revolution in 1917, taking power in the name of the Councils (Soviets) of Workers', Soldiers', and Peasants' Deputies. The Bolsheviks fought challengers on all fronts. Western powers supported Russian monarchists; the United States, France, and Great Britain also sent troops of their own to Siberia, Ukraine and North Russia. The revolution, furthermore, refocused and redivided an international socialist movement already riven by the nationalist upsurge around World War I. Yet the Bolsheviks' efforts in 1919 to create a new international socialist organization—the Third, or Communist, International (later known as the Comintern)—hardly ended conflicts within the left. Among leftists, fierce doctrinal battles dominated political discourse, with foreign and western Russian radicals alike condemning the Bolsheviks. Internationally, too, many socialist organizations across Western Europe and the United States fought with each other for the endorsement of the Comintern, while others bitterly opposed Bolshevism as the wrong sort of revolution, in the wrong place, or at the wrong time.

Soviet Russia (reconstituted as part of the Union of Soviet Socialist Republics in 1924) got off to a rocky start even after defeating its Civil War enemies in late 1920. The year 1921 began with an uprising of sailors at the Kronstadt base (near Petrograd, renamed Leningrad after the leader's death in 1924 and now known once again as St. Petersburg). The Kronstadt sailors lodged complaints over living conditions, but their principal demands were political. The representative councils, or Soviets, they asserted, were not democratic institutions but had become Bolshevized. The Kronstadt rebels called for Soviet power free from Bolshevik dominance. The rebellion was ruthlessly suppressed, leading anarchist Alexander Berkman and others (as Fischer points out) to oppose Bolshevik rule. March 1921 brought the announcement of the New Economic Policy (NEP); this relaxed the tight grip over economic life maintained during the Civil War. While retaining government ownership over the "commanding heights" of the economy—the largest manufacturing and financial institutions—the NEP also ended the policy of requisitioning all the grain from the vast rural population. This policy change, seen by diehards as a concession to the peasantry, was not enough to stave off the famine that affected parts of Russia between 1921 and 1923.

After the tumult of its first half-decade, daily life in Soviet Russia began to stabilize in the mid-1920s. Economic production expanded rapidly, reaching its prewar levels by 1926. Political dissent was dramatically reduced by a combination of repression, deportation, and voluntary exile. At the same time, though, conflicts in the Politburo, the highest Party organ, intensified. With Lenin incapacitated by stroke, many Politburo members started positioning themselves to succeed him. Joseph Stalin, serving in a primarily administrative role as Secretary of the Party, began to outmaneuver two brilliant if tactically ill-equipped Bolsheviks: Leon Trotsky and Nikolai Bukharin. Through a series of temporary alliances with other leading Bolsheviks, Stalin engineered the exile or elimination of his potential rivals.[4]

By 1930, Stalin had taken over the Party apparatus, defeating his Politburo rivals. Trotsky, the leading rival, was subject first to internal exile and later to deportation. Bukharin faced ever-more-difficult circumstances in Moscow before eventually standing trial on trumped-up charges of treason in 1938. His own power secure, Stalin initiated drives for industrialization and cultural revolution. The announcement of the first Five-Year Plan in late 1927 heralded the call for an all-out drive to make the USSR an industrial nation—"a country of metal, a country of automobiles, a country of tractors"—and "to leave behind 'age-old Russian backwardness,' " in Stalin's exhortation.[5] The Plan attracted enthusiastic attention from Western intellectuals even before the Great Depression had begun in the West. Arthur Koestler recalled in an autobiography that he "fell in love with the Five-Year Plan."[6] Louis Fischer described similar emotions in the essay included in this book. These two, and many others, found in Soviet planning the fulfillment of their desires for a well-organized economic system under the firm hand of experts. The very scale of the changes—building new factories and remapping a countryside dotted with peasant villages into huge mechanized collective farms—excited those who wanted to watch a backward nation become modern, centrally planned, and socialist before their very eyes. The costs of industrialization were tremendous: standards of living plummeted below their already-low levels, shortages were rampant. The countryside was especially hard-hit as collectivization resembled a military campaign against the peasants. A famine in 1932–33 left millions in rural areas, especially Ukraine, without any source of food or the means to find it. Soviet sympathizers explained away even such dramatic hardships as part of Russia's attempt to "starve itself great."[7]

As the European economic crises of the late 1920s became the worldwide Great Depression, the Five-Year Plan received even more attention. Propaganda about the Soviet Union's impressive growth made an especially strong impression as Western economies faltered and collapsed. Those concerned about the plight of the workers came to Communism in increasing numbers as the Depression deepened in their own countries. As workers lost their jobs and struggled to survive, many of those guided by the desire to end the suffering they saw joined the Western Communist parties, or at least became "fellow-travelers," an imprecise term referring to those who joined forces with the Communists without ever formally joining the Party. The communist vision of a society in which all would share the fruits of production had special appeal when contrasted with the growing bread lines across the capitalist world.

While the economic programs of the Soviet Union won many converts among Western intellectuals, others were swayed instead by the Soviet cultural revolution in the early 1930s. For authors like Richard Wright, who had struggled to escape the racism of the Jim Crow south by moving to Chicago, the spread of the proletarian literature movement provided a chance to write and publish. Through their John Reed Clubs, the Communist Party of the United States of America (CPUSA) recruited would-be writers—preferably those with authentic proletarian backgrounds—defined to include not just workers but also those of other disadvantaged groups. This broad definition suggests the ways in which opposition to prejudice was visible across Western Communist Parties. Wright's desire to eradicate racism certainly clinched his involvement in the Communist Party; as he wrote one friend, "anyone with common sense could easily guess [that] I was a Communist because I was Negro."[8]

The CPUSA took an especially active role in asserting rights of African-Americans in the early 1930s. In one widely publicized campaign, for instance, the Party organized the defense of the so-called Scottsboro Boys, a group of African-American teenagers in the South accused of raping a white woman. The treatment of ethnic minorities was also important to Arthur Koestler, a Hungarian Jew whose family's fortunes collapsed in the 1920s. Though his essay here makes no mention of this, Koestler had been a committed Zionist for years before joining the German Communist Party (KPD). As he later reflected, he had believed in the 1930s that the "Jewish Question would eventually be solved, together with the Negro question, the Armenian question, and all other questions, in the global context of the Socialist revolution."[9] To many Western followers, Communists' support for minorities—in tune with the optimistic reports of the treatment of national minorities inside the USSR—mattered more than economics.

Threats of racism loomed larger when German President Paul von Hindenburg appointed Nazi chief Adolf Hitler as Chancellor in early 1933. Communists in many nations—and the Comintern overall—challenged Hitler's Fascism in Germany as well as Benito Mussolini's in Italy. In these two nations, the respective Communist parties expanded with anti-Fascist resistors. As the Communists strengthened their opposition to Fascism and particularly to Nazism, they also gained adherents across Western Europe and the United States. Anti-Fascist Italians revered Ignazio Silone, who chronicled the Italian countryside of his youth, for his resistance work as well as his writings. Silone's exile novels, *Fontamara* (1933) and *Bread and Wine* (1936), made a passionate case for Italian anti-Fascism and did much to bolster the cause overseas. Like his essay in this volume, Silone's novels draw on indigenous traditions from Christian-influenced anarchism to the local forms of protest in his native Abruzzi region to explain the need to align with the left and against the Fascists. Documents uncovered in the late 1990s, however, suggest that Silone's affiliations in the 1920s went beyond his leadership role in the Italian Communist Party (PCI)—and that may have been a police informer for much of the decade. His decision to leave the PCI in 1930 may have been as closely related to ending his informer role as to the Comintern machinations he describes in his essay here.[10] This information was unknown until very recently, and thus hardly affected his high reputation in Italian politics from the 1930s until his death in 1978.

The prominence of Communists in Western Europe and the United Sates grew in the 1930s in rough proportion to the rising threat of Nazism. Through the early 1930s, the Comintern treated non-Communist radicals as harshly as Fascists. The German Communists, for instance, allied with the Nazis against their Socialist rivals—whom the Communists derided as "Social Fascists"—and thus helped pave the way for Nazi rule.

Comintern's inauguration of the Popular Front in 1935 brought additional attention to western Communists. This policy replaced intense factionalism with a call for all progressive forces to unite—under Communist leadership—against the Fascist threat. The Popular Front had a parallel in Soviet foreign policy, as the USSR sought to form anti-Fascist alliances with Western nations. Even as that effort foundered, the Soviets offered what support they could to Western anti-Fascists. The most dramatic setting for this policy came in Spain. Not long after the election of a Socialist government in 1936, rightist forces under General Francisco Franco moved to reinstate the Spanish monarchy and rid the country of socialism. While Germany and Italy supported Franco, the Western powers stuck to a policy of strict neutrality, with the United States even banning all forms of interaction with the combatants.

Of the national states in Europe, only the Soviet Union offered open support for the embattled Spanish loyalists, at a price. They provided arms and munitions for the anti-Franco forces. In addition, the Comintern sponsored the International Brigades, recruiting party members and others to join the Loyalists. Communist parties around the world sent more than 50,000 volunteers to oppose Franco's forces—which had in the meantime been armed with German and Italian weapons. It was, in many ways, the first European battleground of World War II. Yet the International Brigades, poorly equipped and ill-trained, suffered tremendous losses. Five hundred American socialists were joined by the American Communist contingent, patriotically named the Abraham Lincoln Battalion, which lost as many as one-third of its 3,000 members.

Spain served as a crucible for Western radicals like British poet and critic Stephen Spender. Spender joined the Communist Party—for less than two months, as it happened—in order to lend support for the Spanish campaign. Longtime Moscow-based correspondent Louis Fischer, his faith in Soviet politics already shaken by intra-party conflicts in the USSR, grasped onto Spain as his next cause. More typical, though, was the political transformation of Arthur Koestler, too, faced political transformation in Spain, though of a different sort. Even before his incarceration in Franco's prisons, Koestler observed the Comintern's violent opposition to a group of Spanish radicals also fighting Franco, the POUM, a collective of labor unions led by Trotskyists. Comintern's actions against the POUM alienated Koestler and many other western leftists. The tolerant atmosphere of the Popular Front did not extend to those aligned with Stalin's most insistent and incisive enemy—as the Moscow Trials demonstrated in the same period.

Beginning in 1936, most Old Bolsheviks who had played significant roles in the 1917 Revolution stood accused in a series of show trials. Prosecutors made outrageous claims about these radicals' treasonous activities: counter-revolutionary wrecking, espionage on behalf of the Germans, plots to overthrow Soviet power, and alliances with Trotsky. Once-fiery revolutionaries typically appeared in court cowed and silenced—except for debasing confessions to the crimes ostensibly committed, irrespective of internal logic, feasibility, or veracity. Even within a cohort of Western radicals reared on the intense factional disputes of the Communists, many questioned their faith—in the Soviet Union or even in communism generally. Most of the figures in this book discuss one or another episode of this conflict; Silone centers his

piece around an earlier effort to eliminate Bukharin's influence in the Comintern; Fischer notes the "black plague" of
the purge trials. During his 1936 Soviet journey, French
writer André Gide saw the trials' effects as they widened to
engulf the nation in the search for spies, saboteurs, and especially Trotskyists. Wright, as he describes in this essay, was
himself a victim of small-scale factional maneuverings in the
Chicago John Reed Club.

Those who continued to defend the Soviet Union during
the purge trials typically did so on one of two grounds. Some
diehards insisted that the USSR was not yet ready for
Western-style democracy; American novelist Upton Sinclair,
for instance, espoused this view. The Russian traditions of
autocracy and violence, so the argument went, meant that
Soviet politics could not justly be compared with Western
democracies.[11] A variety of Western radicals adhered to var-
iants of this notion. Russia's cultural distance from Europe
was a central issue, for instance, in Koestler's views of the
Soviet Union. In his essay here, he refers to Stalin only as
"Djugashwili" in order to emphasize Stalin's—and by extension, the USSR's—"semi-oriental" nature. As Koestler illustrates, Russia's national characteristics were used by Soviet
sympathizers to justify hardships and violence and by critics
to further condemn the USSR. Those going from sympathizer to critic, therefore, were easily able to maintain their
views of Russia's uniqueness.

Other Western observers, when confronted with the Moscow Trials, proposed a more pragmatic defense of the USSR.
Only the USSR, they argued, could offer meaningful opposition to Hitler's expansionism in central Europe, and to
Franco's advancing armies in Spain. Preferring to emphasize
the "Stalin Constitution" of 1936 and its unfilled promises
of Soviet democracy, these radicals placed the Soviet Union's
international role above its domestic imperfections. Louis Fischer often employed such arguments, though his ultimate
disenchantment with the Soviet Union was closely related to

Nazi-Soviet Pact

the purges. As the 1930s waned, however, the situation had again changed. In the spring of 1939, Franco's forces took Madrid, ending the Spanish Civil War. Most dramatically, the USSR signed a nonaggression pact with Nazi Germany later that year. As Fischer indicates, this earth-shattering event served as a final breaking point, even for those resolute enough to have withstood the famine, the cultural revolution, and the purges. Western intellectuals, devastated and confused, fled the Party *en masse*. Only a few rejoined when the Nazis invaded the USSR in June 1941; the faith of the remainder had been irreparably shattered. With the Soviet Union once again fighting Nazism after 1941—this time joined by Britain and the United States—Western Communists offered what support they could to the war effort. For instance, the CPUSA's endorsement of the U.S. Army extended so far that it refused to challenge the military's policy of racial segregation. This lack of opposition convinced Richard Wright that the Party's support for African-American causes was merely tactical, quickly abandoned as the circumstances dictated. Doubting the CPUSA's commitment to African-Americans, Wright quietly resigned from the Party. This feeling of betrayal—so often visible in the decades before the war, as Comintern policy underwent frequent and drastic shifts—as much as anything defined the reason for forsaking the sense of common cause with the Soviet Union.

Western Leftism After World War II

The events of World War II had a profound impact on postwar international politics. Despite the horrendous losses they suffered, Soviets claimed their place among the war's victors. Western leftists, meanwhile, saw their prestige enhanced by this new Soviet position and also by the role of the anti-Fascist Resistance movements in Nazi-occupied France and in Italy. In Britain and the United States, the parties generally served the national cause—as Wright found out, much to his frustration. The Communist International, to emphasize its solidarity with the wartime alliance, formally disbanded in 1943. In spite of vastly different political and economic organizations—not to mention divergent military strategies—Britain, the United States, and the Soviet Union operated as effective allies during the war. With the defeat of their common enemy, the direction of world politics was unknown. The war left behind a new world environment— one in which the United States and the Soviet Union were in ascendence, in which Britain's global role was fading, and in which the atomic bomb heightened fears of international conflict.

The war also put the Western European left in its strongest position ever. The Italy's PCI received almost 20 percent of the vote in 1946 elections, while the French Communists received 26 percent. In Great Britain, meanwhile, the Labour Party won a historic electoral victory, sweeping into power without needing a coalition partner. Crossman's "Keep Left" group ensured that the Labour Party would institute major changes in the aftermath of the war, asserting governmental control over large industries and the health system. Labour's foreign policy was initially oriented toward becoming a third force, a counterweight to both American and Soviet domination in Europe.[12]

This left-of-center strategy did not hold; it was soon overtaken by the eruption of the Cold War and the emergence of a bipolar world. Prompted by civil war in Greece and the inability of the British to support anti-communist forces, American president Harry S. Truman established the Truman Doctrine in 1946, promising American support for those fighting against Communists. By summer 1947, when Secretary of State George Marshall unveiled an aid program to rebuild Europe, American commitment to anti-communism had expanded. In both actions, the United States reoriented its international position against its erstwhile Soviet ally. These moves were undertaken in response to a growing sense of Soviet expansionism. In Iran (1946) and during negotiations over the future status of Poland, Soviet authorities insisted on friendly regimes in states on its borders. Soviet plans for expanding its influence beyond its immediate neighbors, furthermore, was evident in support for Communists in Greece and the eastern zone of occupied Germany.

The crucial events dividing the sides in Europe came in 1948 and 1949—that is, in the years while *The God That Failed* was being assembled and written. The Sovietization of Czechoslovakia in February 1948—with the USSR's insistence that the Czechs not pursue Marshall Plan aid—soon led to the death (in highly suspicious circumstances) of Jan Masaryk, the son of a national hero and the foreign minister in the postwar Czech government. Only months later, the Soviet occupation authorities in Germany announced that they were cutting off all land and water routes to the Western-occupied zones of Berlin. The United States soon thereafter led an airlift to bring food and energy supplies to those in West Berlin.

The arrival of Marshall Plan aid, the Communist coup in Czechoslovakia, and the blockade and airlift in Berlin convinced Crossman to abandon the Third Force in favor of an unabashed pro-American line. Meanwhile in the United States in summer 1948, another factor emerged: the espionage trials of Alger Hiss, a well-regarded establishment figure who had served in a variety of senior government posts and was at that point President-elect of the Carnegie Endowment for International Peace. The evidence against Hiss came from Whittaker Chambers, who alleged that both had worked together in a Soviet espionage ring based in Washington in the 1930s. The trial divided American intellectual and political elites, many of whom sharply resisted the notion that Hiss, a Harvard-educated lawyer, could be guilty of espionage and working with the Soviets.

author of Witness

These national and international events forced a political reevaluation. Communism could no longer be seen as the ideology of liberation, of rapid industrialization, of racial tolerance, or of anti-Fascism which had attracted so many believers in the 1930s. Communism was instead equated with the Soviet Union, which in turn was painted as an international menace, expanding across Eastern Europe and making inroads in Western nations like Greece, France, and Italy. These conclusions, however, were far from universally held and prompted strenuous debate in Western Europe and the United States in the late 1940s.

Those who had been active in leftist politics during what Koestler termed the "pink decade" of the 1930s disagreed strongly about the appropriate course of action. In the United States by the time of the Hiss trial in 1948, any Communist past was enough to initiate an investigation amid spiralling anti-communist sentiment. Across the Atlantic, however, Western European Communists held positions of cultural and political power. These figures offered a serious challenge to American hopes for hegemony in Western Europe. In Italy and France, each of which had powerful Communist parties, the issue was especially divisive, as anti-Americanism outranked anti-communism among intellectuals. Many of France's leading intellectuals, including philosophers Jean-Paul Sartre and Maurice Merleau-Ponty, were active supporters of the Soviet Union. Communists' cultural authority was augmented by their role in the resistance against Nazi occupiers. American policymakers exerted ever-stronger pressures to limit the role of these figures across Europe. Diplomats threatened to cut off Marshall Plan aid to Italy if the Communists won the 1948 election. Even more direct tactics were occasionally employed: American sources secretly facilitated a split in the Italian Socialist Party, with one important faction paid by the CIA for aligning against the Communists.[13]

In spite of British Labour's leftward momentum, the party

quickly sided with the United States in international politics. The British Communist Party, furthermore, had a very limited following. This alone may explain both the origins and the shape of *The God That Failed*. The result of a collaboration between two writers in Britain, Crossman and Koestler, the book sought to convince Western intellectuals—but especially those in continental Europe—to abandon their hopes in the Soviet Union. And they would do so with the ultimate support of American intellectuals and eventually the American government.

Assembling *The God That Failed*

With this goal of conversion in mind, Crossman and Koestler contemplated possible contributors to a volume they had tentatively entitled "Lost Illusions"—after first rejecting options like "Why I Became a Communist" and "We Changed Our Minds."[14] Among the European writers considered for the volume were French philosopher Albert Camus, French novelist André Malraux and German historian Franz Borkenau. Crossman enlisted C. D. Jackson to help select and court American contributors in the spring of 1948; the two had worked together for their respective "psychological warfare" (propaganda) operations during World War II. Ernest Hemingway, whose coverage of the Spanish Civil War had won accolades on the left, was briefly under consideration. Koestler opposed a contribution by Richard Wright, whose reflections on "I Tried to Be a Communist" had already appeared in 1944; he considered Wright neither "sufficiently first-class nor sufficiently reliable politically to be admitted into this most illustrious company." Once Crossman had prevailed over Koestler, however, a new issue arose: Wright insisted that the book include opinions from workers and union leaders as well as intellectuals. But here the organizers got their way, incorporating Wright's contribution without expanding the list of authors.

Crossman, at Jackson's suggestion, also invited Whittaker Chambers to contribute to the volume. Chambers's refusal was overdetermined; his reasons included the impending Hiss trial, his desire to write a book-length reflection on his Communist experiences (which eventually appeared as *Witness* in 1952), and his personal distaste for Jackson.[15]

André Gide presented a special problem for the volume. His highly publicized trip to the Soviet Union in 1936 had resulted in two controversial books and many more heated exchanges, making him something of a *cause célèbre* among Western anti-communists. The Nobel Prize for Literature he received in 1947 made him all the more attractive to Crossman. But his advanced age and ill health meant that his contribution was pulled together from earlier writings by Oxford scholar Dr. Enid Starkie. Both this essay and Wright's, then, were based on writings predating the volume's assembly.

From the time that Crossman began contacting potential authors in early 1948, the march of events made the issues more urgent. The Hiss trials and events in Prague and Berlin made the Soviet threat seem all the more menacing—at the same time that the Communist Party of Italy was a serious force in the upcoming elections. The year 1949 was, if anything even more dramatic. The headlines in the last six months of that year, for instance, made Communism even more pertinent to daily life: the Soviets exploded their first atomic bomb in August; Mao Zedong took power and declared China a People's Republic in October. As Americans sought to make sense of these events, the focus soon turned to Communists in their own midst. President Harry Truman had announced the federal loyalty/security program in early 1948. Subsequent revelations and accusations of Communists in high governmental positions fueled this fire. American anti-communists laid the groundwork for what would be called, somewhat misleadingly, McCarthyism. Even before Senator Joseph McCarthy declared in February 1950 that he knew of 205 Communists in the State Department, a combination of Republican politicians, populists, critics of the New Deal, and communists-turned-right-wingers questioned the loyalty and judgement of anyone with ties—past or present—to communism. Even organizations with strong left-wing traditions—from labor unions to the American Civil Liberties union—had, by the late 1940s, purged their ranks of Communists. The Communist Party itself never regained its prewar position; it adopted a revolutionary strategy and went underground. The rising tide of anti-communism included many who criticized interwar radicals as victims of Soviet duplicity and/or psychological pathologies. Many of these anti-communists sought to explain the interwar radicals as victims of Soviet duplicity and/or psychological pathologies. Amid such explanations, the portraits in *The God That Failed* stand out for their complexity and subtlety.

The Publication of *The God That Failed*

In his introduction, British politico Crossman steers a careful path: convincing European intellectuals to break with their communist past without "swelling the flood of anti-Communist propaganda," an apparent reference to the explosion of that sentiment in the United States. The position was all the more delicate because Crossman's constituents in Coventry were distinctly left-wing; denouncing communism too strongly might cost him his seat in the House of Commons.[16] Crossman seeks to make support for the USSR untenable on the grounds of both culture and international politics. Praising those who have abandoned communism, Crossman also emphasizes the dangers of the Soviet Union to European politics and culture. Intellectuals of the world must unite, he implies, before Western intellectual life is itself threatened. The dangers also spread beyond Europe, with high stakes all around the postwar world. Invoking Richard Wright's essay, the editor reminds Western intellectuals of

the reputation that Communism held "among Colored peoples who make up the great majority of mankind"—thus
foreshadowing Western (especially American) efforts to win
to the "hearts and minds of the Third World."

The reception of these political messages is evident from
the initial reviews of *The God That Failed*. While praising
the power of the autobiographical essays, many reviewers
noted specific political agendas. Arthur M. Schlesinger, Jr.
used the book as a platform to exhort American progressives
to renounce their hopes in the USSR. Similarly, theologian
Reinhold Niebuhr emphasized the need to recognize human
flaws, a recurrent theme of his Cold War writings; Western
societies, he continued, were better suited for such imperfections. *Time Magazine*'s anonymous reviewer called the
book "required reading for democrats." Mainstream reviewers, at least in the United States, did not dismiss the writers
because of their past politics—quite the opposite, in fact.
Many instead called attention to the need to hear out those
who had been believers. One reviewer insisted that, "no one
who has not been a Stalin Communist really knows what the
current world struggle is all about."[17]

This newfound Cassandra role for former Communists facilitated their renewed involvement in politics. There is no
shame, the essays suggest, in a Communist past, which could
have emerged out of a wide range of political and personal
concerns. Indeed, those with such a past, while perhaps suspect in the eyes of the uninformed, were uniquely placed to
make a contribution to the Cold War. As one reviewer put
it, *The God That Failed* should save the FBI from "a good
deal of noisy wrongheadedness." Those "cured" of Communism are "cured permanently," he continued, and will be
actively engaged in the fight against the USSR. They might
even be more likely to spot an undercover Communist.[18] The
Cold War called on intellectuals to take their sides, and the
contributors to *The God That Failed* did just that.

The book, then, functioned as a set of conversion narratives as well as a how-to manual for transforming interwar radicals into Cold-War liberals. Though the autobiographies derive their narrative power from their personal nature, they derive their political power from the close relationship between intellectuals and the interests of national security. Cold War intellectuals were not those who spoke truth to power, but those who saw truth and power as intimately related. Schlesinger stated the goal of political engagement most directly in his extended essay, *The Vital Center* (1949). This young historian accused American progressives (whom he derisively termed "doughfaces") of avoiding power and responsibility. The intellectuals in Schlesinger's vital center, by contrast, were actively bringing once-cloistered intellectual life into the political world. Only months after *The God That Failed* appeared, literary critic Lionel Trilling offered a similar perspective: it was time for intellectuals to acknowledge the "intimate . . . connection between literature and politics." Even Trilling, who himself remained detached from contemporary politics, saw the need for a new relationship between literature and liberalism.[19] Liberal intellectuals, in these powerful statements, would be distinguished by their engagement in political life.

Nowhere was the growing intimacy between intellectual and political life clearer than in the Congress for Cultural Freedom (CCF), an effort to enlist Western intellectuals in the Cold War.[20] This organization reached far beyond *The God That Failed*, but shared both personnel and program with the book. Founded in one of the Cold War's hotspots, Berlin, in 1950, the CCF aimed to sway European intellectuals away from the Soviet Union and toward the Western camp. In the words of Sidney Hook, a sophisticated interpreter of Marx who broke with the Communist Party in 1933, the CCF hoped to deploy these intellectuals to "generate a wave of democratic unrest among the masses . . . of Stalin's own empire."[21]

The CCF quickly established a plethora of national affiliates as well as number of journals of opinion—including some of the most significant ones in Europe: the British *Encounter*, the Italian *Tempo Presente*, and the French *Preuves* all became major forces in their respective nation's cultural lives. An American-sponsored magazine in Germany, *Der Monat*, preceded the formation of the CCF but soon became closely aligned with it. These journals published articles on a wide range of cultural issues, also emphasizing a number of Cold War themes—most notably analyses of Soviet domestic life and foreign policy. Outside of Europe, the CCF operated an even wider array of magazines from Japan to Latin America. These journals printed criticism of everything from Soviet politics to European intellectual life to American popular culture—of everything, it seems, but American foreign policy.

The early history of the CCF overlapped considerably with *The God That Failed*. *Der Monat*, for instance, proudly published translations of all of the book's essays. With the exception of André Gide, who was already in ill health when the book appeared and died in early 1951, all six of the book's authors worked with the CCF or one of its related organs in the 1950s. Arthur Koestler and Ignazio Silone served on the CCF's Executive Committee, though Koestler soon resigned after failing to push the CCF toward a more confrontational position. (One history of the CCF reports that "to Koestlerize" became a verb meaning to "attack contemptuously."[22]) Silone, meanwhile, became co-editor of *Tempo Presente*. Stephen Spender shared the helm of *Encounter* with an American, Irving Kristol. The two American contributors to *The God That Failed* maintained somewhat more distant contacts with the CCF. Richard Wright wrote occasionally for *Encounter*, though his relationship with Cold War anti-communists was one of mutual mistrust. Subject to U.S. government surveillance while living in Paris, Wright felt as used by anti-communists as he had been by the Communists.[23] Louis Fischer pursued an independent writing and journalistic career, though he participated in some CCF events and had joined its General Assembly in time to help preside over the organization's demise in 1967.[24]

The story of the Congress for Cultural Freedom's collapse reveals the extent to which these intellectuals identified with Cold War imperatives. Rumors about secret funding had haunted the CCF for years, though the practice of passing CIA funds through foundations complicated the issue. But in 1966, the *New York Times* reported that the CCF had received the bulk of its funding, especially in its early years, from the CIA. CCF leadership pre-empted mass resignations by folding up shop. Most activists in the CCF claimed no knowledge of the organization's true sponsors, and undoubtedly many did not. Still, one recent biographer claims that Koestler had learned of the CIA involvement as early as 1951. Silone, meanwhile, received U.S. government funding for travel as early as 1949, though whether he knew of its ultimate source is still open to question.[25]

The revelations about CIA sponsorship of the CCF remain a key symbol of the cultural Cold War. Apparent ironies abound: ex-communist intellectuals gathered to fight against their past beliefs; the U.S. government supported dozens of intellectuals whose biographies would have excluded them from most forms of government work; and a government-sponsored organization promoted the virtues of an independent cultural sphere. Yet these ironies fade when considered in historical context. The trajectory from Depression-era communist to postwar anti-communist was a common, even "banal," one. The authors of *The God That Failed*, like the participants in the Congress for Cultural Freedom, were hardly unanimous in their political views. Arthur Koestler became a hard-edged Cold Warrior (like his frequent sparring partner Sidney Hook), while Wright insisted on nonalignment.[26] Koestler's value to American anti-communists is illustrated by his efforts to settle in the United States in 1951. Barred because the recently passed McCarran Act forbade former Communists from becoming permanent residents, Koestler pursued his only option, an act of Congress. The bill allowing him to settle in the United States was sponsored by none other than California Senator Richard Nixon, a firebrand anti-communist who owed his public profile to his energetic pursuit of Alger Hiss.[27] The alliance between aggressive anti-communists and European ex-Communists had reached a peak. Wright, meanwhile, faced continued surveillance and harassment from American authorities.

The question of CIA sponsorship of the non-Communist left—including many Europeans who challenged American foreign policies and cultural expansion—is even more striking. An official CIA history of the CCF termed the promoting the non-Communist left "the theoretical foundation of the Agency's political operations" for much of the Cold War.[28] As government agencies were wracked by accusations of Communist infiltration—a few of which were later confirmed—in the late 1940s and early 1950s, the secrecy of intelligence organs ensured that the recipients of CIA largesse would remain hidden from the U.S. Congress in general and Senator McCarthy in particular.

The third irony, about an organization receiving secret government funding while promoting cultural freedom, is not so easily explained. It serves instead as an apt symbol of Cold War intellectual life. That such a large group of prominent intellectuals could undertake CCF work in apparent ignorance of the origins of the funding is testament to both the CIA's successful management and the intellectuals' own blind spots. After so much time on the margins of political life (especially in the United States), independent of any institutional support, the chance to stand at the center of political life, with foundations sponsoring trips around the world, must have been hard to resist. These intellectuals—in spite of Frances Stonor Saunders's insinuations to this effect—did not sell their souls to the CIA. Instead, as cultural critic Christopher Lasch noted in the wake of the orig-

Who Paid the Piper?

inal revelations, CCF activists "tended to confuse intellectual values with the interests of the intellectuals as a class, just as they confused freedom with the national interests of the United States."[29] Many intellectuals, in other words, were more excited by the links between ideas and politics than by the ideas themselves.

Through books like *The God That Failed* and organizations like the Congress for Cultural Freedom, Western intellectuals were not just present at the creation of the Cold War, but on active service. Information about the CIA connection to the CCF can hardly serve to indict the intellectuals for dishonesty; almost all remained true to their political beliefs. Nor is do these revelations make CCF intellectuals responsible for McCarthyism, which harassed iconoclasts like Richard Wright and claimed many other intellectuals as victims. CCF organs, in fact, produced many powerful articles condemning McCarthyism. But the official connections do suggest that Lasch's observation has merit. Some Western intellectuals were harmed by Cold War politics, especially by virulent anti-communism; yet others rose professionally amid this new political environment.

The God That Failed in the Twenty-first Century

The powerful statements which comprise *The God That Failed* deserve a fresh reading as the twenty-first century opens. For a generation of students, the passions and fears of the Cold War lie in the distant past. The book's essays can shed light on the genuine excitement that greeted the Soviet Union in the 1930s, as well as the climate of uncertainty and apprehension of the early postwar years. Before Senator McCarthy turned anti-communism into a weapon of mass political destruction, a small group of writers offered their own lives as lessons not only about radical hopes betrayed—but also about the need to unite against communism.

The issues raised by *The God That Failed* are not simply

historical—as if history is ever simple. They are relevant to-day, as commentators wield individual biographies and collective histories as weapons in current political conflicts. Just as McCarthy and his allies used anti-communism to strike out against the New Deal, participants in present-day debates seek to re-create the Cold War as a battle between forces of pure good and pure evil—placing themselves, of course, in the appropriate camp. The fierce arguments about Silone's alleged work with the Fascist police, as well as a renewed debate about the CIA sponsorship of the CCF, show that for many intellectuals the Cold War is not over.

Beyond that, *The God That Failed* reveals the political and institutional transformations of Western intellectual life over the last seventy years. Politically, a long-term rightward trend cut across the intellectual traditions of many nations—though of course the upsurge of protest in the 1960s complicates any ideas of a linear trend. The most important works of the 1930s suggested the need for communism in the West and proclaimed the Soviet Union as humanity's future. By the 1990s, in contrast, works dealing with the USSR berated intellectuals for their support for communism, or declared that the demise of the Soviet Union represented "the end of history."[30] *The God That Failed* provides one crucial benchmark for this broad swing. It also suggests the move of cultural life into institutions and the decline of independent intellectuals. The former radicals published in that book were independently employed, but soon thereafter became deeply involved in government-sponsored cultural work. Finally, *The God That Failed* suggests the expansion of American cultural power internationally. Though the book included only two Americans and was organized by Britons, it promoted an American agenda for Europe—or at least a pro-American one. The Cold War brought American dollars to a variety of Western intellectuals, contributing to the Americanization of intellectual life in Europe and around the world. This was especially clear in the case of *The God That Failed*. Billed, however disingenuously, as standing outside of American-Soviet conflict, the book was immediately read as a volley from the American side of the cultural Cold War.

The publication history of the book makes this last point clear: Not only was the book widely distributed through CCF channels—and thus purchased with CIA funds—but both the American and British occupation forces in Germany used the book there. By 1952, the newly formed United States Information Service held all foreign rights to the book.[31] The republication of the book in the 1980s suggests another element of the intellectual transformation. In 1983, three years after the election of Ronald Reagan as President, the last Cold-War edition of the book appeared, this time published by Henry Regnery Publishers, which bills itself as "America's most dedicated conservative publisher."[32] Perhaps, with this first post-Cold War edition, we can return to the book for an education in the history of the Cold War as well as in the responsibilities of intellectuals.

Acknowledgment

Thanks to Daniel Bell, Jim Campbell, Caren Irr, Paul Jankowski, Ethan Pollock, and Stephen Whitfield for their help with this essay, and to Sandy McKinley and Eben Miller for research assistance.

Endnotes

1. Harper and Brothers to Louis Fischer, 26 November 1954, in Louis Fischer Papers (Seeley Mudd Library, Princeton University), series 1, box 4.

2. Spender actually was a Party member for about six weeks; see Spender, *World Within World* (London, 1977 [1951]), 206. I borrow the distinction between capital-c Communism (meaning Soviet-endorsed) and small-c communism (meaning Marxist) from John Dewey; see "Why I Am Not a Communist," *Modern Monthly* 8 (April 1934): 35–37.

3. William Henry Chamberlin, *The Evolution of a Conservative* (Chicago, 1959), 274.

4. Most of the Bolshevik leaders had taken "Party names" to throw off the Tsarist police: Russian Vladimir Il'ich Ul'ianov became Lenin, Russian Jew Lev Davidovich Bronshtein became Leon Trotsky, and Georgian Iosif Vissarionovich Dzhugashvili became Stalin. (Koestler uses a nonstandard spelling of Stalin's name—Djugashwili.

5. Stalin, "A Year of Great Change" (3 November 1929), in *Works* (Moscow, 1955), 12:141.

6. Arthur Koestler, *Arrow in the Blue: An Autobiography* (London, 1952), 279

7. See David C. Engerman, "Modernization from the Other Shore: American Observers and the Costs of Soviet Economic Development," *American Historical Review* 105, no. 2 (April 2000): 383–416.

8. Letter to Edward Aswell, 21 August 1955, quoted in Michel Fabre, *The Unfinished Quest of Richard Wright*, trans. Isabel Barzun (New York, 1973), 230.

9. Koestler, *The Invisible Writing* (London, 1954), 461; David Cesarani, *Arthur Koestler: The Homeless Mind* (London, 1998), 142–43.

10. Mauro Canali, "Ignazio Silone and the Fascist Political Police," *Journal of Modern Italian Studies* 5, no. 1 (2000): 37.

11. See, for instance, Upton Sinclair's contribution to *Terror in Russia? Two Views* (New York, 1938).

12. Kenneth O. Morgan, *The People's Peace: British History, 1945–1990* (Oxford, 1992), 98–99. Donald Sassoon, *One Hundred Years of Socialism: The West European Left in the Twentieth Century* (New York, 1997), chap. 5.

13. Norman Kogan, *A Political History of Italy: The Postwar Years* (New York, 1983), 39; Sassoon, *One Hundred Years*, 135.

14. The eventual title was suggested by Enid Starkie, who assembled and translated André Gide's contribution. This is noted only in the British edition of the book—see Arthur Koestler, et al., *The God That Failed: Six Studies in Communism* (London, 1950), 14 n. 1.

15. Anthony Howard, *Crossman: The Pursuit of Power* (London, 1990), 142–43; Cesarani, *Arthur Koestler*, 341–43; Fabre, *Unfinished Quest*, 331. Whittaker Chambers to William F. Buckley, 15 July 1957, in *Odyssey of a Friend: Whittaker Chambers's Letters to William F. Buckley, Jr., 1954–1961*, ed. William F. Buckley (Washington, 1987), 192; also Sam Tanenhaus, *Whittaker Chambers: A Biography* (New York, 1998), 199. Wright,

"I Tried to Be a Communist," *Atlantic Monthly* 159 (August 1944): 61–70, (September 1944): 48–56.

16. Howard, *Crossman*, 143.

17. Arthur M. Schlesinger, Jr., "Dim Views of the Red Star," *Saturday Review of Literature* 33 (7 January 1950): 11. Niebuhr, "To Moscow—and Back," *The Nation* 170 (28 January 1950): 88–90. "The Ugly Leah," *Time Magazine* 55 (9 January 1950): 86–87. "Books in Brief," *The New Yorker* 25 (14 January 1950): 82.

18. Richard Hatch, "Studies in the Permanent Crisis," *The New Republic* 122 (13 March 1950): 19–20.

19. Arthur M. Schlesinger, Jr., *The Vital Center: The Politics of Freedom* (Boston, 1949); Lionel Trilling, *The Liberal Imagination: Essays on Literature and Society* (New York, 1953), ix.

20. These paragraphs draw from Peter Coleman, *The Liberal Conspiracy: The Congress for Cultural Freedom and the Struggle for the Mind of Postwar Europe* (New York, 1989); Michael Warner, "Origins of the Congress for Cultural Freedom, 1949–1950," *Studies in Intelligence* 38 (Summer 1995): 89–98; and Francis Stonor Saunders, *The Cultural Cold War: The CIA and the World of Arts and Letters* (New York, 2000 [London, 1999]).

21. Quoted in Warner, "Origins," 89.

22. Coleman, *Liberal Conspiracy*, 33.

23. According to one source, organs from the Foreign Service to military intelligence funnelled reports on Wright to the Federal Bureau of Investigation. For this information, along with extensive quotations from the Wright dossier, see Addison Gayle, *Richard Wright: Ordeal of a Native Son* (Garden City, N.Y., 1980).

24. Coleman, *Liberal Conspiracy*, 232.

25. Cesarani, *Arthur Koestler*, 368; Coleman, *Liberal Conspiracy*, 7.

26. Wright, for instance, refused in 1960 to appear on a current-affairs radio program organized around *The God That Failed*—Fabre, *Unfinished Quest*, 517.

27. Cesarani, *Arthur Koestler*, 385.

28. Warner, "Origins," 89.

29. Saunders, *Cultural Cold War*, 5 and *passim;* Lasch, "The Cultural Cold War: The Congress for Cultural Freedom" (1967), in *The Agony of the American Left* (New York, 1969), 69.

30. Compare John Dewey, *Liberalism and Social Action* (New York, 1935) and Stephen Spender, *Forward from Liberalism* (London, 1937) to

Francis Fukuyama, *The End of History and the Last Man* (New York, 1992) and Martin Malia, *Russia Under Western Eyes: From the Bronze Horseman to the Lenin Mausoleum* (Cambridge, Mass., 1999).

31. On CCF distribution of the book, see Saunders, *Cultural Cold War*, 66. On the rights transfer, see Harper and Brothers to Louis Fischer, 26 November 1954, Fischer Papers.

32. On the home page of the Henry Regnery web site, www.regnery.com, accessed 18 January 2001.

Further Reading in English

Major Works by the Authors

Crossman, Richard. *Government and the Governed: A History of Political Ideas and Political Practice*. London, 1939.

Fischer, Louis. *The Soviets in World Affairs: A History of the Relations between the Soviet Union and the Rest of the World*. New York, 1930.

Fischer, Louis. *Gandhi and Stalin: Two Signs at the World's Crossroads*. New York, 1947.

Gide, André. *Afterthoughts on the USSR*. New York, 1938.

Gide, André. *The Immoralist*. Trans. Dorothy Bussy. New York, 1930 [1902].

Gide, André. *Return from the USSR*. New York, 1937.

Gide, André. *The School for Wives*. Trans. Dorothy Bussy. New York, 1950 [1929].

Koestler, Arthur. *Darkness at Noon*. New York, 1941.

Koestler, Arthur. *The Yogi and the Commissar*. New York, 1945.

Silone, Ignazio, *Bread and Wine*. Trans. Gwenda David and Eric Mosbacher. New York, 1937.

Silone, Ignazio. *Fontamara*. Trans. Michael Wharf. New York, 1934 [1930].

Spender, Stephen. *The Destructive Element: A Study of Modern Writers and Beliefs*. London, 1935.

Spender, Stephen. *Collected Poems, 1928–1953*. London, 1954.

Wright, Richard. *Native Son*. New York, 1940.

Wright, Richard. *The Outsider*. New York, 1953.

Biographies and Autobiographies of the Authors

Canali, Mauro. "Ignazio Silone and the Fascist Political Police." *Journal of Modern Italian Studies* 5 (2000): 36–60. (Includes debate with David Ward and Alexander De Grand).

Cesarani, David. *Arthur Koestler: The Homeless Mind*. London, 1998.

David, Hugh. *Stephen Spender: A Portrait with Background*. London, 1992.

Duke, David. *Distant Obligations: Modern American Writers and Foreign Causes*. Oxford, 1983. (Chapter 5 on Louis Fischer.)

Fabre, Michel. *The Unfinished Quest of Richard Wright*. Trans. Isabel Barzun. New York, 1973.

Gide, André. *The Journals of André Gide, 1889–1949*. Ed. and trans. Justin O'Brien. New York, 1956.

Howard, Anthony. *Crossman: The Pursuit of Power*. London, 1990.

Koestler, Arthur. *Arrow in the Blue: An Autobiography*. New York, 1952.

Koestler, Arthur. *The Invisible Writing*. London, 1954.

Raucher, Alan. "Beyond the God That Failed: Louis Fischer, Liberal Internationalist." *The Historian* 44 (February 1982): 174–89.

Sheridan, Alan. *André Gide: A Life in the Present*. Cambridge, Mass., 1999.

Spender, Stephen. *World Within World*. London, 1997 [1951].

Wright, Richard. *Black Boy (American Hunger)*. New York, 1998 [1945].

Western European and American History

Aaron, Daniel. *Writers on the Left: Episodes in American Literary Communism*. New York, 1961

Caute, David. *Communism and the French Intellectuals, 1914–1960*. London, 1964.

Caute, David. *The Fellow-Travellers: A Postscript to the Enlightenment*. London, 1973.

Coleman, Peter. *The Liberal Conspiracy: The Congress for Cultural Freedom and the Struggle for the Mind of Postwar Europe*. New York, 1979.

Diggins, John P. *Up from Communism: Conservative Odysseys in American Intellectual History*. New York, 1975.

Furet, François. *The Passing of an Illusion: The Idea of Communism in the Twentieth Century*. Trans. Deborah Furet. Chicago, 1999.

Judt, Tony. *Past Imperfect: French Intellectuals, 1944–1956*. Berkeley and Los Angeles, 1992.

Klehr, Harvey. *The Heyday of American Communism: The Depression Decade*. New York, 1984.

Kutulas, Judy. *The Long War: The Intellectual People's Front and Anti-Stalinism, 1930–1940*. Durham, N.C., 1995.

Lasch, Christopher. "The Cultural Cold War: The Congress for Cultural Freedom" (1968), in *The Agony of the American Left*. New York, 1969.

Podhoretz, Norman. "Why 'The God That Failed' Failed. . . ." *Encounter* 60 (January 1983): 28–34.

Sassoon, Donald. *One Hundred Years of Socialism: The West European Left in the Twentieth Century*. New York, 1996.

Saunders, Frances Stonor. *The Cultural Cold War: The CIA and the World of Arts and Letters*. New York, 2000.

Schrecker, Ellen. *Many Are the Crimes: McCarthyism in America*. Boston, 1998.

Scott-Smith, Giles. " 'OA Radical Democratic Political Offensive': Melvin J. Lasky, Der Monat, and the Congress for Cultural Freedom." *Journal of Contemporary History* 35 (April 2000): 263–280.

Tanenhaus, Sam. *Whittaker Chambers: A Biography*. New York, 1997.

Warner, Michael. "Origins of the Congress for Cultural Freedom, 1949–1950." *Studies in Intelligence* 38 (Summer 1995): 85–98. [On-line at http://www.odci.gov/csi/studies]

Weinstein, Allen and Alexander Vassiliev. *The Haunted Wood: Soviet Espionage in America—the Stalin Era*. New York, 1999.

Wilkinson, James D. *The Intellectual Resistance in Europe*. Cambridge, Mass., 1981.

Soviet History

Conquest, Robert. *The Great Terror: A Reassessment*. Oxford, 1990.

Dallin, Alexander and F.I. Firsov. *Dimitrov and Stalin, 1934–1943: Letters from the Soviet Archives*. New Haven, 2000.

McDermott, Kevin and Jeremy Agnew. *The Comintern: A History of International Communism from Lenin to Stalin*. London, 1996.

Malia, Martin. *Russia Under Western Eyes: From the Bronze Horseman to the Lenin Mausoleum*. Cambridge, Mass., 1999.

Suny, Ronald Grigor. *The Soviet Experiment: The USSR and Successor States*. Oxford, 1998.

Zubok, Vladislav and Konstantin Pleshakov. *Inside the Kremlin's Cold War: From Stalin to Khrushchev*. Cambridge, Mass., 1996.

Explanations of Some Terms and Names from the Text

11. Palmiro Togliatti (1893–1964)—for forty years the leader of the Italian Communist Party (PCI), building it into western Europe's largest.
27. *Rote Fahne*—Red Flag, the newspaper of the German Communist Party (KPD).
33. Brownshirts—Hitler's storm troops, the Nazi SA.
35. Molotov-Ribbentrop Pact—Nazi-Soviet Pact of 1939, referenced by the foreign ministers' names.
37. OGPU—Soviet secret police, eventually became the GPU, then KGB.
43. Bronislaw Malinowski (1884–1942)—distinguished anthropologist at the University of London.
82. Zimmerwald—site of 1915 meeting of anti-war socialists; less revolutionary than Bolshevism and Third International.
94. *Avanti*—Italy's leading socialist newspaper.
95. *Risorgimento*—unification of Italy in the mid-nineteenth century.
100. André Frossard (1915–95)—French Catholic journalist.
100. Paul Levi (1883–1930)—a German Communist leader.
101. Alexandra Kollontaj (1872–1952)—leading thinker in early Bolshevism; later a Soviet diplomat.
104. Jacques Doriot—former Communist mayor of Saint-Denis, on the outskirts of Paris. Founded the Parti Populaire in France and became a leader in occupation government.
108. Vasil Kolarov (1877–1950)—Bulgarian revolutionary.
110. Matyas Rakosi (1892–1971)—Hungarian Communist Party leader, 1945–56.
110. Antonio Gramsci (1891–1937)—intellectual and political leader who helped found the PCI; imprisoned by Mussolini in 1926. Authored *Prison Letters*.
115. H.L. Mencken (1880–1956)—leading American columnist and critic.
166. Saint Exupéry (1900–44)—French writer, best known for *The Little Prince* (1943).
197. Alexander Kerensky (1881–1970)—head of Provisional Government in late 1917, deposed by Bolshevik revolution.
205. Dnieperstroy and Magnitogorsk—major projects of the Soviets' first Five-Year Plan.

213. Édouard Daladier (1884–1970)—French premier who, along with British premier Neville Chamberlain, signed the Munich Pact, accepting Nazi takeover of Czech land.

216. Genrikh Yagoda (1891–1938)—head of Soviet secret police (GPU) in the 1930s.

224. Pierre Laval (1883–1945)—French politician and statesman who led collaborationist governments in France under Nazi occupation.

230. Harry Pollitt (1890–1960)—British Communist, general secretary of the Party 1929–56 (except 1939–41).

230. Sir George Robey (1869–1954)—British comedian.

239. Otto Braun (1872–1955)—leading member of German Social Democratic Party.

239. Carl Severing (1875–1952)—leading member of German Social Democratic Party.

239. (James) Ramsay MacDonald (1866–1937)—first Labour Party minister in Great Britain.

243. Victor Gollancz (1863–1967)—British writer and publisher.

243. Sir Arthur Bryant (1899–1985)—British historian, biographer of Samuel Pepys.

246. John Strachey (1901–63)—British radical writer.

246. E.M. Forster (1879–1970)—British writer, most famous for *A Passage to India* (1924).

249. Frederico Garcia Lorca (1898–1936)—Spanish poet and dramatist assassinated by Nationalists at outbreak of the Spanish Civil War.

251. Il'ia Ehrenburg (1891–1967)—Soviet writer of the Stalin era.

255. Victor Kravchenko (1905–66)—Soviet defector, author of *I Chose Freedom* (1946).

256. Professor J.B.S. Haldane (1892–1964)—British geneticist and disillusioned Marxist, pioneer in population genetics

THE GOD THAT FAILED

INTRODUCTION

Richard Crossman, M.P.

BIOGRAPHICAL NOTE: *Richard Crossman was born on December 15, 1907.. The son of a barrister, later Mr. Justice Crossman, he was educated at Winchester College and New College, Oxford, where he took first-class honors in classics and philosophy. He remained at Oxford as a Fellow of New College for eight years, teaching Plato and political theory, and simultaneously began his political career as a Socialist on the Oxford City Council.*

In 1937 he became the Labour candidate for Coventry, which he won in the 1945 election.

In 1938 he became Assistant Editor of the New Statesman and Nation, *a position he still holds.*

During the war he served first in the Foreign Office and then on General Eisenhower's Staff, as an expert on Germany in charge of enemy propaganda.

In 1946 he served on the Anglo-American Commission on Palestine, and as a result became the leading English opponent of Mr. Bevin's Palestine policy.

Bibliography: Plato Today, Government and the Governed, Palestine Mission.

This book was conceived in the heat of argument. I was staying with Arthur Koestler in North Wales, and one evening we had reached an unusually barren deadlock in the

1

political discussion of which our friendship seems to consist. "Either you can't or you won't understand," said Koestler. "It's the same with all you comfortable, insular, Anglo-Saxon anti-Communists. You hate our Cassandra cries and resent us as allies—but, when all is said, we ex-Communists are the only people on your side who know what it's all about." And with that the talk veered to why so-and-so had ever become a Communist, and why he had or had not left the Party. When the argument began to boil up again, I said, "Wait. Tell me exactly what happened when *you* joined the Party—not what you feel about it now, but what you felt then." So Koestler began the strange story of his meeting with Herr Schneller in the Schneidemühl paper-mill; and suddenly I interrupted, "This should be a book," and we began to discuss names of ex-Communists capable of telling the truth about themselves.

At first our choice ranged far and wide, but before the night was out we decided to limit the list to half a dozen writers and journalists. We were not in the least interested either in swelling the flood of anti-Communist propaganda or in providing an opportunity for personal apologetics. Our concern was to study the state of mind of the Communist convert, and the atmosphere of the period—from 1917 to 1939—when conversion was so common. For this purpose it was essential that each contributor should be able not to relive the past—that is impossible—but, by an act of imaginative self-analysis, to recreate it, despite the foreknowledge of the present. As I well know, autobiography of this sort is almost impossible for the practical politician: his self-respect distorts the past in terms of the present. So-called scientific analysis is equally misleading; dissecting the personality into a set of psychological and sociological causes, it explains away the emotions, which we wanted described. The objectivity we sought was the power to recollect—if not in tranquillity, at least in "dispassion"— and this power is rarely granted except to the imaginative writer.

It so happens that, in the years between the October Revolution and the Stalin-Hitler Pact, numberless men of letters, both in Europe and America, were attracted to Communism. They were not "typical" converts. Indeed, being people of quite unusual sensitivity, they made most abnormal Communists, just as the literary Catholic is a most abnormal Catholic. They had a heightened perception of the spirit of the age, and felt more acutely than others both its frustrations and its hopes. Their conversion therefore expressed, in an acute and sometimes in a hysterical form, feelings which were dimly shared by the inarticulate millions who felt that Russia was on the side of the workers. The intellectual in politics is always "unbalanced," in the estimation of his colleagues. He peers round the next corner while they keep their eyes on the road, and he risks his faith on unrealized ideas, instead of confining it prudently to humdrum loyalties. He is "in advance," and, in this sense, an extremist. If history justifies his premonitions, well and good. But if, on the contrary, history takes the other turning, he must either march forward into the dead end, or ignominiously turn back, repudiating ideas which have become part of his personality.

In this book, six intellectuals describe the journey into Communism, and the return. They saw it at first from a long way off—just as their predecessors 130 years ago saw the French Revolution—as a vision of the Kingdom of God on earth; and, like Wordsworth and Shelley, they dedicated their talents to working humbly for its coming. They were not discouraged by the rebuffs of the professional revolutionaries, or by the jeers of their opponents, until each discovered the gap between his own vision of God and the reality of the Communist State —and the conflict of conscience reached breaking point.

A very few men can claim to have seen round this particular corner in history correctly. Bertrand Russell has been able to republish his *Bolshevism: Practice and Theory*, written in 1920, without altering a single comma; but most of those, who are now so wise and contemptuous after the event, were either blind, as Edmund Burke in his day was blind, to the meaning of the Russian Revolution, or have merely oscillated with the pendulum—reviling, praising, and then reviling again, according to the dictates of public policy. These six pieces of autobiography should at least reveal the dangers of this facile anti-Communism of expediency. That Communism, as a way of life, should, even for a few years, have captured the profoundly Christian personality of Silone and attracted individualists such as Gide and Koestler, reveals a dreadful deficiency in European democracy. That Richard Wright, as a struggling Negro writer in Chicago, moved almost as a matter of course into the Communist Party, is in itself an indictment of the American way of life. Louis Fischer, on the other hand, represents that distinguished group of British and American foreign correspondents who put their faith in Russia, not so much through respect for Communism, as through disillusionment with Western democracy and—much later—a nausea of appeasement. Stephen Spender, the English poet, was driven by much the same impulses. The Spanish Civil War seemed to him, as it did to nearly all his contemporaries, the touchstone of world politics. It was the cause of his brief sojourn in the Party and also, at a later stage, of his repudiation of it.

The only link, indeed, between these six very different personalities is that all of them—after tortured struggles of conscience—chose Communism because they had lost faith in democracy and were willing to sacrifice "bourgeois liberties" in order to defeat Fascism. Their conversion, in fact, was rooted in despair—a despair of Western values. It is easy enough in retrospect to see that this despair was hysterical. Fascism, after all, *was* overcome, without the surrender of civil liberties which Communism involves. But how could Silone foresee this in the 1920's, when the Democracies were courting Mussolini and only the Communists in Italy were organizing a serious Resistance Movement? Were Gide and Koestler so obviously wrong, at the time when they became Communists, in feeling that German and French democracy were corrupt and would surrender to Fascism? Part of the value of this book is that it jogs our memories so uncomfortably; and reminds us of the terrible loneliness experienced by the "premature anti-Fascists," the men and women who understood Fascism and tried to fight it before it was respectable to do so. It was that loneliness which opened their minds to the appeal of Communism.

This appeal was felt with particular strength by those who were too honest to accept the prevailing belief in an automatic Progress, a steadily expanding capitalism, and the abolition of power politics. They saw that Coolidgism in America, Baldwinism and MacDonaldism in Britain, and the "collective pacifism" of the League of Nations Union, were lazy intellectual shams, which blinded most of us cautious, respectable democrats to the catastrophe into which we were drifting. Because they had a premonition of catastrophe, they looked for a philosophy with which they could analyze it and overcome it—and many of them found what they needed in Marxism.

The intellectual attraction of Marxism was that it exploded liberal fallacies—which really were fallacies. It taught the bitter truth that progress is not automatic, that boom and slump are inherent in capitalism, that social injustice and racial discrimination are not cured merely by the passage of time, and that power politics cannot be "abolished," but only used for good or bad ends. If the choice had to be made between two materialist philosophies, no intelligent man after 1917 could choose the dogma of automatic Progress, which so many influential people then assumed to be the only basis of democracy. The choice seemed to lie between an extreme Right, determined to use power in order to crush human freedom, and a Left which seemed eager to use it in order to free humanity. Western democracy today is not so callow or so materialist as it was in that dreary armistice between the wars. But it has taken two world wars and two totalitarian revolutions to make it begin to understand that its task is not to allow Progress to do its work for it, but to provide an alternative to world revolution by planning the co-operation of free peoples.

If despair and loneliness were the main motives for conversion to Communism, they were greatly strengthened by the Christian conscience. Here again, the intellectual, though he may have abandoned orthodox Christianity, felt its prickings far more acutely than many of his unreflective church-going neighbors. He at least was aware of the unfairness of the status and privileges which he enjoyed, whether by reason of race or class or education. The emotional appeal of Communism lay precisely in the sacrifices—both material and spiritual—which it demanded of the convert. You can call the response masochistic, or describe it as a sincere desire to serve mankind. But, whatever name you use, the idea of an active comradeship of struggle—involving personal sacrifice and abolishing differences of class and race—has had a compulsive power in every Western democracy. The attraction of the ordinary political party is what it offers to its members: the attraction of Communism was that it offered nothing and demanded everything, including the surrender of spiritual freedom.

Here, indeed, is the explanation of a phenomenon which has puzzled many observers. How could these intellectuals accept the dogmatism of Stalinism? The answer is to be found scattered through the pages which follow. For the intellectual, material comforts are relatively unimportant; what he cares most about is spiritual freedom. The strength of the Catholic Church has always been that it demands the sacrifice of that freedom uncompromisingly, and condemns spiritual pride as a deadly sin. The Communist novice, subjecting his soul to the canon law of the Kremlin, felt something of the release which Catholicism also brings to the intellectual, wearied and worried by the privilege of freedom.

Once the renunciation has been made, the mind, instead of operating freely, becomes the servant of a higher and unquestioned purpose. To deny the truth is an act of service. This, of course, is why it is useless to discuss any particular aspect of politics with a Communist. Any genuine intellectual contact which you have with him involves a challenge to his fundamental faith, a struggle for his soul. For it is very much easier to lay the oblation of spiritual pride on the altar of world revolution than to snatch it back again.

This may be one reason why Communism has had much more success in Catholic than in Protestant countries. The Protestant is, at least in origin, a conscientious objector against spiritual subjection to any hierarchy. He claims to know what is right or wrong by the inner light, and democracy for him is not merely a convenient or a just form of government, but a necessity of human dignity. His prototype is Prometheus, who stole the fire from heaven and hangs eternally on the Caucasian mountain, with the eagle pecking out his liver, because he refused to surrender the right to assist his fellow men by intellectual endeavor. I sometimes ask myself why, as a very young man, staying with Willi Münzenberg, the Communist leader, in Berlin, I never felt the faintest temptation to accept his invitation to go with him to Russia. I was captivated by his remarkable personality—described by Arthur Koestler in this book—and Marxism seemed to offer the completion of the Platonic political philosophy which was my main study. I was arrogantly certain—it was the summer of 1931—that German Social Democracy would crumble before the Nazis, and that a war was unavoidable when Hitler had come to power. Then why did I feel no inner response to the Communist appeal? The answer, I am pretty sure, was sheer nonconformist cussedness, or, if you prefer it, pride. No Pope for me, whether spiritual or secular. One can see the same motive at work in Stephen Spender, when, immediately after joining the Party, he wrote a "deviationist" article in the *Daily Worker*, again out of sheer cussedness. I like to think that his experience of Communism is as typically British as that of the comrade, described by Silone, whose innocent reaction to a deliberate lie caused a guffaw which rolled through the whole Kremlin. As a nation, we British produce more than our share of heretics, because we have been endowed with more than our due of conscientious objection to infallibility. After all, in his own period Henry VIII was the prototype of Titoism.

But to return to Europe. One of the strangest revelations of these six autobiographies is the attitude of the professional Communists to the intellectual convert. They not only resented and suspected him, but apparently subjected him to constant and deliberate mental torture. At first, this treatment only confirmed his faith and heightened his sense of humility before the true-born proletarian. Somehow he must achieve by mental training the qualities which, as he fondly imagined, the worker has by nature. But it is clear that, as soon as the intellectual convert began to know more about conditions in Russia, his mood changed. Humility was replaced—Silone describes this very clearly—by a belief (for which Marx, who had an utter contempt for the Slavs, gave plenty of authority) that the West must bring enlightenment to the East, and the middle class to the proletariat. This belief was both the beginning of disillusionment and an excuse for remaining in the Party. Disillusionment, because the main motive for conversion had been despair of Western civilization, which was now found to contain values essential for the redemption of Russian Communism; an excuse, because it could be argued that, if the Western influence were withdrawn, Oriental brutality would turn the defense of human freedom into a loathsome tyranny.

Here was a new and even more terrible conflict of conscience, which André Gide resolved by his classic statement of the Western case against Russian Communism.* Gide's

* After he had expressed his readiness to contribute to this book, M. Gide found that his state of health did not permit him to complete the task. I was most unwilling to lose what I felt to be an essential element in a study of this kind, and was delighted to persuade Dr. Enid Starkie to undertake the task of editing M. Gide's writings on this subject. She has done this in the closest consultation with M. Gide, who approved the final version. The text is her own, but based on paraphrases of the two pamphlets which he wrote in 1936 on his return from the Soviet Union, as well as material from his *Journal* and from a discussion held in Paris at *l'Union pour la Vérité* in 1935. I would like to express here my gratitude and that of the publishers to Dr. Starkie for the skill with which she has completed a most delicate task. R. H. S. C.

withdrawal would have been followed in the late 1930's by that of thousands of other intellectuals, if it had not been for the Spanish War and the Western policy of nonintervention. The tragedy of the Spanish War and the campaign for a Popular Front against Fascism brought a whole new generation of young Westerners either into the Communist Party or into the closest collaboration with it, and delayed the withdrawal of many who were already appalled by their experiences. To denounce Communism now seemed tantamount to supporting Hitler and Chamberlain. For many, however, this conflict was soon resolved by the Stalin-Hitler Pact.

Richard Wright's story has a special interest, because it introduces in an American setting the issues of "imperialism" and race. As a Negro dweller in the Chicago slums, he felt, as no Western intellectual could ever feel, the compelling power of a creed which seemed to provide a complete and final answer to the problems of both social and racial injustice. All the other contributors made a conscious sacrifice of personal status and personal liberty in accepting Communist discipline; for Wright, that discipline was a glorious release of pent-up energies. *His* sacrifice was made when he left the Party.

> For I knew in my heart that I should never be able to write that way again, should never be able to feel with that simple sharpness about life, should never again express such passionate hope, should never again make so total a commitment of faith.

This tragic admission is a reminder that, whatever its failures in the West, Communism still comes as a liberating force among the Colored peoples who make up the great majority of mankind. As an American Negro, Wright both belongs and does not belong to Western democracy. It was as an American writer, imbued with a Western sense of human dignity and artistic values, that he fell afoul of the Communist apparatus. But as a Negro, he utters that tragic sentence after he has left the Party. "I'll be for them, even if they are not for me."

Millions of Colored people are not subjected to the complex conflict through which Richard Wright passed. For them, Western democracy still means quite simply "white ascendancy." Outside the Indian subcontinent, where equality has been achieved through a unique act of Western statesmanship, Communism is still a gospel of liberation among the Colored peoples; and the Chinese or African intellectual can accept it as such without destroying one half of his personality.

Perhaps this explains the indifference shown by the Russians and the Party apparatus towards the Western intelligentsia. In the last resort, the Kremlin may well reckon, the influence of this unreliably conscientious intelligentsia will be negligible, since the coming world struggle will be fought not between class and class inside each nation, but between the proletarian nations and their opponents. Be that as it may, the brutality of the treatment of the Western intellectual is indisputable. If the Comintern had shown only an occasional mark of respect at any time in the last thirty years, it could have won the support of the largest section of progressive thought throughout the Western world. Instead, from the first it seems to have accepted that support reluctantly, and done everything to alienate it. Not one of the contributors to this book, for instance, deserted Communism willingly or with a clear conscience. Not one would have hesitated to return, at any stage in the protracted process of withdrawal which each describes, if the Party had shown a gleam of understanding of his belief in human freedom and human dignity. But no! With relentless selectivity, the Communist machine has winnowed out the grain and retained only the chaff of Western culture.

What happens to the Communist convert when he renounces the faith? Louis Fischer, Stephen Spender and André Gide never worked with the inner hierarchy: Louis Fischer, indeed, at no time joined the Party. All of them were essentially "fellow-travelers," whose personalities were not molded into the life of the Party. Their withdrawal, therefore, though agonizing, did not permanently distort their natures. Silone,

Koestler and Richard Wright, on the other hand, will never escape from Communism. Their lives will always be lived inside its dialectic, and their battle against the Soviet Union will always be a reflection of a searing inner struggle. The true ex-Communist can never again be a whole personality. In the case of Koestler, this inner conflict is the mainspring of his creative work. The Yogi looks in the mirror, sees the Commissar, and breaks the glass in rage. His writing is not an act of purification, which brings tranquillity, but a merciless interrogation of his Western self—and the movements in the outside world which seem to reflect it—by another self, indifferent to suffering. Silone, by moving full circle back to the Christian ethic from which he started, has achieved a moral poise which gives him a certain "distance" from the conflict. His basic faith today is "a feeling of reverence for that which is always trying to excel itself in mankind and lies at the root of his eternal disquiet."

One thing is clear from studying the varied experiences of these six men. Silone was joking when he said to Togliatti that the final battle would be between the Communists and the ex-Communists. But no one who has not wrestled with Communism as a philosophy, and Communists as political opponents can really understand the values of Western Democracy. The Devil once lived in Heaven, and those who have not met him are unlikely to recognize an angel when they see one.

PART I

The Initiates

Arthur Koestler

BIOGRAPHICAL NOTE: *Arthur Koestler was born on September 5, 1905, in Budapest, of Hungarian father and Viennese mother. He was educated in Vienna. After two years' roving in the Near East, he became Near East correspondent for the Ullstein Berlin Liberal newspaper chain.*

He joined the Communist Party on December 31, 1931, and left it in the spring of 1938, after his imprisonment by the Franco authorities during the Civil War in Spain, which he described in Spanish Testament.

Imprisoned once again by the French authorities in 1939, he escaped to England to join the British Army in 1940.

His works include Darkness at Noon, Scum of the Earth, Arrival and Departure, Thieves in the Night, The Yogi and the Commissar, *and* Insight and Outlook.

A faith is not acquired by reasoning. One does not fall in love with a woman, or enter the womb of a church, as a result of logical persuasion. Reason may defend an act of faith—but only after the act has been committed, and the man committed to the act. Persuasion may play a part in a man's conversion; but only the part of bringing to its full and conscious climax a process which has been maturing in regions where no persuasion can penetrate. A faith is not acquired; it grows like a tree. Its crown points to the sky; its roots grow

15

downward into the past and are nourished by the dark sap of the ancestral humus.

From the psychologist's point of view, there is little difference between a revolutionary and a traditionalist faith. All true faith is uncompromising, radical, purist; hence the true traditionalist is always a revolutionary zealot in conflict with pharisaian society, with the lukewarm corrupters of the creed. And vice versa: the revolutionary's Utopia, which in appearance represents a complete break with the past, is always modeled on some image of the lost Paradise, of a legendary Golden Age. The classless Communist society, according to Marx and Engels, was to be a revival, at the end of the dialectical spiral, of the primitive Communist society which stood at its beginning. Thus all true faith involves a revolt against the believer's social environment, and the projection into the future of an ideal derived from the remote past. All Utopias are fed from the sources of mythology; the social engineer's blueprints are merely revised editions of the ancient text.

Devotion to pure Utopia, and revolt against a polluted society, are thus the two poles which provide the tension of all militant creeds. To ask which of the two makes the current flow—attraction by the ideal or repulsion by the social environment—is to ask the old question about the hen and the egg. To the psychiatrist, both the craving for Utopia and the rebellion against the status quo are symptoms of social maladjustment. To the social reformer, both are symptoms of a healthy rational attitude. The psychiatrist is apt to forget that smooth adjustment to a deformed society creates deformed individuals. The reformer is equally apt to forget that hatred, even of the objectively hateful, does not produce that charity and justice on which a utopian society must be based.

Thus each of the two attitudes, the sociologist's and the psychologist's, reflects a half-truth. It is true that the case-history of most revolutionaries and reformers reveals a neurotic conflict with family or society. But this only proves, to paraphrase Marx, that a moribund society creates its own morbid gravediggers.

It is also true that in the face of revolting injustice the only honorable attitude is to revolt, and to leave introspection for better times. But if we survey history and compare the lofty aims, in the name of which revolutions were started, and the sorry end to which they came, we see again and again how a polluted civilization pollutes its own revolutionary offspring.

Fitting the two half-truths—the sociologist's and the psychologist's—together, we conclude that if on the one hand oversensitivity to social injustice and obsessional craving for Utopia are signs of neurotic maladjustment, society may, on the other hand, reach a state of decay where the neurotic rebel causes more joy in heaven than the sane executive who orders pigs to be drowned under the eyes of starving men. This in fact was the state of our civilization when, in December, 1931, at the age of twenty-six, I joined the Communist Party of Germany.

★

I became converted because I was ripe for it and lived in a disintegrating society thirsting for faith. But the day when I was given my Party card was merely the climax of a development which had started long before I had read about the drowned pigs or heard the names of Marx and Lenin. Its roots reach back into childhood; and though each of us, comrades of the Pink Decade, had individual roots with different twists in them, we are products of, by and large, the same generation and cultural climate. It is this unity underlying diversity which makes me hope that my story is worth telling.

I was born in 1905 in Budapest; we lived there till 1919, when we moved to Vienna. Until the First World War we were comfortably off, a typical Continental middle-middle-class family: my father was the Hungarian representative of some old-established British and German textile manufacturers. In September, 1914, this form of existence, like so many others, came to an abrupt end; my father never found his feet again. He embarked on a number of ventures which became the more fantastic the more he lost self-confidence in a changed world. He opened a factory for radioactive soap; he backed several crank-inventions (everlasting electric bulbs, self-heating bed bricks and the like); and finally lost the ɩemains of his capital in the Austrian inflation of the early 'twenties. I left home at twenty-one, and from that day became the only financial support of my parents.

At the age of nine, when our middle-class idyl collapsed, I had suddenly become conscious of the economic Facts of Life. As an only child, I continued to be pampered by my parents; but, well aware of the family crisis, and torn by pity for my father, who was of a generous and somewhat childlike disposition, I suffered a pang of guilt whenever they bought me books or toys. This continued later on, when every suit I bought for myself meant so much less to send home. Simultaneously, I developed a strong dislike of the obviously rich; not because they could afford to buy things (envy plays a much smaller part in social conflict than is generally assumed) but because they were able to do so without a guilty conscience. Thus I projected a personal predicament onto the structure of society at large.

It was certainly a tortuous way of acquiring a social conscience. But precisely because of the intimate nature of the conflict, the faith which grew out of it became an equally intimate part of my self. It did not, for some years, crystallize into a political creed; at first it took the form of a mawkishly sentimental attitude. Every contact with people poorer than myself was unbearable—the boy at school who had no gloves and red chilblains on his fingers, the former traveling salesman of my father's reduced to cadging occasional meals —all of them were additions to the load of guilt on my back. The analyst would have no difficulty in showing that the roots of this guilt-complex go deeper than the crisis in our household budget; but if he were to dig even deeper, piercing through the individual layers of the case, he would strike the archetypal pattern which has produced millions of particular variations on the same theme—"Woe, for they chant to the sound of harps and anoint themselves, but are not grieved for the affliction of the people."

Thus sensitized by a personal conflict, I was ripe for the shock of learning that wheat was burned, fruit artificially spoiled and pigs were drowned in the depression years to keep prices up and enable fat capitalists to chant to the sound of harps, while Europe trembled under the torn boots of hunger-marchers and my father hid his frayed cuffs under the table. The frayed cuffs and drowned pigs blended into one emotional explosion, as the fuse of the archetype was touched off. We sang the "Internationale," but the words might as well have been the older ones: "Woe to the shepherds who feed themselves, but feed not their flocks."

In other respects, too, the story is more typical than it seems. A considerable proportion of the middle classes in central Europe was, like ourselves, ruined by the inflation of the twenties. It was the beginning of Europe's decline. This disintegration of the middle strata of society started the fatal process of polarization which continues to this day. The pauperized bourgeois became rebels of the Right or Left; Schickelgrüber and Djugashwili shared about equally the benefits of the social migration. Those who refused to admit that they had become déclassé, who clung to the empty shell of gentility, joined the Nazis and found comfort in blaming their fate on Versailles and the Jews. Many did not even have that consolation; they lived on pointlessly, like a great black swarm of tired winterflies crawling over the dim windows of Europe, members of a class displaced by history.

The other half turned Left, thus confirming the prophecy of the "Communist Manifesto":

> Entire sections of the ruling classes are . . . precipitated into the proletariat, or are at least threatened in their conditions of existence. They . . . supply the proletariat with fresh elements of enlightenment and progress.

That "fresh element of enlightenment," I discovered to my delight, was I. As long as I had been nearly starving, I had regarded myself as a temporarily displaced offspring of the bourgeoisie. In 1931, when at last I had achieved a comfortable income, I found that it was time to join the ranks of the proletariat. But the irony of this sequence only occurred to me in retrospect.

> The bourgeois family will vanish as a matter of course with the vanishing of Capital. . . . The bourgeois claptrap about the family and education, about the haloed correlation of parent and child, becomes all the more disgusting the more, by the action of modern industry, all family ties among the proletarians are torn asunder. . . .

Thus the "Communist Manifesto." Every page of Marx, and even more of Engels, brought a new revelation, and an intellectual delight which I had only experienced once before, at my first contact with Freud. Torn from its context, the above passage sounds ridiculous; as part of a closed system which made social philosophy fall into a lucid and comprehensive pattern, the demonstration of the historical relativity of institutions and ideals—of family, class, patriotism, bourgeois morality, sexual taboos—had the intoxicating effect of a sudden liberation from the rusty chains with which a pre-1914 middle-class childhood had cluttered one's mind. Today, when Marxist philosophy has degenerated into a Byzantine cult and virtually every single tenet of the Marxist program has become twisted round into its opposite, it is difficult to recapture that mood of emotional fervor and intellectual bliss.

I was ripe to be converted, as a result of my personal case-history; thousands of other members of the intelligentsia and the middle classes of my generation were ripe for it, by virtue of other personal case-histories; but, however much these differed from case to case, they had a common denominator: the rapid disintegration of moral values, of the pre-1914 pattern of life in postwar Europe, and the simultaneous lure of the new revelation which had come from the East.

I joined the Party (which to this day remains "the" Party

for all of us who once belonged to it) in 1931, at the beginning
of that short-lived period of optimism, of that abortive spiritual renaissance, later known as the Pink Decade. The stars
of that treacherous dawn were Barbusse, Romain Rolland,
Gide and Malraux in France; Piscator, Becher, Renn, Brecht,
Eisler, Säghers in Germany; Auden, Isherwood, Spender in
England; Dos Passos, Upton Sinclair, Steinbeck in the United
States. (Of course, not all of them were members of the
Communist Party.) The cultural atmosphere was saturated
with Progressive Writers' congresses, experimental theaters,
committees for peace and against Fascism, societies for cultural relations with the USSR, Russian films and avant-garde
magazines. It looked indeed as if the Western world, convulsed
by the aftermath of war, scourged by inflation, depression,
unemployment and the absence of a faith to live for, was at
last going to

> *Clear from the head the masses of impressive rubbish;*
> *Rally the lost and trembling forces of the will,*
> *Gather them up and let them loose upon the earth,*
> *Till they construct at last a human justice.*
>
> Auden

The new star of Bethlehem had risen in the East; and for
a modest sum, Intourist was prepared to allow you a short and
well-focused glimpse of the Promised Land.

I lived at that time in Berlin. For the last five years, I had
been working for the Ullstein chain of newspapers—first as a
foreign correspondent in Palestine and the Middle East, then
in Paris. Finally, in 1930, I joined the editorial staff in the
Berlin "House." For a better understanding of what follows,
a few words have to be said about the House of Ullstein,
symbol of the Weimar Republic.

Ullstein's was a kind of super-trust; the largest organization
of its kind in Europe, and probably in the world. They published four daily papers in Berlin alone, among these the
venerable *Vossische Zeitung,* founded in the eighteenth century, and the *B. Z. am Mittag,* an evening paper with a record

circulation and a record speed in getting the news out. Apart from these, Ullstein's published more than a dozen weekly and monthly periodicals, ran their own news service, their own travel agency, etc., and were one of the leading book publishers. The firm was owned by the brothers Ullstein—they were five, like the original Rothschild brothers, and like them also, they were Jews. Their policy was liberal and democratic, and in cultural matters progressive to the point of avant-gardism. They were antimilitaristic, antichauvinistic, and it was largely due to their influence on public opinion that the policy of Franco-German rapprochement of the Briand-Stresemann era became a vogue among the progressive part of the German people. The firm of Ullstein was not only a political power in Germany; it was at the same time the embodiment of everything progressive and cosmopolitan in the Weimar Republic. The atmosphere in the "House" in the Kochstrasse was more that of a Ministry than of an editorial office.

My transfer from the Paris office to the Berlin house was due to an article I wrote on the occasion of the award of the Nobel Prize for Physics to the Prince de Broglie. My bosses decided that I had a knack for popularizing science (I had been a student of science in Vienna) and offered me the job of Science Editor of the *Vossische* and adviser on matters scientific to the rest of the Ullstein publications. I arrived in Berlin on the fateful day of September 14, 1930—the day of the Reichstag Election in which the National Socialist Party, in one mighty leap, increased the number of its deputies from 4 to 107. The Communists had also registered important gains; the democratic parties of the Center were crushed. It was the beginning of the end of Weimar; the situation was epitomized in the title of Knickerbocker's best-seller: *Germany,— Fascist or Soviet?* Obviously there was no "third alternative."

I did my job, writing about electrons, chromosomes, rocket-ships, Neanderthal men, spiral nebulae and the universe at large; but the pressure of events increased rapidly. With one-third of its wage-earners unemployed, Germany lived in a state of latent civil war, and if one wasn't prepared to be swept along as a passive victim by the approaching hurricane it became imperative to take sides. Stresemann's party was dead. The Socialists pursued a policy of opportunist compromise. Even by a process of pure elimination, the Communists, with the mighty Soviet Union behind them, seemed the only force capable of resisting the onrush of the primitive horde with its swastika totem. But it was not by a process of elimination that I became a Communist. Tired of electrons and wave-mechanics, I began for the first time to read Marx, Engels and Lenin in earnest. By the time I had finished with *Feuerbach* and *State and Revolution,* something had clicked in my brain which shook me like a mental explosion. To say that one had "seen the light" is a poor description of the mental rapture which only the convert knows (regardless of what faith he has been converted to). The new light seems to pour from all directions across the skull; the whole universe falls into pattern like the stray pieces of a jigsaw puzzle assembled by magic at one stroke. There is now an answer to every question, doubts and conflicts are a matter of the tortured past—a past already remote, when one had lived in dismal ignorance in the tasteless, colorless world of those who *don't know.* Nothing henceforth can disturb the convert's inner peace and serenity—except the occasional fear of losing faith again, losing thereby what alone makes life worth living, and falling back into the outer darkness, where there is wailing and gnashing of teeth. This may explain how Communists, with eyes to see and brains to think with, can still act in subjective *bona fides,* anno Domini 1949. At all times and in all creeds only a minority has been capable of courting excommunication and committing emotional hara-kiri in the name of an abstract truth.

★

The date on which I applied for membership of the Communist Party of Germany is easy to remember: it was the thirty-first of December, 1931. The new life was to start with the new calendar-year. I applied by means of a letter addressed to the Central Committee of the KPD;[1] the letter contained a short *curriculum vitae* and stated my readiness to serve the cause in whatever capacity the Party decided.

It was not usual to apply for membership by writing to the Central Committee; I did it on the advice of friends in close touch with the Party. The normal procedure was to join one of the Party-cells, the basic units of the Party's organizational network. There were two types of cells: "workshop-cells" (*Betriebs-Zellen*), which comprised the Party members of a given factory, workshop, office or any other enterprise; and "street-cells" (*Strassen-Zellen*), organized according to residential blocks. Most wage-earners belonged both to the workshop-cell of the place where they were employed, and to the street-cell of their homes. This system was universal in all countries where the Party led a legal existence. It was an iron rule that each Party member, however high up in the hierarchy, must belong to a cell. There was, so we were told, a "workshop-cell" even in the Kremlin, in which members of the Politbureau, sentries and charwomen discussed the policy of the Party in fraternal democracy at the usual weekly meeting, and where Stalin was told off if he forgot to pay his membership fee.

However, my friend N., who had played a decisive part in my conversion, strongly advised me against joining a cell in the usual way (I call him N., for he left the Party years ago and lives now in a country where even a buried and renounced Communist past might mean trouble for a foreigner). N. was a former plumber's apprentice who, through evening classes and dogged night-reading, had made the grade and become a well-known political writer. He knew his Marx and Lenin backwards and forwards and had that absolute, serene faith which exerts a hypnotic power over other people's minds. "Don't be a fool," he explained to me, "once you join a cell

[1] *Kommunistische Partei Deutschlands.*

and it becomes known that you have become a Party member, you will lose your job with the Ullsteins. And that job is an important asset for the Party."

I must add that in the meantime, while retaining my science job at the *Vossische* I had been appointed Foreign Editor of the *B. Z. am Mittag:* a post which carried a certain political influence and gave access to a good deal of political inside information.

So, on N.'s advice, I wrote direct to the Central Committee.

A week or so later the answer came in the form of a rather puzzling letter. It was typed on a blank sheet of paper without heading, and ran somewhat as follows:

Dear Sir,

  With reference to your esteemed of Dec. 31, we shall be glad if you will meet a representative of our firm, Herr Schneller, at the offices of the Schneidemühl paper-mill, —— strasse, next Monday at 3 P.M.

                              Yours truly,
                                (illegible signature)

The Schneidemühl paper-mills were well-known in Germany, but it had never occurred to me that they had anything to do with the KPD. What exactly the connection was, I do not know; the fact remains that their Berlin offices were used as an inconspicuous rendezvous for confidential interviews. I did not understand the reason for all this conspiratorial secrecy; but I was thrilled and excited. When, at the appointed time, I arrived at Schneidemühl and asked for "Herr Schneller," the girl at the inquiry desk gave me what is commonly called a searching look but might be more correctly described as a fish-eyed stare. Since then I have often met that look in similar situations; whenever the desire for fraternal complicity is checked by distrust and fear, people exchange glances which are neither "penetrating" nor "searching"; they goggle at each other dully, like fish.

"Have you a date with Ernst?" she asked.

"No—with Herr Schneller."

This stupidity seemed somehow to convince her of my *bona fides*. She said Herr Ernst Schneller hadn't arrived yet, and told me to sit down and wait. I waited—for over half an hour. It was my first experience of that unpunctuality which was *de rigueur* in the higher strata of the Party. The Russians, as semi-orientals, are congenitally unpunctual; and as, consciously or unconsciously, every Party bureaucrat tried to live up to Russian style, the habit gradually filtered down from the top Comintern bureaucracy into every national CP in Europe.

At last he turned up. He introduced himself, Continental fashion, by barking out "Schneller"; I barked "Koestler"; we shook hands and after a perfunctory apology for being "a little late" he invited me to a café across the street. He was a thin, bony man of about thirty-five, with a pinched, taut-skinned face and an awkward smile. His manner was equally awkward; he seemed all the time ill at ease. I took him for an insignificant underling in the Party bureaucracy, and learned only later that his name really was Ernst Schneller—and that he was *the* Schneller, member of the German Central Committee and head of the *Agitprop* (Department for Agitation and Propaganda). Again much later, I learned that he was also the head of the "Apparat N"[2]—one of the four or five independent and parallel intelligence organizations, some of which were run by the German Party, some directly by the OGPU. What exactly Schneller's Apparat did, whether military intelligence work or just harmless industrial espionage, I do not know to this day. Schneller himself was sentenced by the Nazis to six years' hard labor, and died, or was killed, in jail.

Of all this of course I knew nothing when I met that insignificant, rather shabby-looking, thin man at the shabby offices of Schneidemühl's, my first contact with the Party. Of our conversation in the little café, I remember that he mentioned that he was a vegetarian and lived mainly on raw

[2] I do not actually remember by which letter Schneller's organization was known.

vegetables and fruit; it seemed to explain that bony, parched face. I also remember that to my question whether he had read a certain article in a newspaper, he answered that he never read bourgeois papers; the only paper he read was the official Party organ, *Rote Fahne*. This confirmed my opinion that the Central Committee had sent me some narrow-minded, sectarian petty-bureaucrat; the absurdity of a propaganda-chief who only reads his own paper did not dawn on me until later, when I learned of Schneller's official function. He did not ask many questions, but inquired in some detail about the exact position I held at Ullstein's. I told him of my desire to throw up my job and to work for the Party only, as a propagandist or, preferably, as a tractor-driver in the Soviet Union. (This was the period of enforced collectivization, and the Soviet Press was calling desperately for tractor-drivers.) My friend N. had already warned me against this idea, which he called "typical petty-bourgeois romanticism," and said that if I talked about it to any Party official, I would make a fool of myself. But I thought him rather cynical and couldn't see what was wrong with being a tractor-driver for a year or two, if that was the most urgent need on the Front of Socialist Reconstruction. Schneller, however, explained to me patiently that the first duty of every Communist was to work for the Revolution in his own country; to be admitted to the Soviet Union, where the Revolution had already triumphed, was a rare privilege, reserved for veterans of the movement. It would be equally wrong to quit my job; I could be much more useful to the Party by carrying on with it and keeping mum about my political convictions. Useful in what way? I asked. After all, I couldn't turn the *B. Z.* into a Communist paper, or change the policy of the House of Ullstein. Schneller said I was "putting the question in a mechanistic form"; there were many ways by which I could influence the policy of the paper through small touches; for instance, by featuring more prominently the dangers to world peace which Japanese aggression against China represented (at that time

Russia's main fear was a Japanese attack). We could, if I wished, meet once a week to discuss these matters, or even better, he could delegate somebody less busy than himself, who would be at my disposal at practically any time for my political guidance. Besides, through this mutual friend, I could hand on to the Party any political information of special interest which came my way. The Party would probably be forced underground quite soon, and, if that happened, people like myself, in respectable positions, untainted by suspicion, would be even more valuable in the life-and-death struggle against Fascism and imperialistic aggression. All this sounded quite reasonable, and my initial aversion for Schneller soon changed into respect for his simple and astute way of arguing. We agreed to meet in a week's time, when he would introduce me to my future political guide. "Who is that going to be?" I asked. "A comrade called Edgar," said Schneller.

After saying goodbye to him, it suddenly occurred to me that nothing had been said about my formal admission to the Party. The whole thing was left in the air; was I henceforth a real Communist or not? I ran after Schneller and put the question to him. He smiled his awkward smile and said: "If you insist, we will make you a Party member, but on condition that your membership remains secret. You won't be attached to any Party-cell and you will be known in the Party under a different name." I agreed to this rather ruefully, for if debarred from admission to a cell, I would not be able to enter the life, atmosphere and fraternity of the Party. "Tell me what cover-name you choose," said Schneller, "and I'll bring along your Party card the next time." The name which occurred to me after the usual blank second was: "Ivan Steinberg." "Ivan," obviously, because it sounded Russian. Steinberg was the name of a friend, a psychoanalyst in Tel Aviv, whom I hadn't seen or heard of for several years. He used to try to persuade me to finish my studies, which I had broken off, at college in Vienna. "If you don't graduate," he once said, "you will always remain a vagabond. Whatever position you achieve, people will always smell out the tramp in you."

I met Schneller again one week later, at the same place. Instead of Edgar, he had brought a girl along, whom he introduced as Comrade Paula, a collaborator of Edgar's. She was a dark, blowsy girl with a slight squint, about twenty-five. Again we went to the little café, and there Schneller explained that Paula was to function as a liaison between Edgar and me; Edgar was "difficult to reach" but I could get Paula any time on the telephone and she in turn could always get hold of Edgar. In other words I was not to be trusted with Edgar's identity and address.

It should be noted that at this time—January, 1932—the Communist Party was still legal in Germany; its Deputies, like Schneller, sat in the Reichstag; its newspapers called every morning openly for strikes and revolution; its mass-meetings were given the usual police protection; its para-military organization, the RFB (*Roter Frontkämpfer Bund*, "League of Red Ex-Servicemen") was one of the four officially recognized private armies in the country (the other three were the Nazi SA, the Nationalist Stahlhelm, and the Social Democratic Reichsbanner).

But at the same time the Party was preparing to go underground; and, apart from this contingency, its activities were for the most part of an illegal, underground character. The new recruit to the Party found himself plunged into a strange world, as if he were entering a deep-sea aquarium with its phosphorescent light and fleeting, elusive shapes. It was a world populated by people with Christian names only—Edgars and Paulas and Ivans—without surname or address. This was true not only of the people of the various Apparat nets—and the majority of the Party members had some indirect contact with one Apparat or the other—but even of the rank and file in the cells. It was a paradoxical atmosphere—a blend of fraternal comradeship and mutual distrust. Its motto might have been: Love your comrade, but don't trust him an inch—both in your own interest, for he may betray you; and in his, because the less he is tempted to betray, the better for him. This, of course, is true of every underground movement; and it was so much taken for granted that nobody seemed to realize the gradual transformation of character and of human relationships which a long Party career infallibly produced.

This second meeting with Schneller was the last one. We again went to the café, where I wrote down Paula's telephone number and arranged to meet her two days later at my flat. Then Schneller produced my Party card, with "Ivan Steinberg" written on it, and we shook hands awkwardly. Paula gave me the same fish-eyed look as the girl at the reception desk. I felt it would be a long time before I would be trusted by girls of this type. They were all dowdily dressed, and their faces had a neglected appearance, as if they disdained the effort to be pretty as a bourgeois convention; and they all had that bold stare which proclaimed that they could not be fooled.

Before we parted, Schneller said with his embarrassed smile: "Now that you are a member of the Party, you must say 'thou' to me and Paula, not 'you.' " I felt like a knight who had just received his accolade.

At the appointed hour, Paula and Edgar appeared at my flat in Neu Westend. They had come by taxi, and Paula had brought her typewriter. Edgar was a smooth and smiling, blond young man of about thirty. We talked about politics. I had qualms about the Party line—why, with Hitler *ante portas*, could we not come to an understanding with the Socialists? Why did we persist in calling them "Social Fascists," which drove them mad and made any collaboration with them impossible? Edgar explained, with great patience, that the Party desired nothing more than to establish a United Proletarian Front with the Social Democratic masses, but unity had to start at the base, not at the top. The Social Democrat leaders were traitors and would betray whatever agreement the Party might conclude with them. The only way to realize the United Front was to unmask the Socialist leaders and to win over the rank and file.

He argued brilliantly and after five minutes I was convinced that only a complete fool could favor collaboration between the two branches of the Workers' Movement against the Nazis. Edgar asked me whether I wanted guidance on any other point; and when I said no, he suggested, with noticeable relief, that I should tell him any bits of political information or confidential gossip that I had picked up in the House of Ullstein. After a minute or two, he asked whether I had any objection to Paula taking down what I said on her typewriter; it would "save work." I had no objection.

During the next few weeks my only Party activities consisted in dictating, once or twice a week, reports to Paula. Sometimes Edgar dropped in too and listened with his smooth, slightly ironical smile, while pacing up and down the room. As I am also in the habit of treading the carpet while dictating, we sometimes both marched at right angles across my sitting-room, which created an atmosphere of fraternal collaboration. That is about as much warmth as I got out of the Party at that stage.

As for Paula, she hardly ever stepped out of her sulky reticence. Once or twice she spoke on the telephone to comrades of hers—always in half-words and half-hints—and then she became a different person: full of vitality, gay, giggly. We had no physical attraction for each other, and I knew that spiritually she would not accept me into her world. I was an outsider—useful to the Party, maybe trustworthy, maybe not, but in any case an outsider, a denizen of the world of bourgeois corruption. She never accepted a drink or refreshment: when we met in a café she insisted on paying for herself; the first time I showed her where to wash, I caught her look of sulky disapproval at my dressing-gown.

Edgar was more smooth and considerate; but whenever I offered him a lift he insisted on being dropped, not at any given address, but at a street corner. When we met in a

much
suspicion
w/i Party

café, I had to let him leave first, on the understanding that I would leave not less than five minutes later, the implication being that otherwise I might trail him to his home. All this, he said smilingly, was mere formality and Party routine; I would soon get into the habit of it and act automatically in the same way.

But, in fact, though I accepted the necessity for conspiratorial vigilance, I felt increasingly frustrated. I was running after the Party, thirsting to throw myself completely into her arms, and the more breathlessly I struggled to possess and be possessed by her, the more elusive and unattainable she became. So, like all rejected suitors, I racked my brain for gifts to make her smile and soften her stony heart. I had offered to sacrifice my job and lead the humble life, driving a tractor in the Russian steppes; that was petty-bourgeois romanticism. I pressed Edgar to let me join a cell where nobody knew me except under my cover-name; he said I might be found out and thereby lose my usefulness to the Party. I asked him what else I could do. He said he would think about it. But weeks passed and nothing happened.

At about that time, a young man was put into my charge at the *B. Z. am Mittag*. Von E. was the son of high-ranking diplomat. He was twenty-one and wished to start on a journalistic career. He was to serve a few months of apprenticeship with only nominal pay, under my tutelage at the foreign desk of the *B. Z.* He had his place opposite mine: when the paper was put to bed, we usually went together to box or to work with the medicine-ball at the gymnasium which the Ullsteins had installed for the physical well-being of their staff. With only five years separating us, we soon became friends. I preached the Marxist gospel to him, and as I was his professional tutor as it were, my arguments were bound to carry added weight. After a fortnight or so I thought he had made sufficient progress to be roped into the service of the cause. I did not, of course, tell him that I was a member of the Party; but I told him that I had friends in the Party to whom

I occasionally passed on political gossip that came my way. It did not even occur to me that this was a somewhat euphemistic description of my work with Edgar and Paula; I was already reaping the reward of all conversions, a blissfully clean conscience.

The von E.'s led a social life and saw a number of German officers and diplomats at their house; so I asked young E. to keep his ears open and report to me, for the good of the common cause, anything of interest—in particular, information relating to the preparation of the war of aggression against the Soviet Union by Germany or other Powers. The young man, rather proud of the trust placed in him, promised to do what he could.

Thus for a while the reports I dictated to Paula became much livelier; they were full of diplomatic gossip, military titbits about rearmament, and information about the complicated and suicidal intrigues between the German parties in this last year of the Weimar Republic. One minor incident has acquired particular vividness in my memory. For weeks the Communist Party Press had sneered at the "Social Fascist" (Laborite) Prussian Government's unwillingness to take any drastic action against the Brownshirts, who were more or less openly preparing for a *putsch.* One day I learned, off the record, from Reiner, the diplomatic correspondent of the *Vossische Zeitung,* that the Prussian police were to carry out a surprise raid at SA headquarters the next morning at 6 A.M., seize their arms and archives, and impose a ban on the wearing of the Nazi uniform. I hurriedly passed on the news to Paula and Edgar. The action was carried out according to plan; but while Berlin feverishly discussed the chances of immediate civil war between Nazis and Socialists, our Communist *Rote Fahne* came out with its usual streamer headline sneer about the Social Democrat Government's tolerance of the Nazis, thus making a complete fool of itself. I asked Edgar why my warning had been disregarded; he explained that the Party's attitude to the Social Democrats was a set, long-term policy which could not be reversed by a small incident. "But every word on the front page is contradicted by the facts," I objected. Edgar gave me a tolerant smile. "You still have the mechanistic outlook," he said, and then proceeded to give me a dialectical interpretation of the facts. The action of the police was merely a feint to cover up their complicity; even if some Socialist leaders were *subjectively* anti-Fascist in their outlook, *objectively* the Socialist Party was a tool of Nazism; in fact the Socialists were the main enemy, for they had split the working class. Already convinced, I objected—to save my face—that after all it was the CP which had split away from the Socialists in 1919. "That's the mechanistic outlook again," said Edgar. "Formally we were in the minority, but it was we who embodied the revolutionary mission of the Proletariat; by refusing to follow our lead, the Socialist leaders split the working class and became lackeys of the reaction."

Gradually I learned to distrust my mechanistic preoccupation with facts and to regard the world around me in the light of dialectic interpretation. It was a satisfactory and indeed blissful state; once you had assimilated the technique you were no longer disturbed by facts; they automatically took on the proper color and fell into their proper place. Both morally and logically the Party was infallible: morally, because its aims were right, that is, in accord with the Dialectic of History, and these aims justified all means; logically, because the Party was the vanguard of the Proletariat, and the Proletariat the embodiment of the active principle in History.

Opponents of the Party, from straight reactionaries to Social Fascists, were products of their environment; their ideas reflected the distortions of bourgeois society. Renegades from the Party were lost souls, fallen out of grace; to argue with them, even to listen to them, meant trafficking with the Powers of Evil.

The days of the Weimar Republic were numbered, and each of us members of the German CP was earmarked for Dachau, Oranienburg, or some other garish future. But we all moved happily through a haze of dialectical mirages which masked the world of reality. The Fascist beasts were Fascist beasts, but our main preoccupation was the Trotskyite heretics and Socialist schismatics. In 1931, CP and Nazis had joined hands in the referendum against the Socialist Prussian Government; in the autumn of 1932 they joined hands again in the Berlin Transport Workers' Strike; Heinz Neumann, the brilliant CP leader, who had coined the slogan "Hit the Fascists wherever you meet them," which sounded orthodox enough, was in disgrace prior to his liquidation, and the Party line was wavering dizzily, just as it did prior to the Molotov-Ribbentrop Pact. But the Party had decreed that 1932 was to be the year that would see the triumph of the Proletarian Revolution in Germany; we had faith—the true faith, which no longer takes divine promises quite seriously—and, the only righteous men in a crooked world, we were happy.

One day Edgar casually asked me whether I had ever been to Japan. I said no. Wouldn't I like to go to Japan? Why, yes, I liked traveling. Couldn't I get Ullstein's to send me as their correspondent to Japan? No—we had our staff there and I did not know the first thing about Japan. But to the Party, Edgar said gently, you could be more useful in Japan than here. Could you get some other paper to send you out? I said that it would be rather difficult; anyway, what was I supposed to do when I got there? Edgar seemed slightly pained by my question. Why, I was to do my job for the paper and earn a good living, just as at present, and continue to pass on information of interest to the Cause to friends with whom I would be put in touch. Would I like to think the matter over? I said there was nothing for me to think over; if the Party wanted me to go, I was prepared to go at once, but the chances of getting a serious newspaper assignment were practically nil. Edgar paused for a moment, then said: "If we get you the assignment through our connections, would you be prepared to take it?" And again he asked me to take time to think it over. By now I was rather excited. I repeated that there was nothing for me to think over; if the Party wanted me to go, I would go.

Edgar said he would let me know in a few days, and dropped the matter. He never took it up again and, by now thoroughly imbued with Party etiquette, I never asked him.

Another curious incident occurred some time later. One day in the office, a Miss Meyer wanted to see me; on the form which visitors had to fill in she had scrawled, as "object of the visit," old friend. She was a puny, plain girl whom I had never seen before; but the deliberately slatternly way in which she was dressed and her provocative air in walking in betrayed her at once as a comrade. She had come to ask me to accept the job of "responsible editor" of a newly founded press agency. According to German law, every publication must have a "responsible editor" who, like the French *gérant*, is legally responsible for the published contents. In little magazines and mushroom publications, the "responsible editor" often has nothing at all to do with editing the paper; he is simply a person of some social standing and with a bank reference who lends his name for the purpose. I asked Miss Meyer to explain the aim, background, etc. of this press agency of which I had never heard. She shrugged impatiently: "But don't you understand—I have been sent by our mutual friends, and it's merely a formality for you to sign." "What mutual friends?" I asked with conspiratorial wariness. She became even more impatient, almost rude. She was the neurotic Cinderella type—the frustrated bourgeois girl turned voluntary proletarian—which abounded in the German Party. I asked her to mention the names of the friends who sent her. "Well, George of course," she said reluctantly, scrutinizing my office as if looking for hidden microphones. Now my only Party contacts at that time were Ernst, Edgar and Paula; I knew of no George and told her so. Miss Meyer was furious. "How dare they make me waste my time with a character like you!" she hissed, and walked out.

The next time I saw Paula, I mentioned the incident to her. She looked puzzled and promised to find out about Miss

Meyer. But when we met again, she said she had as yet had no time to inquire; and the time after that she shrugged my question off ill-humoredly and said there must have been some mix-up and I had better forget about it. There were more such queer incidents, and all of them were neither here nor there. Maybe Edgar's Tokyo proposition was merely meant as a psychological test; maybe he really wanted to send me to Tokyo, but his superiors did not trust me. Maybe Miss Meyer had really come on behalf of Edgar, who was known to her as George (these hyper-conspiratorial hitches occurred constantly); maybe she came from one of the rival party-organs or Apparats which tried to trespass in Edgar's hunting-ground. On this and on many other occasions, in Germany and Russia, I found Communist Apparat-work much less efficient than its scared opponents presume; and the means at their disposal much more restricted. At the same time there are three factors of a psychological nature which are usually underestimated: the idealism, naïveté and unscrupulousness of the legions of voluntary helpers of the SSS—the Silent Soviet Services.

My contact with Ernst Schneller's Apparat lasted only two or three months. It was a peripheral contact; but the fact that it ended there and that I was not drawn into the vortex to become a full-fledged *Apparatchik* (the homely euphemism used in the Party for agents and spies) was due to no merit of mine. As far as I was concerned, I was quite prepared to become one; I was one of those half-virgins of the Revolution who could be had by the SSS, body and soul, for the asking. I mention this, not out of any confessional urge, but because, as a young man of average Central European background, endowed with the average amount of idealism and more than average experience, I consider my case as fairly typical. The Comintern and OGPU carried on a white-slave traffic whose victims were young idealists flirting with violence.

I was saved from the clutches of the Apparat not, I repeat, by my own insight, but by the innocence of young von E.

I have mentioned that he was only twenty-one and that he had for me the affection which one develops at that age for a person who acts both as professional tutor and as Marxist *Guru*. All went well for a few weeks; then I noticed a certain cooling off in von E.'s attitude to me, but did not give the matter much thought. He mentioned once or twice, timidly, that he would like to have "a long, thorough talk"; but I was at that time overworked and unhappily in love; besides, I was getting bored with acting the *Guru*. So I kept putting the "long, thorough talk" off. This turned out to be one of those mistakes arranged by providence, like missing the airplane which is going to crash.

One day, while I was dictating letters to a typist, young von E. burst into the room and asked to talk to me alone at once. He was unshaven, had red, swollen eyes and looked so dramatic that the typist fled in mild panic. "What's the matter?" I asked, with unpleasant forebodings. "I have come to the conclusion," said von E., "that I have either to shoot myself or to denounce our activities. The decision rests with you." "What activities are you talking about?" I asked. "Activities which are called High Treason," young von E. said dramatically. Then he blurted out his story. A week before he had been suddenly assailed by doubts about the propriety of what I had induced him to do. During the previous, sleepless night these doubts had become a certainty: he was a traitor and a spy. The choice before him, he repeated, was either to shoot himself, or to make a full confession and take the consequences.

I told him that he was talking nonsense; that a spy was a man who stole military documents or sold secrets of State to a foreign power; that all he had done was to pass on some parlor-gossip to a friend.

"And what did you do with the information I gave you?" asked von E. with a new, fierce aggressiveness.

"I told it to my friends, for what it was worth."

"Friends! You mean foreign agents."

I told him that the KPD was the Party of the German working class, as German as were the Nazis or the Catholic Center. No, said von E. hotly. Everybody knew that they were tools of Russia.

I wondered what had come over him. Had he turned Nazi overnight? But it transpired that he had not changed his political sympathies. He had merely discovered that to be a Socialist or Marxist was one thing, and to pass information to a foreign power another. He admitted with a shrug that technically we were probably not spies; but that, he said, did not alter the fact that we had acted dishonestly and treacherously. It was impossible for him to live on unless he made a full confession. He had actually written it last night. But he would only hand it in with my consent. . . .

With that, he placed a long, handwritten letter on my desk. There were eight pages of it. It was addressed to the *Verlagsdirektor*, the "Managing Director" of the firm. He asked me to read it.

I read the first two or three lines—"I, the undersigned, hold it to be my duty to bring the following facts to your knowledge, etc."—and then I felt such a reluctance to read on, that I stopped. The boy, standing in front of the desk—he had refused to sit down—looked ghastly with the black stubble on his white face and the swollen, bloodshot eyes. No doubt he was unconsciously dramatizing the situation and getting an adolescent kick out of it; but few suicides are committed for adult motives, and, for all I knew, he was capable of carrying his self-dramatization to the point of really shooting himself.

The situation struck me as half comic, half disgusting. It was comic, because young von E. seemed to me vastly to exaggerate his own importance and what we had done; I still felt that it merely amounted to half-serious, political busybodying. And yet I felt incapable of arguing with him, or even of reading the letter which, after all, directly involved my future. Later on, when I reported the matter to Edgar, I was unable to explain why I had not read on. This was probably why the

Apparat dropped me as a hopeless case. Today of course the matter is simple to explain: I could not face reading in black and white the factual record of actions which I insisted on regarding through a haze of dialectical euphemisms. Besides, though I was convinced that young von E. was a quixotic ass and myself an earnest worker for the cause, I felt guilty towards the boy and frightened of the grand gesture, ending in a bang in front of the mirror. So I stuffed the letter back into his pocket and told him to hand it in with my blessing and to go to hell.

"Do you mean that you agree to my doing it?" he asked. He was so surprised, and seized upon his chance with such alacrity, that I thought for a moment I was really acting like a fool; maybe with a little arguing and dialectics I could talk him out of his dilemma. But I could not face it; my self-confidence as a *Guru* had gone. Young von E. came back from the door and shook my hand with solemn sentiment. Then he pushed off, looking already less unshaven.

That was the end of my career with the Ullsteins and the beginning of seven lean years. I had been prepared to throw up my job for the Party; but not to lose it in such an idiotic way.

It was at the same time the end of my connection with the Apparat. Having lost my usefulness for them—in a manner which proved my total unfitness for intelligence work—they dropped me without ceremony. I never saw Edgar or Paula again. Paula, I later learned, was killed by the Nazis in Ravensbrück; Edgar's identity is unknown to me to this day.

The manner in which the Ullsteins fired me may be called rather decent or an example of bourgeois hypocrisy; it depends on the angle from which you look at it. After von E. had left me, to hand in his eight-page letter, I expected to be called at any minute to *Verlagsdirektor* Müller. I had my defense prepared: yes, I had asked the boy to tell me any political gossip that came to his ears; yes, I occasionally passed such gossip on to friends of mine in the KPD; what on earth

was wrong with that? Everybody discussed politics and exchanged gossip with his friends; and my political sympathies
were no concern of the firm's as long as they did not interfere with the discharge of my professional duties—etc., etc.
This was the line that Edgar suggested; it was all so plausible
that, after the initial shock of the scene with von E. had passed,
I waited impatiently for the showdown, braced with moral
indignation and conscious of being the innocent victim of a
witch-hunt. If one lives in the ambiguity of a deep-sea
aquarium, it is difficult to distinguish substance from shadow.

However, days passed and nothing happened. Then, a week
or ten days after the scene with von E., I found one morning
a letter from the firm on my desk. It stated, with extreme cour-
tesy, that in view of the general reductions of staff made
inevitable by the economic crisis, etc., etc., it was necessary to
dispense with my further services on the editorial staff. It was
up to me whether I preferred to continue writing for the
Ullstein papers as a free-lance with a guaranteed monthly
minimum or to accept a lump sum in settlement of the remaining term of my five-years' contract. Not a word about von E.,
the Communist Party, or breach of confidence. The Ullsteins
were obviously anxious to avoid a scandal. So was the Party,
for Edgar instructed me to accept the settlement and leave it
at that. As already mentioned, I never saw him again in my
life.

★

Having lost my job, I was at last free from all fetters of
the bourgeois world. The lump sum which Ullstein's paid me
I sent to my parents; it was enough to keep them going for
two or three years, and thus free me from my obligation until
after the victorious revolution and the dawn of the New Era.
I retained, however, two hundred marks (about ten pounds
or fifty dollars), to pay my fare to Soviet Russia if and when
the Party gave me permission to emigrate. I gave up my flat
in the expensive district of Neu Westend, and moved into an

apartment house on Bonner Platz; it was mainly inhabited by penniless artists of radical views, and was known as the "Red Block." My three months there were the happiest time in my seven years as a member of the Party.

Now that I had lost my usefulness to the Apparat, there was no longer any objection to my joining a cell and leading the full life of a regular Party member. In actual fact, Edgar had given me permission to join the cell of the Red Block, under my cover-name Ivan Steinberg, some time before I was fired by the Ullsteins. It had been a kind of reward for being a good boy and dictating those long reports to Paula. I then still lived in Neu Westend, miles away from Bonner Platz; so it was assumed that if I joined the Red Block cell nobody would guess the identity of Comrade Ivan Steinberg. It was one of the incredibly crass blunders of the machiavellian Apparat; for, the Red Block being an artists' and writers' colony, the first time I turned up in the cell and was laconically introduced as "a new member—Comrade Ivan," half a dozen familiar faces grinned in welcome.

Having left Ullstein's, I no longer had any reason to keep my Party membership secret. In the Red Block I threw myself body and soul into the fraternal life of the cell. It had about twenty members and met regularly once or twice a week. Like all other Party cells, it was led by a "triangle": *Pol.-Leiter* ("political leader"), *Org.-Leiter* ("administrative organizer") and *Agit-Prop* (the member responsible for "agitation and propaganda"). Our *Pol.-Leiter* was Alfred Kantorowicz, now editor of a Soviet-sponsored literary magazine in Berlin. He was then about thirty, tall, gaunt, squinting, a free-lance critic and essayist and prospective author of the Novel of Our Time, which never saw the light. But he was an exceptionally warm-hearted comrade and a self-sacrificing friend, and he had both dignity and a rich sense of humor; his only shortcoming was lack of moral courage. We remained friends all through the Paris emigré years; when I broke with the Party, he was the only one who did not spit at me. Now he is a literary bigwig under the Soviets—may his innocence and compliance protect him from ever getting caught in the snares of counter-revolutionary formalism, bourgeois cosmopolitanism, neo-Kantian banditism, or just liberal depravity.

Our *Org.-Leiter* was Max Schröder, also a literateur who lived on the reputation he had earned with several remarkable poems published at the age of nineteen, that is to say fifteen years earlier. But he too was a good egg, the lovable type of Munich bohemian, who had found in his devotion to the Party a compensation for his literary, sexual, pecuniary, and other frustrations. The job of *Agitprop* fell to me soon after I had joined the cell; some of the leaflets and broadsheets I produced had, I still believe, a truly Jacobin pathos. Among other members of our cell I remember Dr. Wilhelm Reich, Founder and Director of the *Sex-Pol.* (Institute for Sexual Politics). He was a Freudian Marxist; inspired by Malinowski, he had just published a book called *The Function of the Orgasm*, in which he expounded the theory that the sexual frustration of the Proletariat caused a thwarting of its political consciousness; only through a full, uninhibited release of the sexual urge could the working-class realize its revolutionary potentialities and historic mission; the whole thing was less cock-eyed than it sounds. After the victory of Hitler, Reich published a brilliant psychological study of the Nazi mentality, which the Party condemned; he broke with Communism and is now director of a scientific research institute in the U. S. A. We also had two actors from an avant-garde theater called "The Mouse Trap"; several girls with vaguely intellectual ambitions; an insurance agent; young Ernst, son of our local fruit vendor, and several working men.

Half the activities of the cell were legal, half illegal. All our meetings started with a political lecture which was delivered either by the *Pol.-Leiter* after he had been briefed at the Party's District HQ, or by an instructor from Headquarters itself. The purpose of the lecture was to lay down the political line on the various questions of the day. During that fateful spring and summer of 1932, a series of elections took place which shook the country like a succession of earthquakes—the Presidential elections, two Reichstag elections, and an election for the Prussian Diet; all in all four red-hot election campaigns within eight months in a country on the verge of civil war. We participated in the campaigns by door-to-door canvassing, distributing Party literature and turning out leaflets of our own. The canvassing was the most arduous part of it; it was mostly done on Sunday mornings, when people were supposed to be at home. You rang the doorbell, wedged your foot between door and post and offered your pamphlets and leaflets, with a genial invitation to engage in a political discussion on the spot. In short, we sold the World Revolution like vacuum cleaners. Reactions were mostly unfriendly, rarely aggressive. I often had the door banged in my face but never a fight. However, we avoided ringing the bells of known Nazis. And the Nazis in and round our block were mostly known to us, just as we were all known to the Nazis, through our rival nets of cells and *Blockwarts*. The whole of Germany, town and countryside, was covered by those two elaborate and fine-meshed dragnets. I still believe that, without the wild jerks from Moscow which kept entangling our nets and tearing them from our hands, we would have had a fair chance to win. The idea, the readiness for sacrifice, the support of the masses were all there.

We lost the fight, because we were not fishermen, as we thought, but bait dangling from a hook. We did not realize this, because our brains had been reconditioned to accept any absurd line of action ordered from above as our innermost wish and conviction. We had refused to nominate a joint candidate with the Socialists for the Presidency, and when the Socialists backed Hindenburg as the lesser evil against Hitler, we nominated Thälmann though he had no chance whatsoever—except, maybe, to split off enough proletarian votes to bring Hitler immediately into power. Our instructor gave us a lecture proving that there was no such thing as

Claims brainwashing

a "lesser evil," that it was a philosophical, strategical and tactical fallacy; a Trotskyite, diversionist, liquidatorial and counterrevolutionary conception. Henceforth we had only pity and spite for those who as much as mentioned the ominous term; and, moreover, we were convinced that we had always been convinced that it was an invention of the devil. How could anybody fail to see that to have both legs amputated was better than trying to save one, and that the correct revolutionary policy was to kick the crippled Republic's crutches away? Faith is a wondrous thing; it is not only capable of moving mountains, but also of making you believe that a herring is a race horse.

Not only our thinking, but also our vocabulary was reconditioned. Certain words were taboo—for instance "lesser evil" or "spontaneous"; the latter because "spontaneous" manifestations of the revolutionary class-consciousness were part of Trotsky's theory of the Permanent Revolution. Other words and turns of phrase became favorite stock-in-trade. I mean not only the obvious words of Communist jargon like "the toiling masses"; but words like "concrete" or "sectarian" ("You must put your question into a more concrete form, Comrade"; "you are adopting a Left-sectarian attitude, Comrade"); and even such abstruse words as "herostratic." In one of his works Lenin had mentioned Herostratus, the Greek who burnt down a temple because he could think of no other way of achieving fame. Accordingly, one often heard and read phrases like "the criminally herostratic madness of the counter-revolutionary wreckers of the heroic efforts of the toiling masses in the Fatherland of the Proletariat to achieve the second Five Year Plan in four years."

According to their vocabulary and favorite clichés, you could smell out at once people with Trotskyite, Reformist, Brandlerite, Blanquist and other deviations. And vice versa, Communists betrayed themselves by their vocabulary to the police, and later to the Gestapo. I know of one girl whom the Gestapo had picked up almost at random, without any evidence against

[handwritten margin note: must be anti-Trotsky]

her, and who was caught out on the word "concrete." The Gestapo Commissar had listened to her with boredom, half-convinced that his underlings had blundered in arresting her —until she used the fatal word for the second time. The Commissar pricked his ears. "Where did you pick up that expression?" he asked. The girl, until that moment quite self-possessed, became rattled, and once rattled she was lost.

Our literary, artistic and musical tastes were similarly reconditioned. Lenin had said somewhere that he had learned more about France from Balzac's novels than from all history books put together. Accordingly, Balzac was the greatest of all times, whereas other novelists of the past merely reflected "the distorted values of the decaying society which had produced them." On the Art Front the guiding principle of the period was Revolutionary Dynamism. A picture without a smoking factory chimney or a tractor in it was escapist; on the other hand, the slogan "dynamism" left sufficient scope for cubist, expressionist, and other experimental styles. This changed a few years later when Revolutionary Dynamism was superseded by Socialist Realism; henceforth everything modern and experimental became branded as "bourgeois formalism" expressing "the putrid corruption of capitalist decay." In both music and drama, the chorus was regarded at that time as the highest form of expression, because it reflected a collective, as opposed to a bourgeois-individualistic, approach. As individual *personae* could not be altogether abolished on the stage, they had to be stylized, typified, depersonalized (Meyerhold, Piscator, Brecht, Auden-Isherwood-Spender). Psychology became greatly simplified: there were two recognized emotive impulses: class solidarity and the sexual urge. The rest was "bourgeois metaphysics"; or, like ambition and the lust for power, "products of competitive capitalist economy."

As for the "sexual urge," though it was officially sanctioned, we were in something of a quandary about it. Monogamy, and the whole institution of the family, were a product of the economic system; they bred individualism, hypocrisy, an

escapist attitude to the class struggle and were altogether to
be rejected; bourgeois matrimony was merely a form of prosti-
tution sanctioned by society. But promiscuity was equally a
Bad Thing. It had flourished in the Party, both in Russia and
abroad, until Lenin made his famous pronouncement against
the Glass of Water Theory (that is, against the popular maxim
that the sexual act was of no more consequence than the
quenching of thirst by a glass of water). Hence bourgeois morality was a Bad Thing. But promiscuity was an equally Bad
Thing, and the only correct, concrete attitude towards the
sexual urge was Proletarian Morality. This consisted in getting
married, being faithful to one's spouse, and producing proletarian babies. But then, was this not the same thing as bourgeois morality?—The question, Comrade, shows that you are
thinking in mechanistic, not in dialectical, terms. What is the
difference between a gun in the hands of a policeman and a
gun in the hands of a member of the revolutionary working
class? The difference between a gun in the hands of a policeman and in the hands of a member of the revolutionary
working class is that the policeman is a lackey of the ruling
class and his gun an instrument of oppression, whereas the
same gun in the hands of a member of the revolutionary working class is an instrument of the liberation of the oppressed
masses. Now the same is true of the difference between so-
called bourgeois "morality" and Proletarian Morality. The institution of marriage which in capitalist society is an aspect of
bourgeois decay, is dialectically transformed in its function in
a healthy proletarian society. Have you understood, Comrade,
or shall I repeat my answer in more concrete terms?

Repetitiveness of diction, the catechism technique of asking
a rhetorical question and repeating the full question in the
answer; the use of stereotyped adjectives and the dismissal of
an attitude or fact by the simple expedient of putting words
in inverted commas and giving them an ironic inflection (the
"revolutionary" past of Trotsky, the "humanistic" bleatings of
the "liberal" press, etc.); all these were essential parts of a

style, of which Josef Djugashwili is the uncontested master, and which through its very tedium produced a dull, hypnotic effect. Two hours of this dialectical tom-tom and you didn't know whether you were a boy or a girl, and were ready to believe either as soon as the rejected alternative appeared in inverted commas. You were also ready to believe that the Socialists were: (a) your main enemies, (b) your natural allies; that socialist and capitalist countries: (a) could live peacefully side by side, and (b) could not live peacefully side by side; and that when Engels had written that Socialism in One Country was impossible, he had meant the exact opposite. You further learned to prove, by the method of chain-deduction, that anybody who disagreed with you was an agent of Fascism, because: (a) by his disagreeing with your line he endangered the unity of the Party; (b) by endangering the unity of the Party he improved the chances of a Fascist victory; hence (c) he acted objectively as an agent of Fascism even if subjectively he happened to have his kidneys smashed to pulp by the Fascists in Dachau. Generally speaking, words like "agent of," "Democracy," "Freedom," etc. meant something quite different in Party usage from what they meant in general usage; and as, furthermore, even their Party meaning changed with each shift of the line, our polemical methods became rather like the croquet game of the Queen of Hearts, in which the hoops moved about the field and the balls were live hedgehogs. With this difference, that when a player missed his turn and the Queen shouted "Off with his head," the order was executed in earnest. To survive, we all had to become virtuosos of Wonderland croquet.

A special feature of Party life at that period was the cult of the proletarian and abuse of the intelligentsia. It was the obsession, the smarting complex of all Communist intellectuals of middle-class origin. We were in the Movement on sufferance, not by right; this was rubbed into our consciousness night and day. We had to be tolerated because Lenin had said so, and because Russia could not do without the doctors, en-

Party uses European Jews like it uses American blacks

gineers and scientists of the pre-revolutionary intelligentsia, and without the hated foreign specialists. But we were no more trusted or respected than the category of "Useful Jews" in the Third Reich who were allowed to survive and were given distinctive armlets so that they should not by mistake be pushed into a gas-chamber before their span of usefulness expired. The "Aryans" in the Party were the Proletarians, and the social origin of parents and grandparents was as weighty a factor both when applying for membership and during the biannual routine purges as Aryan descent was with the Nazis. The ideal Proletarians were the Russian factory workers, and the élite among the latter were those of the Putilov Works in Leningrad and of the oil fields in Baku. In all books which we read or wrote, the ideal proletarian was always broad-shouldered, with an open face and simple features; he was fully class-conscious, his sexual urge was kept well under control; he was strong and silent, warmhearted but ruthless when necessary, had big feet, horny hands and a deep baritone voice to sing revolutionary songs with. Proletarians who were not Communists were not real proletarians—they belonged either to the Lumpen-Proletariat or to the Workers' Aristocracy. No movement can exist without a heroic archetype; Comrade Ivan Ivanovich of the Putilov Works was our Buffalo Bill.

A member of the intelligentsia could never become a real proletarian, but his duty was to become as nearly one as he could. Some tried to achieve this by forsaking neckties, by wearing polo sweaters and black fingernails. This, however, was discouraged: it was imposture and snobbery. The correct way was never to write, say, and above all never to think, anything which could not be understood by the dustman. We cast off our intellectual baggage like passengers on a ship seized by panic, until it became reduced to the strictly necessary minimum of stock-phrases, dialectical clichés and Marxist quotations, which constitute the international jargon of Djugashwilese. To have shared the doubtful privilege of a bourgeois education, to be able to see several aspects of a problem and not only one, became a permanent cause of self-reproach. We craved to become single- and simple-minded. Intellectual self-castration was a small price to pay for achieving some likeness to Comrade Ivan Ivanovich.

★

To come back to life in the cell. The meetings, as I have said, started with one, sometimes two, political lectures which laid down the line. This was followed by discussion, but discussion of a peculiar kind. It is a basic rule of Communist discipline that, once the Party has decided to adopt a certain line regarding a given problem, all criticism of that decision becomes deviationist sabotage. In theory, discussion is permissible prior to the decision. But as all decisions are imposed from above, out of the blue, without consulting any representative body of the rank and file, the latter is deprived of any influence on policy and even of the chance of expressing an opinion on it; while at the same time the leadership is deprived of the means of gauging the mood of the masses. One of the slogans of the German Party said: "The front-line is no place for discussions." Another said: "Wherever a Communist happens to be, he is always in the front-line."

So our discussions always showed a complete unanimity of opinion, and the form they took was that one member of the cell after another got up and recited approving variations in Djugashwilese on the theme set by the lecturer. But "recited" is probably not the proper word here. We groped painfully in our minds not only to find justifications for the line laid down, but also to find traces of former thoughts which would prove to ourselves that we had always held the required opinion. In this operation we mostly succeeded. I may have been somewhat bewildered when we were told by the instructor that the Party's main slogan in the coming elections to the Prussian Diet was to be not the seven million German unemployed, or the threats of the Brownshirts, but "the defense of the Chinese proletariat against the aggression of the Japanese pirates." But if I was bewildered, I no longer remember it. I do, however, remember writing a sincere and eloquent election leaflet, which proved just why events in Shanghai were more important to the German working class than events in Berlin; and the pat on the shoulder I received for it from District HQ still makes me feel good—I can't help it.

The proletarian members of the cell usually sat through the lecture with a sleepy expression; they listened, with eyelids slit in mistrust, to the intellectuals expounding the reasons for their agreement; then, after some nudging, one of them would get up and repeat, in a deliberately awkward manner and with an air of defiance, the main slogans from the Inspector's speech without bothering to change the words. He would be listened to in solemn silence, sit down amidst a murmur of approval, and the instructor, winding up the proceedings, would point out that of all the speakers Comrade X had formulated the problem in the happiest and most concrete terms.

As I mentioned before, the summer of 1932 was a period of transition; the Party was preparing to go underground and accordingly regrouping its *cadres*. We might be outlawed overnight; everything had to be ready for this emergency. The moment we were forced into illegality all Party cells would cease to function and would be superseded by a new, nation-wide structure, the "Groups of Five." The cells, whose membership ranged from ten to thirty comrades, were too large for underground work and offered easy opportunities for *agents provocateurs* and informers. The breaking up of the *cadres* into Groups of Five meant organizational decentralization and a corresponding diminution of risks. Only the leader of the Group was to know the identity and addresses of the other four; and he alone had contact with the next higher level of the Party hierarchy. If he was arrested, he could only betray the four individuals in his Group, and his contact man.

So, while the cell still continued to function, each member was secretly allotted to a Group of Five, the idea being that none of the Groups should know the composition of any other. In fact, as we were all neighbors in the Block, we each knew which Group was secretly meeting in whose flat; and on the night of the burning of the Reichstag, when Göring dealt his death blow to the Communist Party, the Groups scattered and the whole elaborate structure collapsed all over the Reich. We had marveled at the conspiratorial ingenuity of our leaders, and, though all of us had read works on the technique of insurrection and civil warfare, our critical faculties had become so numbed that none of us realized the catastrophic implications of the scheme. To prepare for a long underground existence in small decentralized groups meant that our leaders accepted the victory of Nazism as inevitable. And the breaking up of the *cadres* into small units indicated that the Party would offer no open, armed resistance to the ascent of Hitler to power, but was preparing for sporadic small-scale action instead.

But we, the rank and file, knew nothing of this. During that long, stifling summer of 1932 we fought our ding-dong battles with the Nazis. Hardly a day passed without one or two dead in Berlin. The main battlefields were the *Bierstuben*, the smoky little taverns of the working-class districts. Some of these served as meeting-places for the Nazis, some as meeting-places (*Verkehrslokale*) for us. To enter the wrong pub was to venture into the enemy lines. From time to time the Nazis would shoot up one of our *Verkehrslokale*. It was done in the classic Chicago tradition: a gang of SA men would drive slowly past the tavern, firing through the glass-panes, then vanish at breakneck speed. We had far fewer motorcars than the Nazis, and retaliation was mostly carried out in cars either stolen or borrowed from sympathizers. The men who did these jobs were members of the RFB, the League of Communist War Veterans. My car was sometimes borrowed by comrades whom I had never seen before, and returned a few hours later with no questions asked and no explanations offered. It was a tiny, red, open Fiat car, model 509, most unsuitable for such purposes; but nobody else in our cell had one. It was the last relic of my bourgeois past; now it served as a vehicle for the Proletarian Revolution. I spent half my time driving it round on various errands: transporting pamphlets and leaflets, shadowing certain Nazi cars whose numbers had been indicated to us, and acting as a security escort. Once I had to transport the equipment of a complete hand printing press from a railway station to a cellar under a greengrocer's shop.

The RFB men who came to fetch the car for their guerrilla expedition were sometimes rather sinister types from the Berlin underworld. They came, announced by a telephone call or verbal message from District HQ, but the same men rarely turned up twice. Sometimes, on missions of a more harmless nature, I was ordered myself to act as driver. We would drive slowly past a number of Nazi pubs to watch the goings-on, or patrol a pub of our own when one of our informers in the Nazi camp warned us of an impending attack. This latter kind of mission was unpleasant; we would park, with headlights turned off and engine running, in the proximity of the pub; and at the approach of a car I would hear the click of the safety catch on my passengers' guns, accompanied by the gentle advice "to keep my block well down." But I never saw it come to any actual shooting.

Once the RFB men who came to fetch the car disguised themselves in my flat before starting out. They stuck on mustaches, put on glasses, dark jackets and bowler hats. I watched them from the window driving off—four stately, bowler-hatted gents in the ridiculous little red car, looking like a party in a funeral procession. They came back four hours later, changed back to normal, and made off with a silent handshake. My instructions, in case the number of the car was taken by the police during some action, were to say that it had been stolen and that I had found it again in a deserted street.

From time to time a rumor got around that the Nazis were going to attack our Red Block as they had attacked other notorious Communist agglomerations before. Then we were alerted and some RFB men turned up to mount guard. One critical night about thirty of us kept vigil in my tiny flat, armed with guns, lead pipes and leather batons. It happened to be the night when Ernst, a friend of mine, arrived from Vienna to stay for a few days. He was a young scientist with a shy, gentle manner and a razor-sharp mind. The flat was dim with cigarette smoke; men were sitting or sleeping all over the place —on the beds, on the floor, under the kitchen sink, amid lead pipes, beer glasses and batons. When my turn came to patrol the street, I took Ernst with me. "What is all this romantic brigandage about?" he asked me. I explained to him. "I know, I know," he said, "but what do you think you are doing with your life?" "I am helping to prepare the Revolution," I said cheerfully. "It doesn't look like it," he said. "Why?" "I don't know," he said doubtfully. "I know of course nothing about how revolutions are done. But the whole scene upstairs looked to me like a huddle of stragglers from a beaten army."

He was right; we thought of ourselves as the vanguard of the Revolution, and were the rearguard of the disintegrating workers' movement. A few weeks later von Papen staged his *coup d'état*: one lieutenant and eight men chased the Socialist government of Prussia from office. The Socialist Party, with its eight million followers, did nothing. The Socialist-controlled Trade Unions did not even call a protest strike. Only we, the Communists, who a year earlier had joined hands with the Nazis against the same Prussian government and who kept repeating that the Socialists were the main enemy of the working class—we now called for an immediate general strike. The call fell on deaf ears in the whole of Germany. Our verbiage had lost all real meaning for the masses, like inflated currency. And so we lost the battle against Hitler before it was joined. After July 20, 1932, it was evident to all but ourselves that the KPD, strongest among the Communist Parties in Europe, was a castrated giant whose brag and bluster only served to cover its lost virility.

The day after the abortive General Strike, the Party Press

affirmed that it had been a resounding victory: by calling for the strike in the face of Socialist inaction, our Party had definitely unmasked the treachery of the Social Fascist leaders.

A few months later everything was over. Years of conspiratorial training and preparation for the emergency proved within a few hours totally useless. The giant was swept off his feet and collapsed like a Carnival monster. Thälmann, leader of the Party, and the majority of his lieutenants were found in their carefully prepared hide-outs and arrested within the first few days. The Central Committee emigrated. The long night descended over Germany; today, seventeen years later, it has not yet ended.

With Hitler in power, Thälmann in jail, thousands of Party members murdered and tens of thousands in concentration camps, the Comintern at last awoke to its responsibilities. The Party tribunals abroad and the GPU *Collegia* in the USSR sat in merciless judgment over "the enemy within"— the bandits and agents of Fascism who murmured against the official line, according to which the Socialist Party was the Enemy No. 1 of the German working class, and the Communist Party had suffered no defeat, but merely carried out a strategic retreat.

★

As a rule, our memories romanticize the past. But when one has renounced a creed or been betrayed by a friend, the opposite mechanism sets to work. In the light of that later knowledge, the original experience loses its innocence, becomes tainted and rancid in recollection. I have tried in these pages to recapture the mood in which the experiences related were originally lived—and I know that I have failed. Irony, anger and shame kept intruding; the passions of that time seem transformed into perversions, its inner certitude into the closed universe of the drug addict; the shadow of barbed wire lies across the condemned playground of memory. Those who were caught by the great illusion of our time, and have lived through its moral and intellectual debauch, either give themselves up to a new addiction of the opposite type, or are condemned to pay with a lifelong hangover. "They are the ambulant cemeteries of their murdered friends; they carry their shrouds as their banner."[3]

Hence the deep, instinctive resistance of the political dope addict to the cure.

★

In the late summer of 1932 my Soviet visa was granted at last. I obtained it on the strength of an invitation from the International Organization of Revolutionary Writers to tour the country and write a book about it. This was to be called *The Soviet Land Through Bourgeois Eyes.* The idea was to describe how Mr. K., a bourgeois reporter with strong anti-Soviet prejudices, is gradually converted by seeing the results of Socialist Reconstruction during the first Five Year Plan, and ends as Comrade K.

I left for the USSR six months before Hitler came to power in Germany, armed with a recommendation to Comrade Gopner, at that time head of the *Agitprop,* EKKI (Executive Committee of the Communist International), in Moscow. The EKKI, in its turn, provided me with a so-called "strong" letter asking all Soviet authorities to help me to accomplish my mission "as a delegate of the Revolutionary Proletarian Writers of Germany."

A letter of this kind carries in Soviet Russia the weight of a decree. It enabled me to travel unhampered all over the country without a guide, to obtain railway tickets without queuing, sleeping accommodations in government Guest Houses, and food in restaurants reserved for civil servants. It further enabled me to pay for my travels, with several thousand roubles left over at the end of my stay. The procedure was as follows.

When I arrived in a provincial capital, say in Tiflis, I went

[3] *"Et le buisson devint cendre,"* Manes Sperber: Paris, 1949.

to the local Writers' Federation, where I produced my Comintern letter. The Secretary of the Federation thereupon arranged the usual banquets and meetings with the political leaders and members of the intelligentsia of the town, appointed somebody to look after me, and put me in touch with the editor of the local literary magazine and the director of the State Publishing Trust—in this case the Trust of the Georgian Soviet Republic. The editor of the magazine declared that it had been for many years his dearest wish to publish a story by me. I handed him a copy of a story published some time ago in Germany; and the same day a check for two or three thousand roubles was sent to my hotel. The director of the State Publishing Trust asked for the privilege of publishing a Georgian translation of the book I was going to write; I signed a printed agreement form and was sent another check for three or four thousand roubles. (The salary of the average wage-earner was at that time 130 roubles per month.) I thus sold the same short story to eight or ten different literary magazines from Leningrad to Tashkent, and sold the Russian, German, Ukrainian, Georgian and Armenian rights of my unwritten book against advance payments which amounted to a small fortune. And as I did all this with official encouragement, and as other writers did the same, I could wholeheartedly confirm that Soviet Russia was the writer's paradise and that nowhere else in the world was the creative artist better paid or held in higher esteem. Human nature being what it is, it never occurred to me that my contracts and cash advances had been granted not on the strength of my literary reputation, but for reasons of a different nature.

At that time I had not published a single book; my name was completely unknown to those who paid ready cash for a story they had not read and a book that was not written. They were civil servants, acting on instructions. In a country where all publications are State-owned, editors, publishers and literary critics become *ipso facto* part of the Civil Service. They will make or break a writer according to orders received: the publishers, by printing vast editions of his new book or by pulping all his previous works; the critics, by calling him a new Tolstoy or a depraved cosmopolitan vermin, or both within an interval of a few months.

The average visiting foreign author knows little about all this; and the little which his intuition makes him guess, his vanity will quickly make him forget. The people whom he meets at banquets and parties seem to know his works by heart; he would have to be a masochist, with a touch of persecution mania, to assume that they have been specially briefed for the occasion. The Central State Publishing Trust offers him a contract for his next book and an advance covering the royalties on a sale of 150,000 copies. If he is very honest, the honored guest will mention with a blush that this is about fifteen times the number of copies on whose expected sale the cash advances of well-known European writers are calculated. But that, the director points out to him with a smile, is the practice of capitalist publishers. In the Soviet Union all publishing enterprises are owned by the People, and the average Soviet citizen buys 231.57 per cent more books than the average American; at the end of the second Five Year Plan this quotient will reach and outstrip 365 per cent. So it is only natural that honored writers in the Soviet Union, instead of living in garrets as in capitalist countries, own two-room flats with a lavatory all their own, not to mention motorcars and summer *datshas*. Our visitor is slightly nettled by being suspected of living in a garret; but this, he reassures himself, is petty-bourgeois vanity. He signs the contract and a few days later leaves for home, where he will declare that nowhere else in the world is the creative artist held in higher esteem, etc., etc. Though he can't take his roubles with him, as they are not convertible into foreign currency, he can buy some quite decent Bokhara carpets and leave the rest in the State Bank in Moscow; it is a pleasant feeling to have a nest egg in the Socialist sixth of the earth. In exceptional cases the State Publishing Trust is even authorized to convert part of the sum into the author's home currency and to send it to him in monthly installments. I know of two famous exiled German authors in France who for years drew monthly royalty checks of this kind, though one of them never had a book published in Russia. Both were passionate and lucid critics of democratic corruption; neither of them has ever written a word of criticism against the Soviet Regime. I do not mean that they have been bribed; we are not concerned here with such crude machinations, but with the dialectics of the unconscious—with that subtle inner voice which whispers that in the capitalist world publishers are sharks who don't care a damn what you write as long as your books sell, whereas your Soviet publishers are the Soviet People, justifiably resentful of any criticism of their free country.

Russia is indeed the artist's Paradise—but alas a Paradise of forbidden trees guarded by peak-capped angels with flaming swords.

★

I stayed in the Soviet Union for one year, half of which I spent traveling, the other half in Kharkov and Moscow, writing my book. A German edition of it was actually published in Kharkov, under a changed title.[4] The Russian, Georgian, Armenian, etc. editions have, as far as I know, never seen the light.

My travels led me through the industrial centers along the Volga; then southward through the Ukraine and across the Transcaucasian Republics—Georgia, Armenia and Azerbaijan —to Baku; across the Caspian and through the Central Asiatic Republics—Turkmenistan and Uzbekistan—down to the Afghan frontier; then, via Tashkent and across Kazakstan, back to Moscow. What I saw and experienced came as a shock—but a shock with a delayed-action effect, as it were.

[4] *Von Weissen Nächten und Roten Tagen*, UKRDERSHNAZMEN-WYDAW: Kharkov, 1934. (The abbreviation stands for "State Publishing Trust for the National Minorities in the Ukraine.")

Arthur Koestler

My Party education had equipped my mind with such elaborate shock-absorbing buffers and elastic defenses that everything seen and heard became automatically transformed to fit the preconceived pattern.

I spoke Russian fairly fluently but, though I traveled alone, I had little occasion to practice it on people other than official acquaintances; the ordinary Soviet citizen knows that to be seen talking to a foreigner is as unhealthy as touching a leper. Those who did talk to me, in restaurants and railway compartments, used the stereotyped clichés of *Pravda* editorials; one might have thought they were reciting conversation pieces from a phrase-book. All this I registered with approval: it was a healthy sign of revolutionary discipline and Bolshevik vigilance. I saw the ravages of the famine of 1932-33 in the Ukraine: hordes of families in rags begging at the railway stations, the women lifting up to the compartment window their starving brats which—with drumstick limbs, big cadaverous heads, puffed bellies—looked like embryos out of alcohol bottles; the old men with frost-bitten toes sticking out of torn slippers. I was told that these were kulaks who had resisted the collectivization of the land and I accepted the explanation; they were enemies of the people who preferred begging to work. The maid in the Hotel Regina in Kharkov fainted from hunger while doing my room; the manager explained that she was fresh from the countryside and through a technical hitch had not yet been issued her ration cards; I accepted the technical hitch.

I could not help noticing the Asiatic backwardness of life; the apathy of the crowds in the streets, tramways and railway stations; the incredible housing conditions which make all industrial towns appear one vast slum (two or three couples sharing one room divided by sheets hanging from washing lines); the starvation rations handed out by the co-operatives; or the fact that the price of one kilogram of butter on the free market equaled the average worker's monthly wage, the price of a pair of shoes two months' wages. But I had learned that facts had to be appreciated not on their face value, not in a static, but in a dynamic way. Living standards were low, but under the Czarist regime they had been even lower. The working classes in the capitalist countries were better off than in the Soviet Union, but that was a static comparison: for here the level was steadily rising, there steadily falling. At the end of the second Five Year Plan the two levels would be equalized; until that time all comparisons were misleading and bad for the Soviet people's morale. Accordingly, I not only accepted the famine as inevitable, but also the necessity of the ban on foreign travel, foreign newspapers and books, and the dissemination of a grotesquely distorted picture of life in the capitalist world. At first I was shocked when after a lecture I was asked questions like these: "When you left the bourgeois Press was your ration card withdrawn and were you kicked out at once from your room?" "What is the average number per day of French working class families starving to death (a) in rural areas (b) in the towns?" "By what means have our comrades in the West succeeded in temporarily staving off the war of intervention which the finance-capitalists are preparing with the aid of the Social Fascist traitors of the working class?" The questions were always painstakingly formulated in neo-Russian Djugashwilese. After a while I found them quite natural. There was always a small element of truth in them—this had, of course, been exaggerated and simplified according to the accepted technique of propaganda; but propaganda was indispensable for the survival of the Soviet Union, surrounded by a hostile world.

The necessary lie, the necessary slander; the necessary intimidation of the masses to preserve them from shortsighted errors; the necessary liquidation of oppositional groups and hostile classes; the necessary sacrifice of a whole generation in the interest of the next—it may all sound monstrous and yet it was so easy to accept while rolling along the single track of faith. It had all happened before, in the history of the medieval churches, in Byzantium, in the hothouses of

goes back to notion of faith

mystic sects; but the mental world of the drug addict is difficult to explain to the outsider who has never entered the
magic circle and never played Wonderland croquet with himself.

leaves Party before Nazi - Soviet

I left Soviet Russia in the autumn of 1933, yet I stayed in
the Party for another four and a half years, until the early
spring of 1938. My faith had been badly shaken, but thanks
to the elastic shock-absorbers, I was slow in becoming conscious of the damage. A number of external events and inner
rationalizations helped me to carry on and delay the final
crack-up.

The most important of these was the Seventh Congress of
the Comintern in 1934, which inaugurated a new policy, a
complete negation of the previous one—but to be put into
effect, as always, by the same leadership. All revolutionary
slogans, references to the class struggle and to the Dictatorship of the Proletariat were in one sweep relegated to the
lumber room. They were replaced by a brand new façade,
with geranium boxes in the windows, called "Popular Front
for Peace and against Fascism." Its doors were wide open to
all men of good will—Socialists, Catholics, Conservatives,
Nationalists. The notion that we had ever advocated revolution and violence was to be ridiculed as a bogey refuted as a
slander spread by reactionary war-mongers. We no longer
referred to ourselves as "Bolsheviks," nor even as Communists
—the public use of the word was now rather frowned at in the
Party—we were just simple, honest, peace-loving anti-Fascists
and defenders of democracy. On Bastille Day, 1935, in the
Salle Bullier in Paris, acclaimed by a delirious crowd of many
thousands, the veteran Communist Party leader Marcel Cachin
embraced the Social Fascist reptile Léon Blum and kissed
him on both cheeks. Half of the audience cried, the other half
sang the "Marseillaise" followed by the "Internationale." At
last, at last, the working class was united again. In the 1936

elections in Spain and France, the Popular Front scored massive victories.

All this was of course a direct consequence of the change in Soviet foreign policy: of Russia's entry into the League of Nations, the victory of the Litvinov line, the pact negotiations with France and Czechoslovakia. Again, in retrospect, one's memories of the Popular Front days are tainted by the ulterior knowledge of the cynical insincerity behind the façade, and of the bitter aftermath. But while it lasted, the Popular Front had a strong emotional appeal and a fervent *mystique* as a mass-movement. For me, it was a second honeymoon with the Party.

While I was in Russia, Hitler had come to power in Germany; so, in the autumn of 1933 I joined my Party friends in the Paris exile. The whole Red Block, with the exception of those caught by the Gestapo was now reassembled here, in the little hotels of the Left Bank. The next five years were for me years of near-starvation compensated by hectic political activity. Its center and motor was Willi Münzenberg, head of the *Agitprop* for Western Europe and Germany. He was a short, stocky man of proletarian origin; a magnetic personality of immense driving power and a hard, seductive charm. He broke with the Comintern in 1938, six months after myself, and was murdered in the summer of 1940 under the usual lurid and mysterious circumstances; as usual in such cases, the murderers are unknown and there are only indirect clues, all pointing in one direction like magnetic needles to the pole.

Willi was the Red Eminence of the international anti-Fascist movement. He organized the Reichstag Counter-Trial —the public hearings in Paris and London in 1933, which first called the attention of the world to the monstrous happenings in the Third Reich. Then came the series of Brown Books, a flood of pamphlets and emigré newspapers which he financed and directed, though his name nowhere appeared. He produced International Committees, Congresses and Movements as a conjurer produces rabbits out of his hat: the Committee for the Relief of the Victims of Fascism; Committees of Vigilance and Democratic Control; International Youth Congresses and so on. Each of these front organizations had a panel of highly respectable people, from English Duchesses to American columnists and French savants, most of whom had never heard the name of Münzenberg and thought that the Comintern was a bogey invented by Göbbels.

After the change of the general line decreed by the Seventh Congress and the dawn of the Popular Front, Willi's enterprises became truly dazzling. He organized the Committee for Peace and against Fascism (the so-called Amsterdam-Pleyel Movement) presided over by Barbusse; the Writers' Organization for the Defense of Culture; the Committee of Inquiry into Alleged Breaches of the Non-Intervention Agreement on Spain; and a series of other international mushroom growths. He was a genius of organization, an inspired propagandist, and no more unscrupulous in his methods than one had to be if one wanted to maintain one's position amidst the poisoned intrigues in the Comintern. A biography of Willi Münzenberg, if it should ever be written, would be one of the most revealing documents of the period between the two wars.

I worked with Willi at the very beginning of the Paris exile, during the Reichstag Trial and Brown Book period; then again during the Spanish War, and finally in 1938, after his break with the Comintern, when we published together a non-Stalinite anti-Nazi paper, *Die Zukunft*. In between I worked as a free-lance journalist, edited a comic paper for the Party during the Saar Referendum campaign (it was closed down by the Party after the first number as being too frivolous); worked on the staff of a Home for children of Communist underground workers in Germany; then on a news agency run by Alex Rado (later on key-man of Soviet Military Intelligence in Switzerland, and after World War II liquidated in Russia); and for one feverish, hungry and happy year was a kind of managing editor of a set-up called INFA—*Institut pour l'Etude du Fascisme*. It was an anti-Fascist archive and research bureau, run by Party members and controlled, but not financed, by the Comintern. The idea was to create a center for serious study of the inner workings of Fascist regimes, independent of the mass-propaganda methods of the Münzenberg enterprises. We were supported by donations from the French Trade Unions and from French intellectual and academic circles. We all worked unpaid, from ten to twelve hours a day; fortunately our premises, at 25, Rue Buffon, included a kitchen where every day at noon an enormous dish of thick pea soup was produced for the staff. For several weeks this was my only nourishment. At that time I lived in a hayloft in an open-air crank colony of pupils of Raymond Duncan in Meudon-Val Fleuri. This was the only place where I could sleep without paying rent, though it meant walking several miles a day to and from the office.

Work is a potent drug; to make oneself feel that one is doing a useful job anonymously and wholeheartedly is the most effective way of bribing one's conscience. The ignominies of the Djugashwili regime and of the Comintern machine faded into the background; the only thing that mattered was to fight against Nazism and the threatening war. I did not know that it was a shadow fight in which *we* were the shadows.

A second psychological factor helped me to carry on after my return from Russia. It was a conviction shared by the best among my friends who have now either left the Party or been liquidated. Though we wore blinkers, we were not blind, and even the most fanatical among us could not help noticing that all was not well in our movement. But we never tired of telling each other—and ourselves—that the Party could only be changed from inside, not from outside. You could resign from a club and from the ordinary sort of party if its policy no longer suited you; but the Communist Party was something entirely different: it was the vanguard of the Proletariat, the incarnation of the will of History itself. Once you stepped out of it you were *extra muros* and nothing which you said or did had the slightest chance of influencing its course. The only dialectically correct attitude was to remain inside, shut your mouth tight, swallow your bile and wait for the day when, after the defeat of the enemy and the victory of World Revolution, Russia and the Comintern were ready to become democratic institutions. Then and only then would the leaders be called to account for their actions: the avoidable defeats, the wanton sacrifices, the mud-stream of slander and denunciation, in which the pick of our comrades had perished. Until that day you had to play the game—confirm and deny, denounce and recant, eat your words and lick your vomit; it was the price you had to pay for being allowed to continue feeling useful, and thus keep your perverted self-respect.

★

On July 18, 1936, General Franco staged his *coup d'état*. I went to see Willi and asked him to help me to join the Spanish Republican Army; this was before the International Brigades were formed. I had brought my passport along; it was a Hungarian passport. Willi looked at it absentmindedly; as an inveterate propagandist he was not enthusiastic about writers wasting their time digging trenches. In the passport was my press card as a Paris Correspondent of the *Pester Lloyd*. I had never written a word for the *Pester Lloyd*, but every self-respecting Hungarian emigré in Paris was equipped with a press card from one Budapest paper or another, to obtain occasional free theater and movie tickets. Willi's eyes suddenly brightened; he had an idea.

"Why don't you rather make a trip to Franco's headquarters for the *Pester Lloyd*?" he suggested. "Hungary is a semi-Fascist country; they will welcome you with open arms."

I too thought it was an excellent idea, but there were some hitches. Firstly, the *Pester Lloyd* would never agree to sending me; but then why bother to inform them of my going? In the muddle of a civil war, nobody was likely to take the trouble to check my accreditation. Secondly, other foreign correspondents might think it fishy that a poor Hungarian paper was sending a special correspondent to Spain. That difficulty too was overcome. I had friends on the *News Chronicle* in London; the *News Chronicle* was violently anti-Franco and stood no chance of having a staff correspondent of its own admitted to rebel territory; so the Foreign Editor gladly agreed that I should act as his special correspondent provided that I ever got into Franco Spain.

I did get in, via Lisbon to Seville, but my sojourn was short. On the second day in Seville, which was then Franco's headquarters, I was recognized and denounced as a Communist; but thanks to the incredible Spanish muddle, managed to get out in the nick of time via Gibraltar. Even during that short visit however, I had seen the German pilots and German airplanes of Franco's army; I published the facts in the *News Chronicle* and in a pamphlet, and thereby incurred the special hostility of the Franco regime. Accordingly, when I was captured six months later, as a correspondent with the Republican Army, by Franco's troops, I was convinced that to be shot without unpleasant preliminaries was the best I could hope for.

I spent four months in Spanish prisons, in Málaga and Seville, most of the time in solitary confinement and most of the time convinced that I was going to be shot. When, in June, 1937, thanks to the intervention of the British Government, I was unexpectedly set free, my hair had not grayed and my features had not changed and I had not developed religious mania; but I had made the acquaintance of a different kind of reality, which had altered my outlook and values, and altered them so profoundly and unconsciously that during the first days of freedom I was not even aware of it. The experiences responsible for this change were fear, pity and a third one, more difficult to describe. Fear, not of death, but of torture and humiliation and the more unpleasant forms of dying—my companion of patio exercises, Garcia Atadell, was garroted shortly after my liberation. Pity for the little Andalusian and Catalan peasants whom I heard crying and calling for their *madres* when they were led out at night to face the firing squad; and finally, a condition of the mind usually referred to in terms borrowed from the vocabulary of mysticism, which would present itself at unexpected moments and induce a state of inner peace which I have known neither before nor since.

The lesson taught by this type of experience, when put into words, always appears under the dowdy guise of perennial commonplaces: that man is a reality, mankind an abstraction; that men cannot be treated as units in operations of political arithmetic because they behave like the symbols for zero and the infinite, which dislocate all mathematical operations; that the end justifies the means only within very narrow limits; that ethics is not a function of social utility, and charity not a petty-bourgeois sentiment but the gravitational force which keeps civilization in its orbit. Nothing can sound more flat-footed than such verbalizations of a knowledge which is not of a verbal nature; yet every single one of these trivial statements was incompatible with the Communist faith which I held.

★

If this story were fiction, it would end here; the chief character, having undergone a spiritual conversion, takes leave of his comrades of yesterday and goes his own way with a serene smile. But when I was liberated I did not know that I had ceased to be a Communist. The first thing I did after the Guardia Civil put me across the frontier at Gibraltar was to send a cable to the Party. It started with the line from Goethe *"Seid umschlungen, Millionen"*—"I embrace thee, ye millions." And, even more strange, I added the words "am cured of all belly-aches"—"belly-ache" being our slang expression for qualms about the Party line.

It was a short euphoria. I spent three quiet months with friends in England, writing a book on Spain; then, after a short trip to the Middle East for the *News Chronicle*, which offered no points of friction with the Party, the conflict began. There was nothing dramatic about it. I made a lecture tour through England for the Left Book Club; whenever a questioner, in the predominantly Communist audiences, asked for details about the treasonable activities of the POUM—an independent Left-Wing splinter group of Trotskyite leanings in Spain, whom the Party accused of being "agents of Franco"— I answered that their fractional policy might be bad for the cause, but that they were certainly not traitors. Surprisingly enough, I got away with that; the British CP was notoriously lax in denouncing deviations to higher quarters.

Then I learned that, in the Russian mass-purges, my brother-in-law and two of my closest friends had been arrested. All three were members of the German CP; the first, Dr. Ernst Ascher, was a doctor, politically naïve and indifferent, who worked at a State hospital in the Volga German Republic. The accusation against him, as I later learned, was that he was a saboteur who had injected syphilis into his patients,[5] that he had demoralized the people by pretending that venereal diseases were incurable, and thirdly, as a matter of course, that he was the agent of a foreign power. He has never been heard of since his arrest twelve years ago.

The other two were Alex Weissberg and his wife Eva. For reasons which will appear later, I have to tell their story in some detail. Alex, a physicist, was employed at the Ukrainian Institute for Physics and Technology (UFTI); I had known them both for many years and had stayed with them in Kharkov. When I left Russia, in 1933, Alex had seen me to the train; his farewell words had been: "Whatever happens, hold the banner of the Soviet Union high." He was arrested in 1937 on the charge (as I learned much later) of having hired twenty bandits to ambush Stalin and Kaganovitch on their next hunting trip in the Caucasus. He refused to sign a confession, was kept in various prisons for three years, then, after the Ribben-

---

[5] Cf. the charge against Jagoda, former head of the OGPU, and three physicians that they had poisoned Maxim Gorky by quicksilver fumes.

trop-Molotov Pact, was handed over by the GPU to the Gestapo, in 1940, at Brest Litovsk, together with a hundred-odd other Austrian, German and Hungarian Communists. (Among them Grete Neumann Buber, wife of the German Communist leader Heinz Neumann and sister-in-law of Willi Münzenberg, and the physicist Fiesl Hautermans, a former assistant of Professor Blackett.) He survived the Gestapo, took part in the Warsaw Revolt, and has written a book which will shortly be available to English readers.

Alex' wife Eva, was a ceramist; she was arrested about a year before Alex and was at first accused of having inserted swastikas into the pattern on the teacups which she designed for mass-production; then, of having hidden under her bed two pistols which were to serve to kill Stalin at the next Party Congress. She spent eighteen months in the Lubianka, where the GPU tried to brief her as a repentant sinner for the Bukharin show-trial. She cut her veins, was saved, and was released shortly afterwards thanks to the extraordinary exertions of the Austrian Consul in Moscow, who happened to be a friend of her mother.

I met Eva after she had been released and expelled from Russia, in the spring of 1938. Her experiences in Russian prisons, and particularly of the GPU's methods of obtaining confessions, provided me with part of the material for *Darkness at Noon*. I promised her to do what I could to save Alex. Albert Einstein had already intervened on his behalf; so I wrote a carefully worded cable to Stalin, for which I obtained the signatures of the three French Nobel Prize physicists, Perrin, Langevin and Joliot-Curie. The cable, a copy of which was sent to State Attorney Vishinsky, requested that the charges against Weissberg, if any, be made public, and that he be given a public trial. It is characteristic that although both Langevin and Joliot-Curie were Soviet sympathizers who shortly afterward became members of the Party, they obviously did not set great store by the methods of Soviet justice—for, though they had never heard of Alex before, and knew me only slightly, they at once took it for granted that he was innocent. The cable was also signed by Polanyi in Manchester; the only prominent physicist whom I approached and who refused to sign was Professor Blackett. I mention this fact because Blackett did his best to save his former assistant, Hautermans, a close friend of Weissberg's. He was probably afraid that, by signing two protests, he might spoil the chance of saving at least one victim from the mortal embrace of the Socialist Fatherland.

The moral of this story is that Joliot-Curie, Blackett, and the rest of our nuclear Marxists cannot claim starry-eyed ignorance of the goings-on in Russia. They know in detail the case-history of at least these two of their colleagues, both loyal servants of the Soviet Union, arrested on grotesque charges, held for years without trial, and delivered to the Gestapo. They further know that these cases are not exceptional; reliable, second-hand reports of hundreds of similar cases in Russian academic circles are available to them. And the same is true of all Communists or fellow-traveling authors, journalists and other intellectuals. Every single one of us knows of at least one friend who perished in the Arctic subcontinent of forced labor camps, was shot as a spy or vanished without trace. How our voices boomed with righteous indignation, denouncing flaws in the procedure of justice in our comfortable democracies; and how silent we were when our comrades, without trial or conviction, were liquidated in the Socialist sixth of the earth. Each of us carries a skeleton in the cupboard of his conscience; added together they would form galleries of bones more labyrinthine than the Paris catacombs.

At no time and in no country have more revolutionaries been killed and reduced to slavery than in Soviet Russia. To one who himself for seven years found excuses for every stupidity and crime committed under the Marxist banner, the spectacle of these dialectical tight-rope acts of self-deception, performed by men of good will and intelligence, is more disheartening than the barbarities committed by the simple in spirit. Having experienced the almost unlimited possibilities of mental acrobatism on that tight-rope stretched across one's conscience, I know how much stretching it takes to make that elastic rope snap.

About the time when I learned of Alex' arrest, a comrade escaped to Paris from Germany where he had served a term of five years' hard labor. Before his arrest, he had worked for a certain branch of the Apparat whose leaders had meanwhile been liquidated as spies. So, without being given a hearing, without a chance of defending himself, my friend and his wife were denounced as agents of the Gestapo, and their photographs were printed in the Party Press accompanied by a warning not to have any truck with them. Such cases I had heard of before; I had shrugged them off and continued on the tight-rope. Now these two individuals had become more real to me than the cause in the name of which they were to be sacrificed, and I took their side.[6]

The Party did not react. While I had been in jail, they had used me as a martyr for propaganda purposes; some time must be allowed to lapse before I could be denounced as an agent of Franco and the Mikado.

The end came as a curious anticlimax. Some time during the spring of 1938, I had to give a talk on Spain to the German Emigré Writers' Association in Paris. Before the talk, a representative of the Party asked me to insert a passage denouncing the POUM as agents of Franco; I refused. He shrugged, and asked me whether I would care to show him the text of my speech and "to discuss it informally." I refused. The meeting took place in the hall of the Societé des Industries Françaises in the Place St. Germain des Près, before an audience of two or three hundred refugee intellectuals, half of them Communists. I knew it was my last public appearance as a member of the Party. The theme of the speech was the situation in Spain;

[6] They have now entered on a new existence, under a different name, in a British Dominion. Incidentally, it was this girl who was caught out by the Gestapo on the word "concrete."

speech in Paris

it contained not a single word of criticism of the Party or of Russia. But it contained three phrases, deliberately chosen because to normal people they were platitudes, to Communists a declaration of war. The first was: "No movement, party or person can claim the privilege of infallibility." The second was: "Appeasing the enemy is as foolish as persecuting the friend who pursues your own aim by a different road." The third was a quotation from Thomas Mann: "A harmful truth is better than a useful lie."

That settled it. When I had finished, the non-Communist half of the audience applauded, the Communist half sat in heavy silence, most of them with folded arms. This was not done by order, but as a spontaneous reaction to those fatal commonplaces. You might as well have told a Nazi audience that all men are born equal regardless of race and creed.

A few days later I wrote my letter of resignation to the Central Committee of the Party. *dnt get the boot*

★

This is the second occasion where the story should end; and yet there was a second anticlimax. My letter was a farewell to the German CP, the Comintern and the Djugashwili regime. But it ended with a declaration of loyalty to the Soviet Union. I stated my opposition to the system, to the cancerous growth of the bureaucracy, the suppression of civil liberties. But I professed my belief that the foundations of the Workers and Peasants State had remained unshaken, that the nationalization of the means of production was a guarantee of her eventual return to the road of Socialism; and that, in spite of everything, the Soviet Union still "represented our last and only hope on a planet in rapid decay."

The tight-rope had snapped, but there was a safety net spread under it. When I landed there, I found myself in a mixed company—veteran acrobats who had lost their dialectical balance, Trotskyites, critical sympathizers, independent "cryptos," new statesmen, new republicans, totalitarian liberals

breaks support of soviets w/ 1939 Pact

and so on—who were sprawling in the net in various contorted positions. We were all hellishly uncomfortable, suspended in no man's land, but at least we did not have to regard ourselves as completely fallen angels. I remained in that state of suspended animation until the day when the swastika was hoisted on Moscow Airport in honor of Ribbentrop's arrival and the Red Army band broke into the *Horst Wessel Lied*. That was the end; from then onward I no longer cared whether Hitler's allies called me a counter-revolutionary.

Elsewhere I have tried to expose "the fallacy of the unshaken foundations,"[7] the belief that a State-capitalist economy must of necessity lead to a Socialist regime. I shall not repeat the argument; I have only mentioned this epilogue to my Party days, my clinging to the last shred of the torn illusion, because it was typical of that intellectual cowardice which still prevails on the Left. The addiction to the Soviet myth is as tenacious and difficult to cure as any other addiction. After the Lost Weekend in Utopia the temptation is strong to have just one last drop, even if watered down and sold under a different label. And there is always a supply of new labels on the Cominform's black market in ideals. They deal in slogans as bootleggers deal in faked spirits; and the more innocent the customer, the more easily he becomes a victim of the ideological hooch sold under the trade-mark of Peace, Democracy, Progress or what you will.

★

I served the Communist Party for seven years—the same length of time as Jacob tended Laban's sheep to win Rachel his daughter. When the time was up, the bride was led into his dark tent; only the next morning did he discover that his ardors had been spent not on the lovely Rachel but on the ugly Leah.

I wonder whether he ever recovered from the shock of

[7] *The Yogi and the Commissar*, New York: The Macmillan Company, 1945.

having slept with an illusion. I wonder whether afterwards he believed that he had ever believed in it. I wonder whether the happy end of the legend will be repeated; for at the price of another seven years of labor, Jacob was given Rachel too, and the illusion became flesh.

And the seven years seemed unto him but a few days, for the love he had for her.

Ignazio Silone

BIOGRAPHICAL NOTE: *Ignazio Silone was born on May 1, 1900, at Pescina dei Marsi, a village in the Abruzzi Apennines. His father was a small landowner, his mother a weaver. During the First World War, at the age of seventeen, he was appointed secretary of the land workers for the Abruzzi district, and had to appear in court for having organized a violent demonstration against the war. In 1921, he took part in the foundation of the Italian Communist Party; he edited the weekly* Avanguardia *of Rome and the* Lavoratore, *a daily of Trieste. He remained in Italy even after the enforcement of the special laws against opponents of Fascism, printing illegal newspapers. In 1930, after having been imprisoned in and expelled from various European countries, he settled down in Switzerland, where he remained till 1944, when he returned to Italy. He had left the Communist Party in 1930. Ten years later, in 1940, he accepted the direction of the Foreign Center of the Italian Socialist Party, for which he formulated the political platform of the "Third Front."*

Bibliography: Fontamara, *novel, 1930;* Bread and Wine, *novel, 1937;* The School for Dictators, *dialogues, 1938;* The Seed beneath the Snow, *novel, 1940;* And He did Hide Himself, *play, 1944.*

That evening in November, immediately after the promulgation of the "special laws," several of us escaped arrest by taking refuge in a little villa in a suburb of Milan, recently rented by one of our comrades who was masquerading as a painter. In the working-class quarters the streets were deserted, the taverns closed or silent, the houses in darkness. This gave the damp, cold time of the year an atmosphere of gloom. The police, in full war order, were carrying out a series of raids on suspected blocks of houses, as if they were enemy strong-points. The number of people arrested was already very considerable and was growing day by day as more names and addresses came to light, either as the result of these raids, or of denunciations by spies and *agents provocateurs*, or of statements from the feebler people arrested, who had not been able to stand up to threats or torture.

Much the same was happening in other cities and provinces. The newspapers which could still be published (those in open opposition had been suppressed just about that time) had been ordered not to mention the arrests, and to report, instead, the tributes to the Italian dictatorship which eminent representatives of democracy and liberalism in other countries had been expressing. But reports based on the information which the three or four Party couriers collected from our local representatives in the most important areas, and brought to the central underground offices, left no doubt that the dictatorship intended to exterminate every trace of opposition. The Communists alone possessed a clandestine organization of any efficiency. But in various provinces the police, sometimes not realizing it themselves, had already by their raids destroyed our network of communications. Numerous comrades who had escaped arrest came in asking us for a permanent refuge in a city other than their own, and for false documents to enable them to travel and to make a fresh start.

Those of us who had been living under false names for some time—hiding our illegal activities under some banal or innocent cloak—were now in a much more advantageous position. But we were none too safe, either, as betrayal or carelessness on the part of anyone who had been arrested might at any time give the police a clue and put them on our tracks. So that evening I, too, had suddenly been warned not to return home, because it looked as if the police were picketing the house. With others in the same condition, we had found temporary refuge in the pretended painter's little country villa. After putting a man on guard near by and arranging what to do if surprised by the police, we resigned ourselves to spending the night on chairs, as the little house was very sparsely furnished and had only one bed. With the bogus painter and his wife, we had a bogus Spanish tourist, a bogus dentist, a bogus architect and a German girl, a bogus student. We had already known each other for a couple of years; but, up to that day, our relations had been entirely confined to technical collaboration in various branches of the illegal organization; we had not yet had the time or opportunity to become friends. At most we knew each other's social origins and family situation, because of the inevitable repercussions these things have in the complicated circumstances of life outside the law. Why, then, did that evening's casual encounter make such a deep impression on my memory?

The dentist happened to remark:

"I passed La Scala this afternoon. There was a big crowd queuing up to buy tickets for the next concert. I stopped a while to look at them and got the clear impression of a procession of madmen."

"Why madmen?" asked the Spanish tourist. "Is music madness, in your opinion?"

"Not in normal circumstances," admitted the dentist. "But in times like these, how can people amuse themselves with music? They must really be maniacs."

"Music isn't always a mere amusement," observed the Spanish tourist.

"If the music maniacs could see us now, and hear who we are and what we're doing," added the painter, "they in their turn would almost certainly consider us mad. It isn't so easy to discover who the really mad people are; that's one of the most difficult of sciences."

The dentist did not like the turn the conversation was taking.

"One can't risk one's life and liberty as we are doing," he replied severely, "and then reason like someone who's above the struggle."

"You can throw yourself into the struggle," replied the painter, "and kick and hit out at your opponent, but it's not absolutely necessary to butt him. Isn't it better to reserve your head for other uses?"

"Isn't our struggle a struggle of ideas?" asked the Spanish tourist. "Doesn't it involve your head?"

"It involves my head, of course, but not my eyes," the painter explained with a smile. "In other words," he added, "I'd like to go on seeing things with my own eyes."

"I don't understand," declared the dentist. "The risk you run by staying with us seems to me very much out of proportion to the small amount of work you do."

There was an embarrassing pause. Through the window we could see three trucks full of militiamen passing on the main road. Our hostess closed the shutters and gave us some excellent coffee.

"In our era all roads lead to Communism," said the Spanish tourist, to restore harmony among his comrades. "But we can't all be Communists in the same way."

"I've staked my life on the Proletarian Revolution," explained the painter. "If I haven't staked my eyes as well, it's only to reserve myself the right of seeing what happens to my life. But the life itself is already staked. In the same way, to put it more clearly, a dear school friend of mine has become a nun, and staked her life on Paradise. On the heavenly Paradise, I mean, not to be confused with ours. I can assure you I shan't withdraw my stake. Why should I? No one has the right to doubt my honor."

"But the Proletarian Revolution," the dentist commented severely, "isn't a game of chance."

"I know perfectly well," explained the painter, "that winning the game doesn't depend on chance, but on the strength and skill of the players, and on everything else one reads about in the manuals of our Party schools. And that's why I'm taking part, not only as a gambler, but as a player too; as a player who is entirely wrapped up in the game and has staked himself. Entirely, I say, except for the eyes."

"I don't understand," declared the dentist.

"In short, I refuse to blindfold myself," the painter concluded. "I'll do absolutely everything you expect me to do, but with my eyes open."

"All right," said the Spanish tourist in his turn, "but I don't understand if you are really interested in what you are gambling on. Forgive the question, but, in other circumstances, mightn't you have gambled on something completely different, war, for instance, exploring the South Pole, tending lepers, the white-slave traffic, or forging money?"

"Why not?" the other replied, laughing. "But in all these possible professions of mine, I would certainly have tried to keep my eyes open. I'd have tried to understand."

"One's born a Communist," declared the German girl.

"But one becomes a man," commented the painter.

"Well," the dentist asked him, "could you tell us what the circumstances are which led you to put your stake on Communism?"

"That would be a long story," the other replied gravely. "And some things, to be frank, would be incomprehensible to you."

"Tell us your long incomprehensible story," insisted the German girl. "We'll drink coffee and keep awake to listen to you."

"And will you all tell your stories too?" the painter asked us with a smile.

"Agreed," said the dentist, "and we'll all keep awake and drink coffee."

"Think about it seriously before you begin," the painter warned us. "It may be dangerous for you to look backward. It may be dangerous for anyone in the thick of the struggle, myself included, to analyze the 'whys' and the 'wherefores,' to look back. At a certain moment, the game is set and *rien ne va plus.* You can't leave off dancing in the middle of the dance."

"But can one separate the struggle," said the Spanish tourist, "from the motives that have led one into it? Is it dangerous to remind oneself of the motives which have led one to Communism?"

"The night is long," said the German girl. "Let's tell our incomprehensible stories. We'll drink coffee and keep ourselves awake."

So we spent that night trying to explain to each other how and why we had become Communists. The explanations were anything but exhaustive; but by morning we had all become friends. "It's really true," we said to each other as we separated, "that any road can lead to Communism nowadays."

Next year the bogus dentist was arrested; he was tortured, refused to denounce his collaborators and died in prison. The bogus painter went on carrying out his political duties until the fall of Fascism and the end of the war; I think he afterward retired into private life. Nothing more was heard of the German girl.

I often thought later about the confidences shared during that meeting. By then the imperious necessity of understanding, of realizing, of comparing the development of the action in which I was engaged with the motives which had originally led me into it, had taken entire possession of me and left me no more peace. And if my poor literary work has any meaning, in the ultimate analysis, it consists of this: a time came when writing meant, for me, an absolute necessity to testify, an urgent need to free myself from an obsession, to state the meaning and define the limits of a painful but decisive break, and of a vaster allegiance that still continues. For me writing has not been, and never could be, except in a few favored moments of grace, a serene aesthetic enjoyment, but rather the painful and lonely continuation of a struggle. As for the difficulties and imperfections of self-expression with which I sometimes have to wrestle, they arise, not from lack of observation of the rules of good writing, but rather from a conscience which, while struggling to heal certain hidden and perhaps incurable wounds, continues obstinately to demand that its integrity be respected. For to be sincere is obviously not enough, if one wants to be truthful.

★

At the foundation congress of the Italian Communist Party (Leghorn, 1921) I brought with me the adherence of the greater part of the Socialist Youth, to which I had belonged since 1917. Our attitude, as far back as the war years, had been so strongly critical of reformist Social Democracy that our adherence aroused no surprise.

That November evening in Milan, when I wanted to explain to my friends why, at the age of seventeen and still a schoolboy, I had adhered to the Socialism of Zimmerwald, I had to go back, in my memory, step by step, to the beginning of my adolescence; I even had to mention episodes of my childhood, to rediscover the very earliest origins of a view of society which, as it later on assumed a political form, was bound to reveal itself as radical. At the age of seventeen, and in time of war, one does not join a revolutionary movement which is persecuted by the government, unless one's motives are serious.

I grew up in a mountainous district of southern Italy. The phenomenon which most impressed me, when I arrived at the age of reason, was the violent contrast, the incomprehensible, absurd, monstrous contrast between family and private life— in the main decent, honest, and well-conducted—and social relations, which were very often crude and full of hatred and deceit. Many terrifying stories are known of the misery and desperation of the southern provinces (I have told some myself), but I do not intend to refer now to events that caused a stir, so much as to the little occurrences of daily life. It was these commonplace minor events that showed up the strange double existence of the people among whom I grew up, the observation of which was one of the agonizing secrets of my adolescence.

I was a child just five years old when, one Sunday, while crossing the little square of my native village with my mother leading me by the hand, I witnessed the cruel, stupid spectacle of one of the local gentry setting his great dog at a poor woman, a seamstress, who was just coming out of church. The wretched woman was flung to the ground, badly mauled, and her dress was torn to ribbons. Indignation in the village was general, but silent. I have never understood how the poor woman ever got the unhappy idea of taking proceedings against the squire; but the only result was to add a mockery of justice to the harm already done. Although, I must repeat, everybody pitied her and many people helped her secretly, the unfortunate woman could not find a single witness prepared to give evidence before the magistrate, nor a lawyer to conduct the prosecution. On the other hand, the squire's supposedly Left-Wing lawyer turned up punctually, and so did a number of bribed witnesses who perjured themselves by giving a grotesque version of what had happened, and accusing the woman of having provoked the dog. The magistrate—a most worthy, honest person in private life—acquitted the squire and condemned the poor woman to pay the costs.

"It went very much against the grain with me," he excused himself a few days later at our house. "On my word of honor, I do assure you, I was very sorry about it. But even if I had been present at the disgusting incident as a private citizen and couldn't have avoided blaming him, still as a judge I had to go by the evidence of the case, and unfortunately it was in favor of the dog." "A real judge," he used to love to say, sententiously, "must be able to conceal his own egoistic feelings, and be impartial." "Really, you know," my mother used to comment, "it's a horrible profession. Better to keep ourselves to ourselves at home. My son," she used to say to me, "when you're grown up, be whatever you like, but not a judge."

I can remember other typical little incidents like that of

the squire, the dog, and the seamstress. But I should not like to suggest, by quoting such episodes, that we were ignorant of the sacred concepts of Justice and Truth or that we held them in contempt. On the contrary; at school, in church, and at public celebrations they were often discussed with eloquence and veneration, but in rather abstract terms. To define our curious situation more exactly, I should add that it was based on a deception of which all of us, even the children, were aware; and yet it still persisted, being built on something quite apart from the ignorance and stupidity of individuals.

I remember a lively discussion one day in my catechism class between the boys who were being prepared for confirmation and the parish priest. The subject was a marionette show at which we boys had been present with the priest the day before. It was about the dramatic adventures of a child who was persecuted by the devil. At one point the child-marionette had appeared on the stage trembling with fear and, to escape the devil who was searching for him, had hidden under a bed in a corner of the stage; shortly afterward the devil-marionette arrived and looked for him in vain. "But he *must* be here," said the devil-marionette. "I can smell him. Now I'll ask these good people in the audience." And he turned to us and asked: "My dear children, have you by any chance seen that naughty child I'm looking for, hiding anywhere?" "No, no, no," we all chorused at once, as energetically as possible. "Where is he then? I can't see him," the devil insisted. "He's left, he's gone away," we all shouted. "He's gone to Lisbon." (In our part of Italy, Lisbon is still the furthermost point of the globe, even today.) I should add that none of us, when we went to the theater, had expected to be questioned by a devil-marionette; our behavior was therefore entirely instinctive and spontaneous. And I imagine that children in any other part of the world would have reacted in the same way. But our parish priest, a most worthy, cultured and pious person, was not altogether pleased. We had told a lie,

he warned us with a worried look. We had told it for good
ends, of course, but still it remained a lie. One must never tell
lies. "Not even to the devil?" we asked in surprise. "A lie is
always a sin," the priest replied. "Even to the magistrate?"
asked one of the boys. The priest rebuked him severely. "I'm
here to teach you Christian doctrine and not to talk nonsense.
What happens outside the church is no concern of mine." And
he began to explain the doctrine about truth and lies in general
in the most eloquent language. But that day the question of
lies *in general* was of no interest to us children; we wanted to
know, "Ought we to have told the devil where the child was
hiding, yes or no?" "That's not the point," the poor priest kept
repeating to us rather uneasily. "A lie is always a lie. It might
be a big sin, a medium sin, an average sort of sin, or a little tiny
sin, but it's always a sin. Truth must be honored."

"The truth is," we said, "that there was the devil on one side
and the child on the other. We wanted to help the child, that's
the real truth." "But you've told a lie," the parish priest kept
on repeating. "For good ends, I know, but still a lie." To end it,
I put forward an objection of unheard-of perfidy, and, considering my age, considerable precocity: "If it'd been a priest
instead of a child," I asked, "what ought we to have replied
to the devil?" The parish priest blushed, avoided a reply, and,
as a punishment for my impertinence, made me spend the rest
of the lesson on my knees beside him. "Are you sorry?" he
asked me at the end of the lesson. "Of course," I replied. "If the
devil asks me for your address, I'll give it to him at once."

It was certainly unusual for a discussion in such terms to take
place in a catechism class, although free discussion was quite
frequent in our family circle and among our friends. But this
intellectual liveliness did not even create a stir in the humiliating and primitive stagnation of our social life.

★

Some time earlier the so-called democratic system had, however, introduced a new technical detail into the relations be-

tween citizen and State. This was the secret vote, which though not in itself enough to change things radically, sometimes produced results which were surprising, and, as far as public order was concerned, scandalous. Though these incidents were isolated and had no immediate sequel, they were none the less disturbing.

I was seven years old when the first election campaign, which I can remember, took place in my district. At that time we still had no political parties, so the announcement of this campaign was received with very little interest. But popular feeling ran high when it was disclosed that one of the candidates was "the Prince." There was no need to add Christian and surname to realize which Prince was meant. He was the owner of the great estate formed by the arbitrary occupation of the vast tracts of land reclaimed in the previous century from the Lake of Fucino. About eight thousand families (that is, the majority of the local population) are still employed today in cultivating the estate's fourteen thousand hectares. The Prince was deigning to solicit "his" families for their vote so that he could become their deputy in parliament. The agents of the estate, who were working for the Prince, talked in impeccably liberal phrases: "Naturally," said they, "naturally, no one will be forced to vote for the Prince, that's understood; in the same way that no one, naturally, can force the Prince to allow people who don't vote for him to work on his land. This is the period of real liberty for everybody; you're free, and so is the Prince." The announcement of these "liberal" principles produced general and understandable consternation among the peasants. For, as may easily be guessed, the Prince was the most hated person in our part of the country. As long as he remained in the invisible Olympus of the great feudal proprietor (none of the eight thousand tenants had seen him, up to then, even from afar) public hatred for him was allowed, and belonged to the same category as curses against hostile deities; such curses, though useless, are satisfying. But now the clouds were being rent, and the Prince was coming down within reach of mortal men. From now on, consequently, they would have to keep their expressions of hatred within the narrow circle of private life and get ready to welcome him with due honors in the village streets.

My father seemed reluctant to accept this kind of logic. He was the youngest of several brothers, all of them peasant proprietors; the youngest, the most restless, and the only one with any inclinations toward insubordination. One evening his older brothers came and urged him, in the common interest, to be prudent and careful. For me (to whom no one paid any attention, for grown-ups think that children don't understand such things) it was a most instructive evening. "The Prince being a candidate is a real farce," the eldest brother admitted. "Political candidatures should be reserved for lawyers and other such windbags. But as the Prince is a candidate, all we can do is support him." "If the Prince's candidature is a farce," replied my father, "I don't understand why we should support him." "Because we're his dependents, as you know perfectly well." "Not in politics," said my father. "In politics we're free." "We don't cultivate politics, we cultivate the land," they answered him. "As cultivators of the land we depend on the Prince." "There's no mention of politics in our contracts for the land, only of potatoes and beetroots. As voters we're free." "The Prince's bailiff will also be free not to renew our contracts," they answered him. "That's why we're forced to be on his side." "I can't vote for someone merely because I'm forced to," said my father. "I'd feel humiliated." "No one will know how you vote," they answered him. "In the secrecy of the polling booth you can vote as you like, freely. But during the electioneering campaign we must be on the Prince's side, all of us together." "I'd be pleased to do it if I wasn't ashamed to," said my father, "but, do believe me, I'd be too much ashamed." To settle it, my uncles and my father reached this compromise: he would not come out either on the Prince's side or against him.

The Prince's election tour was prepared by the civil

authorities, the police, the carabineers, and the agents of the estate. One Sunday, the Prince deigned to pass through the principal villages in the constituency, without stopping and without making any speeches. This tour of his was remembered for a long time in our district, mainly because he made it in a motorcar, and it was the first time we had seen one. The word "motorcar" itself had not yet found a place in our everyday language, and the peasants called it a "horseless carriage." Strange legends were current among the people about the invisible motive force which took the place of the horses, about the diabolical speed which the new vehicle could reach, and about the ruinous effect, particularly on the vines, of the stink it left behind it. That Sunday the entire population of the village had gone to meet the Prince on the road by which he was due to arrive. There were numerous visible signs of the collective admiration and affection for the Prince. The crowds were dressed up in their best, and were in a perfectly understandable state of excitement. The "horseless carriage" arrived late, and roared through the crowd and the village, without stopping and without even slowing down, leaving a thick white dust cloud behind it. The Prince's agents then explained, to anyone who cared to listen, that the "horseless carriage" went by "petrol vapor" and could only stop when the petrol had finished. "It isn't like horses," they explained, "where all one need do is to pull on the reins. There aren't any reins at all. Did you notice any reins?"

Two days later a strange little old man arrived from Rome; he wore glasses, and had a black stick and a small suitcase. Nobody knew him. He said he was an oculist and had put himself up as candidate against the Prince. A few people gathered round him out of curiosity, mainly children and women, who had not the right to vote. I was among the children, in my short trousers and with my schoolbooks under my arm. We begged the old man to make a speech. He said to us: "Remind your parents that the vote is secret. Nothing else." Then he said, "I am poor; I live by being an oculist; but if any of you have anything wrong with your eyes I'm willing to treat them for nothing." So we brought him an old woman who sold vegetables. She had bad eyes, and he cleaned them up and gave her a little phial with drops in it and explained how to use it. Then he said to us (we were only a group of children): "Remind your parents that the vote is secret," and he went away. But the Prince's election was so certain, to judge by the festive throngs which had welcomed him during his electioneering tour, that the authorities and the agents of the estate had announced in advance a whole program for the celebration of the inevitable victory. My father, according to the agreement with his brothers, did not side with either candidate, but managed to get himself included among the scrutineers of the ballot-papers. Great was everybody's surprise when it became known that in the secrecy of the polling booths an enormous majority had voted against the Prince and for the unknown oculist. It was a great scandal; the authorities called it sheer treachery. But the treachery was of such proportions that the agents of the estate could not take any reprisals against anyone.

After this, social life went back to normal. Nobody asked himself: Why can the will of the people only express itself sporadically? Why can it not become a permanent and stable basis for the reorganization of public life? And yet, it would be incorrect to conclude, from a false interpretation of the episode I have just recorded, that the major obstacle was fear. Our people have never been cowardly or spineless or weak. On the contrary; the rigors of the climate, the heaviness of the work, the harsh conditions of the struggle for existence, have made them into one of the toughest, hardest, and most enduring peoples in the whole of Italy. So much so, that there are fewer references in our local annals to political surprises resulting from the secret vote than there are to revolts, localized and shortlived, but violent, destructive and almost savage. These humiliated and downtrodden people could endure the worst abuses without complaint, but then they would break out on unforeseen occasions.

My native village, at the period to which I am now referring, had some five thousand inhabitants, and public order was in the keeping of about twenty carabineers, commanded by a lieutenant. This excessive number of police is in itself revealing. There was not much sympathy between the soldiers and the carabineers during the First World War, because the latter were on duty in the rear areas, and some of them, it was said, took too much interest in the wives and fiancées of the men at the front. In small places, rumors of this kind are immediately given a very exact personal application. So it happened one evening that three soldiers, home from the front on short leave, had a quarrel with some carabineers and were arrested by them. This action was ridiculous and ungallant to begin with, but it became absolutely monstrous when the commanding officer of the carabineers canceled the three soldiers' leave and sent them back to the front. I was a close friend of one of them (he was killed in the war afterward), and his old mother came sobbing to me to tell me about the affair. I begged the mayor, the magistrate and the parish priest to intervene, but they all declared it was outside their province. "If that's the way things are," I said, "there's nothing for it but *revolution!*" We have always used this fateful historical term, in our dialect, in order to describe a mere violent demonstration. In those wartime years, for example, two "revolutions" had already taken place in my native village, the first against the town council because of bread rationing, the second against the church because the seat of the bishopric had been transferred to another township. The third, which I am about to describe, went down in history as "the revolution of the three soldiers." The men were to be escorted to the train at five o'clock, so the revolution was arranged for half an hour earlier, in front of the barracks. Unfortunately it took a more serious turn than had been intended. It began as a joke, which three of us boys were bold enough to start.

One of us, at the agreed moment, went up the bell-tower and began hammering away at the great bell, the signal in our part of the country denoting a serious fire or other public danger. The other two went off to meet the peasants to explain what was happening. Alarmed by the ringing of the tocsin, they had at once stopped working in the fields, and were hurrying anxiously toward the village.

In a few minutes a threatening and tumultuous crowd had collected in front of the barracks. They began by shouting abuse, then they threw stones, and finally shots were fired. The siege of the barracks lasted until late at night. Rage had made my fellow-villagers unrecognizable. In the end, the windows and gates of the barracks were broken open; the carabineers fled across the orchards and fields under cover of darkness; and the three soldiers, whom everyone had forgotten, went back to their homes unobserved. So we boys found ourselves absolute masters of the place for an entire night. "Now what are we going to do?" the other boys asked me. (My authority came, mainly, from the fact that I knew Latin.) "Tomorrow morning," I said, "the village is sure to be reoccupied by hundreds and hundreds of armed men, carabineers and police, who'll arrive from Avezzano, Sulmona, Aquila, and perhaps even from Rome." "But what are we going to do tonight, before they arrive?" the other boys insisted. "Obviously one night is not enough to create a new order of things," I said, thinking I had guessed what they were after. "Couldn't we take advantage of the fact that the whole village is asleep, to make Socialism?"

That was what the other boys wanted me to suggest. Perhaps they were still overexcited from their riotous evening; perhaps they really believed that anything was possible now. "I don't think," I said, "I honestly don't think that, even if the whole village is asleep, one can make Socialism in a single night." I must mention in my own justification that at that time the theory of Socialism overnight had not yet been propounded. "One night, though, might be enough to sleep in one's own bed before going to prison," one of the others finally suggested. And as we were tired, we all found this advice both sensible and acceptable.

Such episodes of violence—with their inevitable sequel of mass arrests, trials, legal expenses, and prison sentences—reinforced distrust, diffidence, and skepticism in the peasants' minds. For them, the State became the irremediable creation of the devil. A good Christian, if he wanted to save his soul, should avoid, as far as possible, all contact with the State. The State always stands for swindling, intrigue and privilege, and could not stand for anything else. Neither law nor force can change it. If retribution occasionally catches up with it, this can only be by the dispensation of God.

★

In 1915 an earthquake of exceptional violence destroyed a large part of our province and killed, in thirty seconds, about fifty thousand people. I was surprised to see how much my fellow-villagers took this appalling catastrophe as a matter of course. The geologists' complicated explanations, reported in the newspapers, aroused their contempt. In a district like ours, where so many injustices go unpunished, people regarded the recurrent earthquakes as a phenomenon requiring no further explanation. In fact, it was astonishing that earthquakes were not more frequent. An earthquake buries rich and poor, learned and illiterate, authorities and subjects alike beneath its ruined houses. Here lies, moreover, the real explanation of the Italians' well-known powers of endurance when faced with the cataclysms of nature. An earthquake achieves what the law promises but does not in practice maintain—the equality of all men. A neighbor of ours, a woman who kept a bakery, lay buried, but not hurt, for several days after the earthquake, when her house was completely destroyed. Not realizing that the disaster was general, and imagining that it was only her own house which had fallen down, either because of some defect in its construction or because someone had put a curse on it, the poor woman was greatly distressed; so much so that when a rescue party wanted to drag her out of the ruins she absolutely refused. She calmed down, however, and quickly regained her strength and her wish to live and to rebuild her house, the moment she was told there had been an earthquake and that an enormous number of other houses had collapsed as well.

What seemed to the poor people of our part of the world a much more serious calamity than any natural cataclysm was what happened *after* the earthquake. The State reconstruction program was carried out to the accompaniment of innumerable intrigues, frauds, thefts, swindles, embezzlements, and dishonesty of every kind. An acquaintance of mine, who had been sacked by one of the government departments concerned, gave me some information of this sort about certain criminal acts which were being committed by the head engineers of the department. Impressed rather than surprised, I hastened to pass on the facts to some persons in authority, whom I knew to be upright and honest, so that they could denounce the criminals. Far from denying the truth of what I told them, my honorable friends were in a position to confirm it. But, even then, they advised me not to get mixed up in it or to get worked up, in my simplicity, about things of that kind. "You're young," they said to me affectionately, "you must finish your studies, you've got your career to think of, you shouldn't compromise yourself with things that don't concern you." "Of course," I said, "it would be better for the denunciation to come from grown-up people like yourselves, people with authority, rather than from a boy of seventeen."

They were horrified. "We are not madmen," they answered. "We shall mind our own business and nobody else's."

I then talked the matter over with some reverend priests, and then with some of my more courageous relations. All of them, while admitting that they were already aware of the shameful things that were happening, begged me not to get mixed up in that hornets' nest, but to think of my studies, of my career, and of my future. "With pleasure," I replied, "but isn't one of you ready to denounce the thieves?" "We are not madmen," they replied, scandalized, "these things have nothing to do with us."

I then began to wonder seriously whether it mightn't be a good thing to organize, together with some other boys, a new "revolution" that would end up with a good bonfire of the corrupt engineers' offices; but I was dissuaded by the acquaintance who had given me the proof of their crooked dealings: a bonfire, he pointed out, would destroy the proofs of the crimes. He was older and more experienced than myself; he suggested I should get the denunciation printed in some newspaper. But which newspaper? "There's only one," he explained, "which could have any interest in publishing your denunciation, and that's the Socialist paper." So I set to work and wrote three articles, the first of my life, giving a detailed exposure of the corrupt behavior of State engineers in my part of the country, and sent them off to *Avanti*. The first two were printed at once and aroused much comment among the readers of the paper, but none at all among the authorities. The third article did not appear, because, as I learned later, a leading Socialist intervened with the editorial staff. This showed me that the system of deception and fraud oppressing us was much vaster than at first appeared, and that its invisible ramifications extended even into Socialism. However, the partial denunciation which had appeared unexpectedly in the press contained enough material for a number of law-suits, or at least for a board of enquiry; but nothing happened. The engineers, whom I had denounced as thieves and bandits and against whom quite specific charges had been leveled, did not even attempt to justify themselves or to issue a general denial. There was a short period of expectancy, and then everyone went back to his own affairs.

★

The student who had dared to throw down the challenge was considered, by the most charitably-minded, an impulsive and strange boy. One must remember that the economic

poverty of the southern provinces offers small scope for a
career to the youths leaving school by the thousand every year.
Our only important industry is State employment. This does
not require exceptional intelligence, merely a docile disposition
and a readiness to toe the line in politics. The young men of
the South, who have grown up in the atmosphere I have briefly
described, tend naturally, if they have a minimum of sensitive-
ness in human relationships, toward anarchy and rebellion.
For those still on the threshold of youth, to become a civil
servant means renunciation, capitulation, and the mortification
of their souls. That is why people say: anarchists at twenty,
conservatives at thirty. Nor is the education imparted in the
schools, whether public or private, designed to strengthen
character. Most of the later years of my school-life I spent in
private Catholic institutions. Latin and Greek were excellently
taught there; the education in private or personal habits was
simple and clean; but civic instruction and training were
deplorable. Our history teachers were openly critical of the
official views; the mythology of the Risorgimento and its heroes
(Mazzini, Garibaldi, Victor Emmanuel II, Cavour) were the
objects of derision and disparagement; the literature prevalent
at the time (Carducci, D'Annunzio) was despised.

Insofar as this method of teaching developed the pupils'
critical spirit, it had its advantages. But the same priestly
schoolmasters, since they had to prepare us for the State
school examinations—and the fame and prosperity of their
academies depended on the results we achieved—also taught
us, and recommended us to uphold in our examinations, the
points of view completely opposed to their own convictions.
Meanwhile, the State examiners, who knew we came from
confessional schools, enjoyed questioning us on the most controversial subjects, and then praising us ironically for the
liberal and unprejudiced way in which we had been taught.
The falseness, hypocrisy, and double-facedness of all this
were so blatant that they could not but perturb anyone with
the slightest inborn respect for culture. But it was equally

inevitable that the average unfortunate student ended by considering diplomas, and his future job in a government office, as the supreme realities of life.

★

"People who are born in this district are really out of luck," Dr. F. J., a doctor in a village near mine, used to say. "There's no halfway house here; you've got either to rebel or become an accomplice." He rebelled. He declared himself an anarchist. He made Tolstoyan speeches to the poor. He was the scandal of the entire neighborhood, loathed by the rich, despised by the poor, and secretly pitied by a few. His post as panel-doctor was finally taken away from him, and he literally died of hunger.

★

I realize that the progress which I have been tracing in these pages is too summary to seem anything but strained. And if I touch on this objection now, it is not to refute it or to swear to the absolute truth of my explanations; I can guarantee their sincerity, not their objectivity. I am myself sometimes astonished to find, when I go back over that remote, almost prehistoric, period of our lives with my contemporaries, how they cannot remember at all, or only very vaguely, incidents which had a decisive influence on me; whereas on the contrary, they can clearly recall other circumstances which to me were pointless and insignificant. Are they, these contemporaries of mine, all "unconscious accomplices"? And by what destiny or virtue does one, at a certain age, make the important choice, and become "accomplice" or "rebel"? From what source do some people derive their spontaneous intolerance of injustice, even though the injustice affects only others? And that sudden feeling of guilt at sitting down to a well-laden table, when others are having to go hungry? And that pride which makes poverty and prison preferable to contempt?

I don't know. Perhaps no one knows. At a certain point, even the fullest and deepest confession becomes a mere statement of fact and not an answer. Anyone who has reflected seriously about himself or others knows how profoundly secret are certain decisions, how mysterious and unaccountable certain vocations.

There was a point in my rebellion where hatred and love coincided; both the facts which justified my indignation and the moral motives which demanded it stemmed directly from the district where I was born. This explains, too, why everything I have happened to write up to now, and probably everything I shall ever write, although I have traveled and lived abroad, is concerned solely with this same district, or more precisely with the part of it which can be seen from the house where I was born—not more than thirty or forty kilometers on one side or the other. It is a district, like the rest of the Abruzzi, poor in secular history, and almost entirely Christian and medieval in its formation. The only buildings worthy of note are churches and monasteries. Its only illustrious sons for many centuries have been saints and stone-carvers. The conditions of human existence have always been particularly difficult there; pain has always been accepted there as first among the laws of nature, and the Cross welcomed and honored because of it. Franciscanism and anarchy have always been the two most accessible forms of rebellion for lively spirits in our part of the world. The ashes of skepticism have never suffocated, in the hearts of those who suffered most, the ancient hope of the Kingdom of God on earth, the old expectation of charity taking the place of law, the old dream of Gioacchino da Fiore, of the "Spirituali," of the Celestimisto.* And this is a fact of enormous, fundamental importance; in a disappointed, arid, exhausted, weary country such as ours, it constitutes real riches, it is a miraculous reserve. The politi-

* Followers of Pope Celestine V, an Abruzzi hermit who, elected Pope in August, 1294, abdicated three and a half months later. He was canonized in 1313.

cians are unaware of its existence, the clergy are afraid of it; only the saints, perhaps, know where to find it. What for us has always been much more difficult, if not impossible, has been to discern the ways and means to a political revolution, *hic et nunc*, to the creation of a free and ordered society.

I thought I had reached this discovery, when I moved to the town and made my first contact with the workers' movement. It was a kind of flight, a safety exit from unbearable solitude, the sighting of *terra firma*, the discovery of a new continent. But it was not easy to reconcile a spirit in moral mutiny against an unacceptable long-established social reality with the "scientific" demands of a minutely codified political doctrine.

For me to join the Party of Proletarian Revolution was not just a simple matter of signing up with a political organization; it meant a conversion, a complete dedication. Those were still the days when to declare oneself a Socialist or a Communist was equivalent to throwing oneself to the winds, and meant breaking with one's parents and not finding a job. If the material consequences were harsh and hard, the difficulties of spiritual adaptation were no less painful. My own internal world, the "Middle Ages," which I had inherited and which were rooted in my soul, and from which, in the last analysis, I had derived my initial aspiration to revolt, were shaken to their foundations, as though by an earthquake. Everything was thrown into the melting-pot, everything became a problem. Life, death, love, good, evil, truth, all changed their meaning or lost it altogether. It is easy enough to court danger when one is no longer alone; but who can describe the dismay of once and for all renouncing one's faith in the individual immortality of the soul? It was too serious for me to be able to discuss it with anyone; my Party comrades would have found it a subject for mockery, and I no longer had any other friends. So, unknown to anyone, the whole world took on a different aspect. How men are to be pitied!

The conditions of life imposed on the Communists by the Fascist conquest of the State were very hard. But they also served to confirm some of the Communists' political theses, and provided an opportunity to create a type of organization which was in no way incompatible with the Communist mentality. So I too had to adapt myself, for a number of years, to living like a foreigner in my own country. One had to change one's name, abandon every former link with family and friends, and live a false life to remove any suspicion of conspiratorial activity. The Party became family, school, church, barracks; the world that lay beyond it was to be destroyed and built anew. The psychological mechanism whereby each single militant becomes progressively identified with the collective organization is the same as that used in certain religious orders and military colleges, with almost identical results. Every sacrifice was welcomed as a personal contribution to the "price of collective redemption"; and it should be emphasized that the links which bound us to the Party grew steadily firmer, not in spite of the dangers and sacrifices involved, but because of them. This explains the attraction exercised by Communism on certain categories of young men and of women, on intellectuals, and on the highly sensitive and generous people who suffer most from the wastefulness of bourgeois society. Anyone who thinks he can wean the best and most serious-minded young people away from Communism by enticing them into a well-warmed hall to play billiards, starts from an extremely limited and unintelligent conception of mankind.

★

It is not surprising that the first internal crises which shook the Communist International left me more or less indifferent. These crises originated from the fact that the main parties which had adhered to the new International, even after the formal acceptance of the twenty-one conditions laid down by Lenin to govern admission, were far from homogeneous.

They had in common a hatred of imperialist war and of its results; they united in criticizing the reformist ideas of the Second International; but, as to the rest, for good or ill, each reflected its own country's unequal degree of historical development. That is why there were notable differences of opinion between Russian Bolshevism, formed in an atmosphere in which political liberty and a differentiated social structure were both alien concepts, and the Left-Wing Socialist groups of the Western countries. The history of the Communist International was therefore a history of schisms, a history of intrigues and of arrogance on the part of the directing Russian group toward every independent expression of opinion by the other affiliated parties. One after another, they were forced to break with the Communist International: the currents most attached to democratic and parliamentary forms (Frossard), the groups most attached to legality and most opposed to attempts at *coups d'état* (Paul Levi), the libertarian elements who deluded themselves about Soviet Democracy (Roland-Holst), the revolutionary trade-unionists who opposed the bureaucratic submission of the trade unions to the Communist Party (Pierre Monatte, Andres Nin), the groups most reluctant to break off all collaboration with Social Democracy (Brandier, Bringolf, Tasca), and the extreme Left Wing which was intolerant of any opportunist move (Bordiga, Ruth Fischer, Boris Souvarine).

These internal crises took place in a sphere far removed from my own and so I was not involved. I do not say this boastfully; on the contrary, I am merely trying to explain the situation. The increasing degeneration of the Communist International into a tyranny and a bureaucracy filled me with repulsion and disgust, but there were some compelling reasons which made me hesitate to break with it: solidarity with comrades who were dead or in prison, the nonexistence at that time of any other organized anti-Fascist force in Italy, the rapid political, and in some cases also moral, degeneration of many who had already left Communism, and finally the illusion that the International might be made healthy again by the proletariat of the West, in the event of some crisis occurring within the Soviet regime.

Between 1921 and 1927, I had repeated occasion to go to Moscow and take part, as a member of Italian Communist delegations, in a number of congresses and meetings of the Executive. What struck me most about the Russian Communists, even in such really exceptional personalities as Lenin and Trotsky, was their utter incapacity to be fair in discussing opinions that conflicted with their own. The adversary, simply for daring to contradict, at once became a traitor, an opportunist, a hireling. *An adversary in good faith* is inconceivable to the Russian Communists. What an aberration of conscience this is, for so-called materialists and rationalists absolutely in their polemics to uphold the primacy of morals over intelligence! To find a comparable infatuation one has to go back to the Inquisition.

Just as I was leaving Moscow, in 1922, Alexandra Kollontaj said to me: "If you happen to read in the papers that Lenin has had me arrested for stealing the silver spoons in the Kremlin, that simply means that I'm not entirely in agreement with him about some little problem of agricultural or industrial policy." Kollontaj had acquired her sense of irony in the West and so only used it with people from the West. But even then, in those feverish years of building the new regime, when the new orthodoxy had not yet taken complete possession of cultural life, how difficult it was to reach an understanding with a Russian Communist on the simplest, and for us most obvious, questions; how difficult, I don't say to agree, but at least to understand each other, when talking of what liberty means for a man of the West, even for a worker. I spent hours one day trying to explain to one of the directors of the State publishing house, why she ought at least to be ashamed of the atmosphere of discouragement and intimidation in which Soviet writers lived. She could not understand what I was trying to tell her.

"Liberty"—I had to give examples—"is the possibility of doubting, the possibility of making a mistake, the possibility of searching and experimenting, the possibility of saying 'no' to any authority—literary, artistic, philosophic, religious, social, and even political." "But that," murmured this eminent functionary of Soviet culture in horror, "that is counter-revolution." Then she added, to get a little of her own back, "We're glad we haven't got your liberty, but we've got the sanatoria in exchange." When I observed that the expression "in exchange" had no meaning, "liberty not being merchandise that could be exchanged," and that I had seen sanatoria in other countries, she laughed in my face. "You're in the mood for joking with me today," she said to me. And I was so taken aback by her candor that I no longer dared to contradict her.

The spectacle of the enthusiasm of Russian youth in those first years of the creation of a new world, which we all hoped would be more humane than the old one, was utterly convincing. And what a bitter disillusionment it was, as the years went by and the new regime strengthened itself and its economic system got into shape and the armed attacks from abroad ceased, to see the long-promised ultimate democratization failing to come, and, instead, the dictatorship accentuating its repressive character.

One of my best friends, the head of the Russian Communist Youth, Lazar Schatzky, one evening confided to me how sad he was to have been born too late, and not to have taken part either in the 1905 or the 1917 Revolutions. "But there'll still be revolutions," I said to console him, "there'll always be need of revolutions, even in Russia." We were in the Red Square, not far from the tomb of Lenin. "What kind?" he wanted to know. "And how long have we got to wait?" Then I pointed to the tomb, which was still made of wood at that time, and before which we used every day to see an interminable procession of poor ragged peasants slowly filing.

"I presume you love Lenin," I said to him. "I knew him

Silone resents idolatrization of Lenin

too and have a very vivid recollection of him. You must admit with me that this superstitious cult of his mummy is an insult to his memory and a disgrace to a revolutionary city like Moscow." I suggested to him, in short, that we should get hold of a tin or two of petrol and make a "little revolution" on our own, by burning the totem-hut. I did not, to be frank, expect him to accept my proposal there and then, but at least I thought he would laugh about it; instead of which my poor friend went very pale and began to tremble violently. Then he begged me not to say dreadful things of that kind, either to him or still less to others. (Ten years later, when he was being searched for as an accomplice of Zinoviev, he committed suicide by throwing himself from the fifth floor of the house he lived in.) I have been present at the march post of immense parades of people and armies in the Red Square, but, in my mind, the recollection of that young friend's emotion and of his frightened and affectionate voice, has remained stronger than any other image. It may be that that memory is "objectively" more important.

It is not easy to trace the history of the Communist International, and it would be undoubtedly premature. How can one separate the fatuous from the essential in the interminable discussions at its congresses and meetings? What speeches should be left to the mice in the archives to criticize, and which should be recommended to intelligent people anxious to understand? I do not know. What my memory prefers to recall may to some people seem only bizarre. They were discussing one day, in a special commission of the Executive, the ultimatum issued by the central committee of the British trade unions, ordering its local branches not to support the Communist-led minority movement, on pain of expulsion. After the representative of the English Communist Party had explained the serious disadvantages of both solutions—because one meant the liquidation of the minority movement and the other the exit of the minority from the Trades Unions—the Russian delegate Piatnisky put forward a suggestion which seemed as obvious to him as Columbus' egg. "The branches," he suggested, "should declare that they submit to the discipline demanded, and then, in practice, should do exactly the contrary." The English Communist interrupted, "But that would be a lie." Loud laughter greeted this ingenuous objection, frank, cordial, interminable laughter, the like of which the gloomy offices of the Communist International had perhaps never heard before. The joke quickly spread all over Moscow, for the Englishman's entertaining and incredible reply was telephoned at once to Stalin and to the most important offices of State, provoking new waves of mirth everywhere. The general hilarity gave the English Communist's timid, ingenuous objection its true meaning. And that is why, in my memory, the storm of laughter aroused by that short, almost childishly simple little expression—"But that would be a lie"—outweighs all the long, heavy oppressive speeches I heard during sittings of the Communist International, and has become a kind of symbol for me.

My visits to Moscow, as I have already said, were few, and limited to my functions as a member of the Italian Communist delegations. I have never been part of the organization of the Communist International, but I could follow its rapid corruption by observing a few acquaintances of mine who belonged to it. Among them, an outstanding example was the Frenchman Jacques Doriot. I had met him for the first time in Moscow in 1921; he was then a modest, willing and sentimental young working-man, and it was for his obvious docility and easy-going nature that he was chosen for the international organization in preference to other young French Communists, who were more intelligent and better educated than himself, but also less conventional. He lived up fully to expectation. Year by year, he became an increasingly important figure in the hierarchy of International Communism, and, year by year, each time I came across him, I found him changed for the worse, skeptical, cynical, unscrupulous, and rapidly becoming Fascist in his political attitude toward men and the State. If I could triumph over my natural repugnance and write a biography of Jacques Doriot, my theme would be: "Militant Communist into Fascist."

Once I met Doriot in Moscow, just after his return from a political mission in China. He gave a few friends and myself a disturbing account of the mistakes of the Communist International in the Far East. The next day, however, speaking before the Executive in full session, he affirmed the exact opposite. "It was an act of political wisdom," he confided to me after the meeting with a slight and superior smile. His case is worth mentioning because it was not isolated. Internal changes in French Communism later led Jacques Doriot to leave the Communist International, and gave him a chance to show himself openly in what had already been, for a long time, his true colors; but many others, who basically are no different from Doriot, have remained at the head of Communist Parties. Palmiro Togliatti, the Italian, referred to this phenomenon of duplicity and demoralization among the personnel of the Communist International in his speech before its Sixth Congress, and asked permission to repeat the words of the dying Goethe: "Light, more light."

In a certain sense, that speech was Togliatti's swan-song; for another year or two he kept up the effort to follow his inmost promptings and to reconcile being a Communist with speaking his mind frankly, but, in the end, even he had to capitulate and submit.

Besides internal differences resulting from its own heterogeneous composition, the Communist International felt the repercussions of every difficulty of the Soviet State. After Lenin's death, it was clear that the Soviet State could not avoid what seems to be the destiny of every dictatorship: the gradual and inexorable narrowing of its political pyramid. The Russian Communist Party, which had suppressed all rival parties and abolished any possibility of general political discussion in the Soviet assemblies, itself suffered a similar fate, and its members' political views were rapidly ousted by the policy of the

Party machine. From that moment, every difference of opinion in the controlling body was destined to end in the physical extinction of the minority. The Revolution, which had extinguished its enemies, began to devour its favorite sons. The thirsty gods gave no more truce.

In May, 1927, as a representative of the Italian Communist Party, I took part with Togliatti in an extraordinary session of the enlarged Executive of the Communist International. Togliatti had come from Paris, where he was running the political secretariat of the Party, and I from Italy, where I was in charge of the underground organization. We met in Berlin and went on to Moscow together. The meeting—ostensibly summoned for an urgent discussion of what direction should be given to the Communist Parties in the struggle "against the imminent imperialist war"—was actually designed to begin the "liquidation" of Trotsky and Zinoviev, who were still members of the International Executive. As usual, to avoid surprises, the full session had been preceded and every detail prepared by the so-called Senior-convent, consisting of the heads of the most important delegations. Togliatti, on that occasion, insisted that I should accompany him to these restricted sittings. According to the rules, only he had a right to attend on behalf of the Italian delegation; but, rightly foreseeing what complications were about to arise, he preferred to have the support of the representative of the clandestine organization. At the first sitting which we attended, I had the impression that we had arrived too late. We were in a small office in the Communist International Headquarters. The German Thälmann was presiding, and immediately began reading out a proposed resolution against Trotsky, to be presented at the full session. This resolution condemned, in the most violent terms, a document which Trotsky had addressed to the Political Office of the Russian Communist Party. The Russian delegation at that day's session of the Senior-convent was an exceptional one: Stalin, Rikov, Bukharin and Manuilsky. At the end of the reading Thälmann asked if we were in agreement with the proposed resolution. The Finn Ottomar Kuusinen found that it was not strong enough. "It should be said openly," he suggested, "that the document sent by Trotsky to the Political Office of the Russian Communist Party is of an entirely counter-revolutionary character and constitutes clear proof that the man who wrote it no longer has anything in common with the working class." As no one else asked to speak, after consulting Togliatti, I made my apologies for having arrived late and so not having been able to see the document which was to be condemned. "To tell the truth," Thälmann declared candidly, "we haven't seen the document either."

Preferring not to believe my ears, I repeated my objection in other words: "It may very well be true," I said, "that Trotsky's document should be condemned, but obviously I cannot condemn it before I've read it."

"Neither have we," repeated Thälmann, "neither have the majority of the delegates present here, except for the Russians, read the document." Thälmann spoke in German and his words were translated into Russian for Stalin, and into French for two or three of us. The reply given to me was so incredible that I rounded on the translator. "It's impossible," I said, "that Thälmann should have said that. I must ask you to repeat his answer word for word."

At this point Stalin intervened. He was standing over at one side of the room, and seemed the only person present who was calm and unruffled.

"The Political Office of the Party," said Stalin, "has considered that it would not be expedient to translate and distribute Trotsky's document to the delegates of the International Executive, because there are various allusions in it to the policy of the Soviet State." (The mysterious document was later published abroad by Trotsky himself, in a booklet entitled *Problems of the Chinese Revolution*, and as anyone can today still see for himself, it contains no mention of the policy of the Soviet State, but a closely reasoned attack on the policy practiced in China by Stalin and the Communist International.

In a speech of April 15, 1927, in the presence of the Moscow Soviets, Stalin had sung the praises of Chiang Kai-shek, and confirmed his personal confidence in the Kuomintang; this was barely a week before the famous anti-Communist *volte face* of the Chinese Nationalist leader and of his party; the Communists were expelled from the Kuomintang overnight, tens of thousands of workers were massacred in Shanghai and, a month later, in Wuhan. It was natural therefore that Stalin should have been anxious to avoid a debate on these matters, seeking to protect himself behind a screen of *raison d'état*.

Ernst Thälmann asked me if I were satisfied with Stalin's explanation. "I do not contest the right of the Political Office of the Russian Communist Party to keep any document secret," I said. "But I do not understand how others can be asked to condemn an unknown document." At this, indignation against myself and Togliatti, who appeared to agree with what I had said, knew no bounds; it was especially violent on the part of the Finn, whom I have already mentioned, a Bulgarian and one or two Hungarians.

"It's unheard-of," cried Kuusinen, very red in the face, "that we still have such petty bourgeois in the fortress of the World Revolution." He pronounced the words petty bourgeois with an extremely comical expression of contempt and disgust. The only person who remained calm and imperturbable was Stalin. He said, "If a single delegate is against the proposed resolution, it should not be presented." Then he added, "Perhaps our Italian comrades are not fully aware of our internal situation. I propose that the sitting be suspended until tomorrow and that one of those present should be assigned the task of spending the evening with our Italian comrades and explaining our internal situation to them." The Bulgarian Vasil Kolarov was given this ungrateful task.

He carried it out with tact and good humor. He invited us

to have a glass of tea that evening in his room at the Hotel Lux. And he faced up to the thorny subject without much preamble. "Let's be frank," he said to us with a smile. "Do you think I've read that document? No, I haven't. To tell you the whole truth, I can add that that document doesn't even interest me. Shall I go further? Even if Trotsky sent me a copy here, secretly, I'd refuse to read it. My dear Italian friends, this isn't a question of documents. I know that Italy is the classic country of academies, but we aren't in an academy here. Here we are in the thick of a struggle for power between two rival groups of the Russian Central Directorate. Which of the two groups do we want to line up with? That's the point. Documents don't come into it. It's not a question of finding the historic truth about an unsuccessful Chinese revolution. It's a question of a struggle for power between two hostile, irreconcilable groups. One's got to choose. I, for my part, have already chosen, I'm for the majority group. Whatever the minority says or does, whatever document it draws up against the majority, I repeat to you that I'm for the majority. Documents don't interest me. We aren't in an academy here." He refilled our glasses with tea and scrutinized us with the air of a schoolmaster obliged to deal with two unruly youngsters. "Do I make myself clear?" he asked, addressing me specifically.

"Certainly," I replied, "very clear indeed." "Have I persuaded you?" he asked again. "No," I said. "And why not?" he wanted to know. "I should have to explain to you," I said, "why I'm against Fascism." Kolarov pretended to be indignant, while Togliatti expressed his opinion in more moderate, but no less succinct, terms. "One can't just declare oneself for the majority or for the minority in advance," he said. "One can't ignore the political basis of the question."

Kolarov listened to us with a benevolent smile of pity. "You're still too young," he explained, as he accompanied us to the door. "You haven't yet understood what politics are all about."

Next morning, in the Senior-convent, the scene of the day

before was repeated. An unusual atmosphere of nervousness pervaded the little room into which a dozen of us were packed. "Have you explained the situation to our Italian comrades?" Stalin asked Kolarov. "Fully," the Bulgarian assured him. "If a single delegate," Stalin repeated, "is against the proposed resolution, it cannot be presented in the full session. A resolution against Trotsky can only be taken unanimously. Are our Italian comrades," he added, turning to us, "favorable to the proposed resolution?"

After consulting Togliatti, I declared: "Before taking the resolution into consideration, we must see the document concerned." The Frenchman Albert Treint and the Swiss Jules Humbert-Droz made identical declarations. (Both of them, a few years later, also ended outside the Communist International.)

"The proposed resolution is withdrawn," said Stalin. After which, we had the same hysterical scene as the day before, with the indignant, angry protests of Kuusinen, Rakosi, Pepper and the others. Thälmann argued from our "scandalous" attitude that the whole trend of our anti-Fascist activity in Italy was most probably wrong, and that if Fascism was still so firmly entrenched in Italy it must be our fault. He asked because of this that the policy of the Italian Communist Party should be subjected to a thorough sifting. This was done; and as a reprisal for our "impertinent" conduct those fanatical censors discovered that the fundamental guiding lines of our activity, traced in the course of the previous years by Antonio Gramsci, were seriously contaminated by a petty-bourgeois spirit. Togliatti decided that it would be prudent for us both to address a letter to the Political Office of the Russian Communist Party explaining the reason for our attitude at that meeting of the Executive. No Communist, the letter said in effect, would presume to question the historical pre-eminence of our Russian comrades in the leadership of the International; but this pre-eminence imposed special duties on our Russian comrades; they could not apply the rights it gave them in a mechanical and authoritarian way. The letter was received by Bukharin, who sent for us at once and advised us to withdraw it so as not to worsen our already appalling political situation.

Days of somber discouragement followed for me. I asked myself: Have we sunk to this? Those who are dead, those who are dying in prison, have sacrificed themselves for this? The vagabond, lonely, perilous lives that we ourselves are leading, strangers in our own countries—is it all for this? My depression soon reached that extreme stage when the will is paralyzed and physical resistance suddenly gives way.

Before I left Moscow an Italian working-man came to see me. He had been a refugee in Russia for some years to avoid the long term of imprisonment to which a Fascist tribunal had sentenced him. (He is still, I believe, a Communist today.) He came to complain of the humiliating conditions of the workers in the Moscow factory to which he was attached. He was ready to put up with the material shortages of every kind, since to remedy them was clearly beyond the power of individuals, but he could not understand why the workmen were entirely at the mercy of the factory directorate and had no effective organization to protect their interests; why, in this respect also, they should be much worse off than in capitalist countries. Most of the much-vaunted rights of the working class were purely theoretical.

In Berlin, on my way back, I read in the paper that the Executive of the Communist International had severely rebuked Trotsky for a document he had prepared about recent events in China. I went to the offices of the German Communist Party and asked Thälmann for an explanation. "This is untrue," I said to him sharply.

But he explained that the statutes of the International authorized the Presidium, in case of urgency, to adopt any resolution in the name of the Executive. During the few days I had to stay in Berlin, while waiting for my false documents to be put in order, I read in the papers that the American,

Hungarian and Czechoslovakian Communist Parties had energetically deplored Trotsky's letter. "Has the mysterious document finally been produced, then?" "No," he answered me. "But I hope the example set by the American, Hungarian and Czechoslovakian Communists has shown you what Communist discipline means." These´ things were said with no hint of irony, but indeed with dismal seriousness that befitted the nightmare reality to which they referred.

★

For reasons of health I had to go straight into a Swiss sanatorium, and all political decisions were suspended. One day, in a village not far from where I was taking my cure, I had a meeting with Togliatti. He explained to me at great length, clearly and frankly, the reasons for the line of conduct he had chosen. The present state of the International, he said in brief, was certainly neither satisfactory nor agreeable. But all our good intentions were powerless to change it; objective historical conditions were involved and must be taken into account. The forms of the Proletarian Revolution were not arbitrary. If they did not accord with our preferences, so much the worse for us. And besides, what alternative remained? Other Communists who had broken with the Party, how had they ended up? Consider, he said, the appalling condition of Social Democracy.

My objections to these arguments were not very coherent, mainly because Togliatti's arguments were purely political, whereas the agitation which my recent experiences had aroused in me went far beyond politics. These "inexcusable historical forms" to which we must bow down—what were they but a new version of the inhuman reality against which, in declaring ourselves Socialists, we had rebelled? I felt at that time like someone who has had a tremendous blow on the head and keeps on his feet, walking, talking and gesticulating, but without fully realizing what has happened.

Realization came, however, slowly and with difficulty during the course of the succeeding years. And to this day I go on thinking it over, trying to understand better. If I have written books, it has been to try and understand and to make others understand. I am not at all certain that I have reached the end of my efforts. The truth is this: the day I left the Communist Party was a very sad one for me, it was like a day of deep mourning, the mourning for my lost youth. And I come from a district where mourning is worn longer than elsewhere. It is not easy to free oneself from an experience as intense as that of the underground organization of the Communist Party. Something of it remains and leaves a mark on the character which lasts all one's life. One can, in fact, notice how recognizable the ex-Communists are. They constitute a category apart, like ex-priests and ex-regular officers. The number of ex-Communists is legion today. "The final struggle," I said jokingly to Togliatti recently, "will be between the Communists and the ex-Communists."

However, I carefully avoided, after I had left the Communist Party, ending up in one of the many groups and splinter-groups of ex-Communists; and I have never regretted this in any way, as I know well the kind of fate which rules over these groups and splinter-groups, and makes little sects of them which have all the defects of official Communism— the fanaticism, the centralization, the abstraction—without the qualities and advantages which the latter derives from its vast working-class following. The logic of opposition at all costs has carried many ex-Communists far from their starting-points, in some cases as far as Fascism.

Consideration of the experience I have been through has led me to a deepening of the motives for my separation which go very much further than the circumstantial ones by which it was produced. But my faith in Socialism (to which I think I can say my entire life bears testimony) has remained more alive than ever in me. In its essence, it has gone back to what it was when I first revolted against the old social order; a refusal to admit the existence of destiny, an extension of the ethical impulse from the restricted individual and family sphere to the whole domain of human activity, a need for effective brotherhood, an affirmation of the superiority of the human person over all the economic and social mechanisms which oppress him. As the years have gone by, there has been added to this an intuition of man's dignity and a feeling of reverence for that which in man is always trying to outdistance itself, and lies at the root of his eternal disquiet. But I do not think that this kind of Socialism is in any way peculiar to me. The "mad truths" recorded above are older than Marxism; toward the second half of the last century they took refuge in the workers' movement born of industrial capitalism, and continue to remain one of its most enduring founts of inspiration. I have repeatedly expressed my opinion on the relations between the Socialist Movement and the theories of Socialism; these relations are by no means rigid or immutable. With the development of new studies, the theories may go out of fashion or be discarded, but the movement goes on. It would be inaccurate, however, with regard to the old quarrel between the doctrinaires and the empiricists of the workers' movement, to include me among the latter. I do not conceive Socialist policy as tied to any particular theory, but to a faith. The more Socialist theories claim to be "scientific," the more transitory they are; but Socialist values are permanent. The distinction between theories and values is not sufficiently recognized, but it is fundamental. On a group of theories one can found a school; but on a group of values one can found a culture, a civilization, a new way of living together among men.

also, "faith"

Richard Wright

BIOGRAPHICAL NOTE: *Richard Wright was born on September 4, 1908, on a plantation twenty-five miles from Natchez, Mississippi, of poor Negro parents. Deserted by his father, his mother, a washerwoman, brought him up until she was stricken with paralysis, when his grandmother took charge and sent him to a Seventh Day Adventist school. At fifteen he left home and worked for two years in Memphis where he read H. L. Mencken's* A Book of Prefaces *and decided to become a writer. With $150 in his pocket he went to Chicago and earned his living by odd jobs until the depression put him out of work. He joined the Communist Party through the John Reed Club.*

His books are: Uncle Tom's Children *(short stories),* How Bigger was Born, Native Son *and* Black Boy.

One Thursday night I received an invitation from a group of white boys I had known when I was working in the post office to meet in one of Chicago's South Side hotels and argue the state of the world. About ten of us gathered, and ate salami sandwiches, drank beer, and talked. I was amazed to discover that many of them had joined the Communist Party. I challenged them by reciting the antics of the Negro Communists I had seen in the parks, and I was told that those antics were "tactics" and were all right. I was dubious.

Then one Thursday night Sol, a Jewish chap, startled us by announcing that he had had a short story accepted by a little magazine called the *Anvil*, edited by Jack Conroy, and that he had joined a revolutionary artist organization, the John Reed Club. Sol repeatedly begged me to attend the meetings of the club.

"You'd like them," Sol said.

"I don't want to be organized," I said.

"They can help you to write," he said.

"Nobody can tell me how or what to write," I said.

"Come and see," he urged. "What have you to lose?"

I felt that Communists could not possibly have a sincere interest in Negroes. I was cynical and I would rather have heard a white man say that he hated Negroes, which I could have readily believed, than to have heard him say that he respected Negroes, which would have made me doubt him.

One Saturday night, bored with reading, I decided to appear at the John Reed Club in the capacity of an amused spectator. I rode to the Loop and found the number. A dark stairway led upward; it did not look welcoming. What on earth of importance could happen in so dingy a place? Through the windows above me I saw vague murals along the walls. I mounted the stairs to a door that was lettered: THE CHICAGO JOHN REED CLUB.

I opened it and stepped into the strangest room I had ever seen. Paper and cigarette butts lay on the floor. A few benches ran along the walls, above which were vivid colors depicting colossal figures of workers carrying streaming banners. The mouths of the workers gaped in wild cries; their legs were sprawled over cities.

"Hello."

I turned and saw a white man smiling at me.

"A friend of mine, who's a member of this club, asked me to visit here. His name is Sol—" I told him.

"You're welcome here," the white man said. "We're not having an affair tonight. We're holding an editorial meeting. Do you paint?" He was slightly gray and he had a mustache.

"No," I said. "I try to write."

"Then sit in on the editorial meeting of our magazine, *Left Front*," he suggested.

"I know nothing of editing," I said.

"You can learn," he said.

I stared at him, doubting.

"I don't want to be in the way here," I said.

"My name's Grimm," he said.

I told him my name and we shook hands. He went to a closet and returned with an armful of magazines.

"Here are some back issues of the *Masses*," he said. "Have you ever read it?"

"No," I said.

"Some of the best writers in America publish in it," he explained. He also gave me copies of a magazine called *International Literature*. "There's stuff here from Gide, Gorky—"

I assured him that I would read them. He took me to an office and introduced me to a Jewish boy who was to become one of the nation's leading painters, to a chap who was to become one of the eminent composers of his day, to a writer who was to create some of the best novels of his generation, to a young Jewish boy who was destined to film the Nazi occupation of Czechoslovakia. I was meeting men and women whom I should know for decades to come, who were to form the first sustained relationships in my life.

I sat in a corner and listened while they discussed their magazine, *Left Front*. Were they treating me courteously because I was a Negro? I must let cold reason guide me with these people, I told myself. I was asked to contribute something to the magazine, and I said vaguely that I would consider it. After the meeting I met an Irish girl who worked for an advertising agency, a girl who did social work, a schoolteacher, and the wife of a prominent university professor. I had once worked as a servant for people like these and I was skeptical. I tried to fathom their motives, but I could detect no condescension in them.

★

I went home full of reflection, probing the sincerity of the strange white people I had met, wondering how they *really* regarded Negroes. I lay on my bed and read the magazines and was amazed to find that there did exist in this world an organized search for the truth of the lives of the oppressed and the isolated. When I had begged bread from the officials, I had wondered dimly if the outcasts could become united in action, thought, and feeling. Now I knew. It was being done in one-sixth of the earth already. The revolutionary words leaped from the printed page and struck me with tremendous force.

It was not the economics of Communism, nor the great power of trade unions, nor the excitement of underground politics that claimed me; my attention was caught by the similarity of the experiences of workers in other lands, by the possibility of uniting scattered but kindred peoples into a whole. It seemed to me that here at last, in the realm of revolutionary expression, Negro experience could find a home, a functioning value and role. Out of the magazines I read came a passionate call for the experiences of the disinherited, and there were none of the lame lispings of the missionary in it. It did not say: "Be like us and we will like you, maybe." It said: "If you possess enough courage to speak out what you are, you will find that you are not alone." It urged life to believe in life.

I read on into the night; then, toward dawn, I swung from bed and inserted paper into the typewriter. Feeling for the first time that I could speak to listening ears, I wrote a wild, crude poem in free verse, coining images of black hands playing, working, holding bayonets, stiffening finally in death. I felt that in a clumsy way it linked white life with black, merged two streams of common experience.

I heard someone poking about the kitchen.

"Richard, are you ill?" my mother called.

"No. I'm reading."

My mother opened the door and stared curiously at the pile of magazines that lay upon my pillow.

"You're not throwing away money buying those magazines, are you?" she asked.

"No. They were given to me."

She hobbled to the bed on her crippled legs and picked up a copy of the *Masses* that carried a lurid May Day cartoon. She adjusted her glasses and peered at it for a long time.

"My God in heaven," she breathed in horror.

"What's the matter, Mama?"

"What is this?" she asked, extending the magazine to me, pointing to the cover. "What's wrong with that man?"

With my mother standing at my side, lending me her eyes, I stared at a cartoon drawn by a Communist artist; it was the figure of a worker clad in ragged overalls and holding aloft a red banner. The man's eyes bulged; his mouth gaped as wide as his face; his teeth showed; the muscles of his neck were like ropes. Following the man was a horde of nondescript men, women, and children, waving clubs, stones and pitchforks.

"What are those people going to do?" my mother asked.

"I don't know," I hedged.

"Are these Communist magazines?"

"Yes."

"And do they want people to act like this?"

"Well—" I hesitated.

My mother's face showed disgust and moral loathing. She was a gentle woman. Her ideal was Christ upon the cross. How could I tell her that the Communist Party wanted her to march in the streets, chanting, singing?

"What do Communists think people are?" she asked.

"They don't quite mean what you see there," I said, fumbling with my words.

"Then what do they mean?"

"This is symbolic," I said.

"Then why don't they speak out what they mean?"

"Maybe they don't know how."

"Then why do they print this stuff?"

"They don't quite know how to appeal to people yet," I admitted, wondering whom I could convince of this if I could not convince my mother.

"That picture's enough to drive a body crazy," she said, dropping the magazine, turning to leave, then pausing at the door. "You're not getting mixed up with those people?"

"I'm just reading, Mama," I dodged.

My mother left and I brooded upon the fact that I had not been able to meet her simple challenge. I looked again at the cover of the *Masses* and I knew that the wild cartoon did not reflect the passions of the common people. I reread the magazine and was convinced that much of the expression embodied what the *artists* thought would appeal to others, what they thought would gain recruits. They had a program, an ideal, but they had not yet found a language.

Here, then, was something that I could do, reveal, say. The Communists, I felt, had oversimplified the experience of those whom they sought to lead. In their efforts to recruit masses, they had missed the meaning of the lives of the masses, had conceived of people in too abstract a manner. I would try to put some of that meaning back. I would tell Communists how common people felt, and I would tell common people of the self-sacrifice of Communists who strove for unity among them.

The editor of *Left Front* accepted two of my crude poems for publication, sent two of them to Jack Conroy's *Anvil*, and sent another to the *New Masses*, the successor of the *Masses*. Doubts still lingered in my mind.

"Don't send them if you think they aren't good enough," I said to him.

"They're good enough," he said.

"Are you doing this to get me to join up?" I asked.

"No," he said. "Your poems are crude, but good for us. You see, we're all new in this. We write articles about Negroes, but we never see any Negroes. We need your stuff."

I sat through several meetings of the club and was impressed by the scope and seriousness of its activities. The club was demanding that the government create jobs for unemployed artists; it planned and organized art exhibits; it raised funds for the publication of *Left Front*; and it sent scores of speakers to trade-union meetings. The members were fervent, democratic, restless, eager, self-sacrificing. I was convinced, and my response was to set myself the task of making Negroes know what Communists were. I got the notion of writing a series of biographical sketches of Negro Communists. I told no one of my intentions, and I did not know how fantastically naïve my ambition was.

★

I had attended but a few meetings before I realized that a bitter factional fight was in progress between two groups of members of the club. Sharp arguments rose at every meeting. I noticed that a small group of painters actually led the club and dominated its policies. The group of writers that centered in *Left Front* resented the leadership of the painters. Being primarily interested in *Left Front*, I sided in simple loyalty with the writers.

Then came a strange development. The *Left Front* group declared that the incumbent leadership did not reflect the wishes of the club. A special meeting was called and a motion was made to re-elect an executive secretary. When nominations were made for the office, my name was included. I declined the nomination, telling the members that I was too ignorant of their aims to be seriously considered. The debate lasted all night. A vote was taken in the early hours of morning by a show of hands, and I was elected.

Later I learned what had happened: the writers of the club had decided to use me to oust the painters, who were Party members, from the leadership of the club. Without my knowledge and consent, they confronted the members of the Party with a Negro, knowing that it would be difficult for Com-

munists to refuse to vote for a man representing the largest
single racial minority in the nation, inasmuch as Negro equality was one of the main tenets of Communism.

As the club's leader, I soon learned the nature of the fight.
The Communists had secretly organized a "fraction" in the
club; that is, a small portion of the club's members were secret
members of the Communist Party. They would meet outside
of the club and decide what policies the club should follow;
in club meetings the sheer strength of their arguments usually
persuaded non-Party members to vote with them. The crux of
the fight was that the non-Party members resented the excessive demands made upon the club by the local Party authorities through the fraction.

The demands of the local Party authorities for money,
speakers, and poster painters were so great that the publication of *Left Front* was in danger. Many young writers had
joined the club because of their hope of publishing in *Left
Front*, and when the Communist Party sent word through the
fraction that the magazine should be dissolved, the writers
rejected the decision, an act which was interpreted as hostility
toward Party authority.

I pleaded with the Party members for a more liberal program for the club. Feeling waxed violent and bitter. Then the
showdown came. I was informed that if I wanted to continue
as secretary of the club I should have to join the Communist
Party. I stated that I favored a policy that allowed for the
development of writers and artists. My policy was accepted.
I signed the membership card.

One night a Jewish chap appeared at one of our meetings
and introduced himself as Comrade Young of Detroit. He told
us that he was a member of the Communist Party, a member
of the Detroit John Reed Club, that he planned to make his
home in Chicago. He was a short, friendly, black-haired, well-
read fellow with hanging lips and bulging eyes. Shy of forces
to execute the demands of the Communist Party, we welcomed
him. But I could not make out Young's personality; whenever

I asked a simple question, he looked off and stammered a confused answer. I decided to send his references to the Communist Party for checking and forthwith named him for membership in the club. He's O.K., I thought. Just a queer artist.

After the meeting Comrade Young confronted me with a problem. He had no money, he said, and asked if he could sleep temporarily on the club's premises. Believing him loyal, I gave him permission. Straightway Young became one of the most ardent members of our organization, admired by all. His painting—which I did not understand—impressed our best artists. No report about Young had come from the Communist Party, but since Young seemed a conscientious worker, I did not think the omission a serious one in any case.

At a meeting one night Young asked that his name be placed upon the agenda; when his time came to speak, he rose and launched into one of the most violent and bitter political attacks in the club's history upon Swann, one of our best young artists. We were aghast. Young accused Swann of being a traitor to the workers, an opportunist, a collaborator with the police, and an adherent of Trotsky. Naturally most of the club's members assumed that Young, a member of the Party, was voicing the ideas of the Party. Surprised and baffled, I moved that Young's statement be referred to the executive committee for decision. Swann rightfully protested; he declared that he had been attacked in public and would answer in public.

It was voted that Swann should have the floor. He refuted Young's wild charges, but the majority of the club's members were bewildered, did not know whether to believe him or not. We all liked Swann, did not believe him guilty of any misconduct; but we did not want to offend the Party. A verbal battle ensued. Finally the members who had been silent in deference to the Party rose and demanded of me that the foolish charges against Swann be withdrawn. Again I moved that the matter be referred to the executive committee and again my proposal was voted down. The membership had now begun to distrust the Party's motives. They were afraid to let an executive committee, the majority of whom were Party members, pass upon the charges made by Party-member Young.

A delegation of members asked me later if I had anything to do with Young's charges. I was so hurt and humiliated that I disavowed all relations with Young. Determined to end the farce, I cornered Young and demanded to know who had given him authority to castigate Swann.

"I've been asked to rid the club of traitors."

"But Swann isn't a traitor," I said.

"We must have a purge," he said, his eyes bulging, his face quivering with passion.

I admitted his great revolutionary fervor, but I felt that his zeal was a trifle excessive. The situation became worse. A delegation of members informed me that if the charges against Swann were not withdrawn, they would resign in a body. I was frantic. I wrote to the Communist Party to ask why orders had been issued to punish Swann, and a reply came back that no such orders had been issued. Then what was Young up to? Who was prompting him? I finally begged the club to let me place the matter before the leaders of the Communist Party. After a violent debate, my proposal was accepted.

One night ten of us met in an office of a leader of the Party to hear Young restate his charges against Swann. The Party leader, aloof and amused, gave Young the signal to begin. Young unrolled a sheaf of papers and declaimed a list of political charges that excelled in viciousness his previous charges. I stared at Young, feeling that he was making a dreadful mistake, but fearing him because he had, by his own account, the sanction of high political authority.

When Young finished, the Party leader asked, "Will you allow me to read these charges?"

"Of course," said Young, surrendering a copy of his indictment. "You may keep that copy. I have ten carbons."

"Why did you make so many carbons?" the leader asked.

"I didn't want anyone to steal them," Young said.

"If this man's charges against me are taken seriously," Swann said, "I'll resign and publicly denounce the club."

"You see!" Young yelled. "He's with the police!"

I was sick. The meeting ended with a promise from the Party leader to read the charges carefully and render a verdict as to whether Swann should be placed on trial or not. I was convinced that something was wrong, but I could not figure it out. One afternoon I went to the club to have a long talk with Young; but when I arrived, he was not there. Nor was he there the next day. For a week I sought Young in vain. Meanwhile the club's members asked his whereabouts and they would not believe me when I told them that I did not know. Was he ill? Had he been picked up by the police?

One afternoon Comrade Grimm and I sneaked into the club's headquarters and opened Young's luggage. What we saw puzzled us. First of all, there was a scroll of paper twenty yards long—one page pasted to another—which had drawings depicting the history of the human race from a Marxist point of view. The first page read: "A Pictorial Record Of Man's Economic Progress."

"This is terribly ambitious," I said.

"He's very studious," Grimm said.

There were long dissertations written in long-hand; some were political and others dealt with the history of art. Finally we found a letter with a Detroit return address and I promptly wrote asking news of our esteemed member. A few days later a letter came which said in part:—

Dear Sir:

In reply to your letter, we beg to inform you that Mr. Young who was a patient in our institution and who escaped from our custody a few months ago, has been apprehended and returned to this institution for mental treatment.

I was thunderstruck. Was this true? Undoubtedly it was. Then what kind of club did we run that a lunatic could step into it and help run it? Were we all so mad that we could not detect a madman when we saw one?

I made a motion that all charges against Swann be dropped, which was done. I offered Swann an apology, but as the leader of the Chicago John Reed Club I was a sobered and chastened Communist.

★

The Communist Party fraction in the John Reed Club instructed me to ask my party cell—"unit," as it was called—to assign me to full duty in the work of the club. I was instructed to give my unit a report of my activities, writing, organizing, speaking. I agreed and wrote the report.

A unit, membership in which is obligatory for all Communists, is the Party's basic form of organization. Unit meetings are held on certain nights which are kept secret for fear of police raids. Nothing treasonable occurs at these meetings; but once one is a Communist, one does not have to be guilty of wrongdoing to attract the attention of the police.

I went to my first unit meeting—which was held in the Black Belt of the South Side—and introduced myself to the Negro organizer.

"Welcome, comrade," he said, grinning. "We're glad to have a writer with us."

"I'm not much of a writer," I said.

The meeting started. About twenty Negroes were gathered. The time came for me to make my report and I took out my notes and told them how I had come to join the Party, what few stray items I had published, what my duties were in the John Reed Club. I finished and waited for comment. There was silence. I looked about. Most of the comrades sat with bowed heads. Then I was surprised to catch a twitching smile on the lips of a Negro woman. Minutes passed. The Negro woman lifted her head and looked at the organizer. The organizer smothered a smile. Then the woman broke into unrestrained laughter, bending forward and burying her face in her hands. I stared. Had I said something funny?

"What's the matter?" I asked.

The giggling became general. The unit organizer, who had been dallying with his pencil, looked up.

"It's all right, comrade," he said. "We're glad to have a writer in the Party."

There was more smothered laughter. What kind of people were these? I had made a serious report and now I heard giggles.

"I did the best I could," I said uneasily. "I realize that writing is not basic or important. But, given time, I think I can make a contribution."

"We know you can, comrade," the black organizer said.

His tone was more patronizing than that of a Southern white man. I grew angry. I thought I knew these people, but evidently I did not. I wanted to take issue with their attitude, but caution urged me to talk it over with others first.

During the following days I learned through discreet questioning that I seemed a fantastic element to the black Communists. I was shocked to hear that I, who had been only to grammar school, had been classified as an *intellectual*. What was an intellectual? I had never heard the word used in the sense in which it was applied to me. I had thought that they might refuse me on the ground that I was not politically advanced; I had thought they might say I would have to be investigated. But they had simply laughed.

I learned, to my dismay, that the black Communists in my unit had commented upon my shined shoes, my clean shirt, and the tie that I had worn. Above all, my manner of speech had seemed an alien thing to them.

"He talks like a book," one of the Negro comrades had said. And that was enough to condemn me forever as bourgeois.

★

In my Party work I met a Negro Communist, Ross, who was under indictment for "inciting to riot." Ross typified the effective street agitator. Southern-born, he had migrated North and his life reflected the crude hopes and frustrations of the peasant in the city. Distrustful but aggressive, he was a bundle of the weaknesses and virtues of a man struggling blindly between two societies, of a man living on the margin of a culture. I felt that if I could get his story, I could make known some of the difficulties inherent in the adjustment of a folk people to an urban environment; I should make his life more intelligible to others than it was to himself.

I approached Ross and explained my plan. He was agreeable. He invited me to his home, introducing me to his Jewish wife, his young son, his friends. I talked to Ross for hours, explaining what I was about, cautioning him not to relate anything that he did not want to divulge.

"I'm after the things that made you a Communist," I said.

Word spread in the Communist Party that I was taking notes on the life of Ross, and strange things began to happen. A quiet black Communist came to my home one night and called me out to the street to speak to me in private. He made a prediction about my future that frightened me.

"Intellectuals don't fit well into the Party, Wright," he said solemnly.

"But I'm not an intellectual," I protested. "I sweep the streets for a living." I had just been assigned by the relief system to sweep the streets for thirteen dollars a week.

"That doesn't make any difference," he said. "We've kept records of the trouble we've had with intellectuals in the past. It's estimated that only 13 per cent of them remain in the Party."

"Why do they leave, since you insist upon calling me an intellectual?" I asked.

"Most of them drop out of their own accord."

"Well, I'm not dropping out," I said.

"Some are expelled," he hinted gravely.

"For what?"

"General opposition to the Party's policies," he said.

"But I'm not opposing anything in the Party."

"You'll have to prove your revolutionary loyalty."

"How?"

"The Party has a way of testing people."

"Well, talk. What is this?"

"How do you react to police?"

"I don't react to them," I said. "I've never been bothered by them."

"Do you know Evans?" he asked, referring to a local militant Negro Communist.

"Yes. I've seen him; I've met him."

"Did you notice that he was injured?"

"Yes. His head was bandaged."

"He got that wound from the police in a demonstration," he explained. "That's proof of revolutionary loyalty."

"Do you mean that I must get whacked over the head by cops to prove that I'm sincere?" I asked.

"I'm not suggesting anything," he said. "I'm explaining."

"Look. Suppose a cop whacks me over the head and I suffer a brain concussion. Suppose I'm nuts after that. Can I write then? What shall I have proved?"

He shook his head. "The Soviet Union has had to shoot a lot of intellectuals," he said.

"Good God!" I exclaimed. "Do you know what you're saying? You're not in Russia. You're standing on a sidewalk in Chicago. You talk like a man lost in a fantasy."

"You've heard of Trotsky, haven't you?" he asked.

"Yes."

"Do you know what happened to him?"

"He was banished from the Soviet Union," I said.

"Do you know why?"

"Well," I stammered, trying not to reveal my ignorance of politics, for I had not followed the details of Trotsky's fight against the Communist Party of the Soviet Union, "it seems that after a decision had been made, he broke that decision by organizing against the Party."

"It was for counter-revolutionary activity," he snapped impatiently; I learned afterward that my answer had not been satisfactory, had not been couched in the acceptable phrases of bitter, anti-Trotsky denunciation.

"I understand," I said. "But I've never read Trotsky. What's his stand on minorities?"

"Why ask me?" he asked. "I don't read Trotsky."

"Look," I said. "If you found me reading Trotsky, what would that mean to you?"

"Comrade, you don't understand," he said in an annoyed tone.

That ended the conversation. But that was not the last time I was to hear the phrase: "Comrade, you don't understand." I had not been aware of holding wrong ideas. I had not read any of Trotsky's works; indeed, the very opposite had been true. It had been Stalin's *Marxism and the National and Colonial Question* that had captured my interest.

Of all the developments in the Soviet Union, the way scores of backward peoples had been led to unity on a national scale was what had enthralled me. I had read with awe how the Communists had sent phonetic experts into the vast regions of Russia to listen to the stammering dialects of peoples oppressed for centuries by the czars. I had made the first total emotional commitment of my life when I read how the phonetic experts had given these tongueless people a language, newspapers, institutions. I had read how these forgotten folk had been encouraged to keep their old cultures, to see in their ancient customs meanings and satisfactions as deep as those contained in supposedly superior ways of living. And I had exclaimed to myself how different this was from the way in which Negroes were sneered at in America.

Then what was the meaning of the warning I had received from the black Communist? Why was I a suspected man because I wanted to reveal the vast physical and spiritual ravages of Negro life, the profundity latent in these rejected people, the dramas as old as man and the sun and the mountains and the seas that were taking place in the poverty of black America? What was the danger in showing the kinship between the sufferings of the Negro and the sufferings of other people?

★

I sat one morning in Ross's home with his wife and child. I was scribbling furiously upon my yellow sheets of paper. The doorbell rang and Ross's wife admitted a black Communist, one Ed Green. He was tall, taciturn, soldierly, square-shouldered. I was introduced to him and he nodded stiffly.

"What's happening here?" he asked bluntly.

Ross explained my project to him, and as Ross talked I could see Ed Green's face darken. He had not sat down, and when Ross's wife offered him a chair he did not hear her.

"What're you going to do with these notes?" he asked me.

"I hope to weave them into stories," I said.

"What're you asking the Party members?"

"About their lives in general."

"Who suggested this to you?" he asked.

"Nobody. I thought of it myself."

"Were you ever a member of any other political group?"

"I worked with the Republicans once," I said.

"I mean, revolutionary organizations?" he asked.

"No. Why do you ask?"

"What kind of work do you do?"

"I sweep the streets for a living."

"How far did you go in school?"

"Through the grammar grades."

"You talk like a man who went further than that," he said.

"I've read books. I taught myself."

"I don't know," he said, looking off.

"What do you mean?" I asked. "What's wrong?"

"To whom have you shown this material?"

"I've shown it to no one yet."

What was the meaning of his questions? Naïvely I thought

that he himself would make a good model for a biographical
sketch.

"I'd like to interview you next," I said.

"I'm not interested," he snapped.

His manner was so rough that I did not urge him. He called
Ross into a rear room. I sat feeling that I was guilty of something. In a few minutes Ed Green returned, stared at me wordlessly, then marched out.

"Who does he think he is?" I asked Ross.

"He's a member of the Central Committee," Ross said.

"But why does he act that way?"

"Oh, he's always like that," Ross said uneasily.

There was a long silence.

"He's wondering what you're doing with this material,"
Ross said finally.

I looked at him. He, too, had been captured by suspicion.
He was trying to hide the fear in his face.

"You don't have to tell me anything you don't want to," I
said.

That seemed to soothe him for a moment. But the seed of
doubt had already been planted. I felt dizzy. Was I mad? Or
were these people mad?

"You see, Dick," Ross's wife said, "Ross is under an indictment. Ed Green is the representative of the International
Labor Defense for the South Side. It's his duty to keep track
of people he's trying to defend. He wanted to know if Ross
has given you anything that could be used against him in
court."

I was speechless.

"What does he think I am?" I demanded.

There was no answer.

"You lost people!" I cried and banged my fist on the table.

Ross was shaken and ashamed. "Aw, Ed Green's just super-
cautious," he mumbled.

"Ross," I asked, "do you trust me?"

"Oh, yes," he said uneasily.

We two black men sat in the same room looking at each

other in fear. Both of us were hungry. Both of us depended upon public charity to eat and for a place to sleep. Yet we had more doubt in our hearts of each other than of the men who had cast the mold of our lives.

I continued to take notes on Ross's life, but each successive morning found him more reticent. I pitied him and did not argue with him, for I knew that persuasion would not nullify his fears. Instead I sat and listened to him and his friends tell tales of Southern Negro experience, noting them down in my mind, not daring to ask questions for fear they would become alarmed.

In spite of their fears, I became drenched in the details of their lives. I gave up the idea of the biographical sketches and settled finally upon writing a series of short stories, using the material I had got from Ross and his friends, building upon it, inventing. I wove a tale of a group of black boys trespassing upon the property of a white man and the lynching that followed. The story was published in an anthology under the title of "Big Boy Leaves Home," but its appearance came too late to influence the Communists who were questioning the use to which I was putting their lives.

My fitful work assignments from the relief officials ceased, and I looked for work that did not exist. I borrowed money to ride to and fro on the club's business. I found a cramped attic for my mother and aunt and brother behind some railroad tracks. At last the relief authorities placed me in the South Side Boys' Club, and my wages were just enough to provide a bare living for my family.

Then political problems rose to plague me. Ross, whose life I had tried to write, was charged by the Communist Party with "anti-leadership tendencies," "class collaborationist attitudes," and "ideological factionalism"—phrases so fanciful that I gaped when I heard them. And it was rumored that I, too, would face similar charges. It was believed that I had been politically influenced by him.

One night a group of black comrades came to my house and ordered me to stay away from Ross.

"But why?" I demanded.

"He's an unhealthy element," they said. "Can't you accept a decision?"

"Is this a decision of the Communist Party?"

"Yes," they said.

"If I were guilty of something, I'd feel bound to keep your decision," I said. "But I've done nothing."

"Comrade, you don't understand," they said. "Members of the Party do not violate the Party's decisions."

"But your decision does not apply to me," I said. "I'll be damned if I'll act as if it does."

"Your attitude does not merit our trust," they said.

I was angry.

"Look," I exploded, rising and sweeping my arms at the bleak attic in which I lived. "What is it here that frightens you? You know where I work. You know what I earn. You know my friends. Now, what in God's name is wrong?"

They left with mirthless smiles which implied that I would soon know what was wrong.

But there was relief from these shadowy political bouts. I found my work in the South Side Boys' Club deeply engrossing. Each day black boys between the ages of eight and twenty-five came to swim, draw, and read. They were a wild and homeless lot, culturally lost, spiritually disinherited, candidates for the clinics, morgues, prisons, reformatories, and the electric chair of the state's death house. For hours I listened to their talk of planes, women, guns, politics, and crime. Their figures of speech were as forceful and colorful as any ever used by English-speaking people. I kept pencil and paper in my pocket to jot down their word-rhythms and reactions. These boys did not fear people to the extent that every man looked like a spy. The Communists who doubted my motives did not know these boys, their twisted dreams, their all too clear destinies; and I doubted if I should ever be able to convey to them the tragedy I saw here.

★

Party duties broke into my efforts at expression. The club decided upon a conference of all the Left-Wing writers of the Middle West. I supported the idea and argued that the conference should deal with craft problems. My arguments were rejected. The conference, the club decided, would deal with political questions. I asked for a definition of what was expected from the writers—books or political activity. Both, was the answer. Write a few hours a day and march on the picket line the other hours.

The conference convened with a leading Communist attending as adviser. The question debated was: What does the Communist Party expect from the club? The answer of the Communist leader ran from organizing to writing novels. I argued that either a man organized or he wrote novels. The Party leader said that both must be done. The attitude of the Party leader prevailed and *Left Front*, for which I had worked so long, was voted out of existence.

I knew now that the club was nearing its end, and I rose and stated my gloomy conclusions, recommending that the club dissolve. My "defeatism," as it was called, brought upon my head the sharpest disapproval of the Party leader. The conference ended with the passing of a multitude of resolutions dealing with China, India, Germany, Japan, and conditions afflicting various parts of the earth. But not one idea regarding writing had emerged.

The ideas I had expounded at the conference were linked with the suspicions I had roused among the Negro Communists on the South Side, and the Communist Party was now certain that it had a dangerous enemy in its midst. It was whispered that I was trying to lead a secret group in opposition to the Party. I had learned that denial of accusations was useless. It was now painful to meet a Communist, for I did not know what his attitude would be.

Following the conference, a national John Reed Club Congress was called. It convened in the summer of 1934 with Left-Wing writers attending from all states. But as the sessions got under way, there was a sense of looseness, bewilderment, and dissatisfaction among the writers, most of whom were young, eager, and on the verge of doing their best work. No one knew what was expected of him, and out of the congress came no unifying idea.

As the congress drew to a close, I attended a caucus to plan the future of the clubs. Ten of us met in a Loop hotel room, and to my amazement the leaders of the clubs' national board confirmed my criticisms of the manner in which the clubs had been conducted. I was excited. Now, I thought, the clubs will be given a new lease on life.

Then I was stunned when I heard a nationally known Communist announce a decision to dissolve the clubs. Why? I asked. Because the clubs do not serve the new People's Front policy, I was told. That can be remedied; the clubs can be made healthy and broad, I said. No; a bigger and better organization must be launched, one in which the leading writers of the nation could be included, they said. I was informed that the People's Front policy was now the correct vision of life and that the clubs could no longer exist. I asked what was to become of the young writers whom the Communist Party had implored to join the clubs and who were ineligible for the new group, and there was no answer. "This thing is cold!" I exclaimed to myself. To effect a swift change in policy, the Communist Party was dumping one organization, then organizing a new scheme with entirely new people!

I found myself arguing alone against the majority opinion, and then I made still another amazing discovery. I saw that even those who agreed with me would not support me. At that meeting I learned that when a man was informed of the wish of the Party he submitted, even though he knew with all the strength of his brain that the wish was not a wise one, was one that would ultimately harm the Party's interests.

It was not courage that made me oppose the Party. I simply did not know any better. It was inconceivable to me, though bred in the lap of Southern hate, that a man could not have his say. I had spent a third of my life traveling from the place of my birth to the North just to talk freely, to escape the pressure of fear. And now I was facing fear again.

Before the congress adjourned, it was decided that another congress of American writers would be called in New York the following summer, 1935. I was lukewarm to the proposal and tried to make up my mind to stand alone, write alone. I was already afraid that the stories I had written would not fit into the new, official mood. Must I discard my plot-ideas and seek new ones? No. I could not. My writing was my way of seeing, my way of living, my way of feeling; and who could change his sight, his sense of direction, his senses?

refusal to submit

★

The spring of 1935 came and the plans for the writers' congress went on apace. For some obscure reason—it might have been to "save" me—I was urged by the local Communists to attend and I was named as a delegate. I got time off from my job at the South Side Boys' Club and, along with several other delegates, hitchhiked to New York.

We arrived in the early evening and registered for the congress sessions. The opening mass meeting was being held at Carnegie Hall. I asked about housing accommodations, and the New York John Reed Club members, all white members of the Communist Party, looked embarrassed. I waited while one white Communist called another white Communist to one side and discussed what could be done to get me, a black Chicago Communist, housed. During the trip I had not thought of myself as a Negro; I had been mulling over the problems of the young Left-Wing writers I knew. Now, as I stood watching one white comrade talk frantically to another about the color of my skin, I felt disgusted. The white comrade returned.

"Just a moment, comrade," he said to me. "I'll get a place for you."

"But haven't you places already?" I asked. "Matters of this sort are ironed out in advance."

"Yes," he admitted in an intimate tone. "We have some addresses here, but we don't know the people. You understand?"

"Yes, I understand," I said, gritting my teeth.

"But just wait a second," he said, touching my arm to reassure me. "I'll find something."

"Listen, don't bother," I said, trying to keep anger out of my voice.

"Oh, no," he said, shaking his head determinedly. "This is a problem and I'll solve it."

"It oughtn't to be a problem," I could not help saying.

"Oh, I didn't mean that," he caught himself.

I cursed under my breath. Several people standing nearby observed the white Communist trying to find a black Communist a place to sleep. I burned with shame. A few minutes later the white Communist returned, frantic-eyed, sweating.

"Did you find anything?" I asked.

"No, not yet," he said, panting. "Just a moment. I'm going to call somebody I know. Say, give me a nickel for the phone."

"Forget it," I said. My legs felt like water. "I'll find a place. But I'd like to put my suitcase somewhere until after the meeting tonight."

"Do you really think you can find a place?" he asked, trying to keep a note of desperate hope out of his voice.

"Of course I can," I said.

He was still uncertain. He wanted to help me, but he did not know how. He locked my bag in a closet, and I stepped to the sidewalk wondering where I would sleep that night. I stood on the sidewalks of New York with a black skin and practically no money, absorbed, not with the burning questions of the Left-Wing literary movement in the United States, but with the problem of how to get a bath. I presented my credentials at Carnegie Hall. The building was jammed with people. As I listened to the militant speeches, I found myself wondering why in hell I had come.

I went to the sidewalk and stood studying the faces of the people. I met a Chicago club member.

"Didn't you find a place yet?" he asked.

"No," I said. "I'd like to try one of the hotels, but, God, I'm in no mood to argue with a hotel clerk about my color."

"Oh, hell, wait a minute," he said.

He scooted off. He returned in a few moments with a big, heavy white woman. He introduced us.

"You can sleep in my place tonight," she said.

I walked with her to her apartment and she introduced me to her husband. I thanked them for their hospitality and went to sleep on a cot in the kitchen. I got up at six, dressed, tapped on their door, and bade them goodbye. I went to the sidewalk, sat on a bench, took out a pencil and paper, and tried to jot down notes for the argument I wanted to make in defense of the John Reed Clubs. But the problem of the clubs did not seem important. What did seem important was: Could a Negro ever live halfway like a human being in this goddamn country?

That day I sat through the congress sessions, but what I heard did not touch me. That night I found my way to Harlem and walked pavements filled with black life. I was amazed, when I asked passers-by, to learn that there were practically no hotels for Negroes in Harlem. I kept walking. Finally I saw a tall, clean hotel; black people were passing the doors and no white people were in sight. Confidently I entered and was surprised to see a white clerk behind the desk. I hesitated.

"I'd like a room," I said.

"Not here," he said.

"But isn't this Harlem?" I asked.

"Yes, but this hotel is for white only," he said.

"Where is a hotel for colored?"

"You might try the Y," he said.

Half an hour later I found the Negro Young Men's Christian Association, that bulwark of Jim Crowism for young black men, got a room, took a bath, and slept for twelve hours. When I awakened, I did not want to go to the congress. I lay in bed thinking. "I've got to go it alone. . . . I've got to learn how again. . . ."

I dressed and attended the meeting that was to make the final decision to dissolve the clubs. It started briskly. A New York Communist writer summed up the history of the clubs and made a motion for their dissolution. Debate started, and I rose and explained what the clubs had meant to young writers and begged for their continuance. I sat down amid silence. Debate was closed. The vote was called. The room filled with uplifted hands to dissolve. Then came a call for those who disagreed and my hand went up alone. I knew that my stand would be interpreted as one of opposition to the Communist Party, but I thought: "The hell with it."

willing to go against the Party

With the John Reed Clubs now dissolved, I was free of all Party relations. I avoided unit meetings for fear of being subjected to discipline. Occasionally, a Negro Communist—defying the code that enjoined him to shun suspect elements—came to my home and informed me of the current charges that Communists were bringing against one another. To my astonishment I heard that Buddy Nealson had branded me a "smuggler of reaction."

Buddy Nealson was the Negro who had formulated the Communist position for the American Negro; he had made speeches in the Kremlin; he had spoken before Stalin himself.

"Why does Nealson call me that?" I asked.

"He says that you are a petty bourgeois degenerate," I was told.

"What does that mean?"

"He says that you are corrupting the Party with your ideas."

"How?"

There was no answer. I decided that my relationship with the Party was about over; I should have to leave it. The attacks were growing worse, and my refusal to react incited Nealson into coining more absurd phrases. I was termed a "bastard intellectual," an "incipient Trotskyite"; it was claimed that I possessed an "anti-leadership attitude" and that I was manifesting "seraphim tendencies," a phrase meaning that one has withdrawn from the struggle of life and considers oneself infallible.

Working all day and writing half the night brought me down with a severe chest ailment. While I was ill, a knock came at my door one morning. My mother admitted Ed Green, the man who had demanded to know what use I planned to make of the material I was collecting from the comrades. I stared at him as I lay abed, and I knew that he considered me a clever and sworn enemy of the Party. Bitterness welled up in me.

"What do you want?" I asked bluntly. "You see I'm ill."

"I have a message from the Party for you," he said.

I had not said good day, and he had not offered to say it. He had not smiled, and neither had I. He looked curiously at my bleak room.

"This is the home of a bastard intellectual," I cut at him.

He stared without blinking. I could not endure his standing there so stonelike. Common decency made me say, "Sit down."

His shoulders stiffened.

"I'm in a hurry." He spoke like an army officer.

"What do you want to tell me?"

"Do you know Buddy Nealson?" he asked.

I was suspicious. Was this a political trap?

"What about Buddy Nealson?" I asked, committing myself to nothing until I knew the kind of reality I was grappling with.

"He wants to see you," Ed Green said.

"What about?" I asked, still suspicious.

"He wants to talk with you about your Party work," he said.

"I'm ill and can't see him until I'm well," I said.

Green stood for a fraction of a second, then turned on his heel and marched out of the room.

When my chest healed, I sought an appointment with Buddy Nealson. He was a short, black man with an ever ready smile, thick lips, a furtive manner, and a greasy, sweaty look. His bearing was nervous, self-conscious; he seemed always to be hiding some deep irritation. He spoke in short, jerky sentences, hopping nimbly from thought to thought, as though his mind worked in a free, associational manner. He suffered from asthma and would snort at unexpected intervals. Now and then he would punctuate his flow of words by taking a nip from a bottle of whiskey. He had traveled half around the world and his talk was pitted with vague allusions to European cities. I met him in his apartment, listened to him intently, observed him minutely, for I knew that I was facing one of the leaders of World Communism.

"Hello, Wright," he snorted. "I've heard about you."

As we shook hands, he burst into a loud, seemingly causeless laugh; and as he guffawed, I could not tell whether his mirth was directed at me or was meant to hide his uneasiness.

"I hope what you've heard about me is good," I parried.

"Sit down," he laughed again, waving me to a chair. "Yes, they tell me you write."

"I try to," I said.

"You can write," he snorted. "I read that article you wrote for the *New Masses* about Joe Louis. Good stuff. First political treatment of sports we've yet had. Ha-ha."

I waited. I had thought that I should encounter a man of ideas, but he was not that. Then perhaps he was a man of action? But that was not indicated either.

"They tell me that you are a friend of Ross," he shot at me.

I paused before answering. He had not asked me directly, but had hinted in a neutral, teasing way. Ross, I had been told, was slated for expulsion from the Party on the ground that he was "anti-leadership"; and if a member of the Communist International was asking me if I was a friend of a man about to be expelled, he was indirectly asking me if I was loyal or not.

"Ross is not particularly a friend of mine," I said frankly. "But I know him well; in fact, quite well."

"If he isn't your friend, how do you happen to know him so

well?" he asked, laughing to soften the hard threat of his question.

"I was writing an account of his life and I know him as well, perhaps, as anybody," I told him.

"I heard about that," he said. "Wright. Ha-ha. Say, let me call you Dick, huh?"

"Go ahead," I said.

"Dick," he said, "Ross is a nationalist." He paused to let the weight of his accusation sink in. He meant that Ross's militancy was extreme. "We Communists don't dramatize Negro nationalism," he said in a voice that laughed, accused and drawled.

"What do you mean?" I asked.

"We're not advertising Ross." He spoke directly now.

"We're talking about two different things," I said. "You seem worried about my making Ross popular because he is your political opponent. But I'm not concerned about Ross's politics at all. The man struck me as one who typified certain traits of the Negro migrant. I've already sold a story based upon an incident in his life."

Nealson became excited.

"What was the incident?" he asked.

"Some trouble he got into when he was thirteen years old," I said.

"Oh, I thought it was political," he said, shrugging.

"But I'm telling you that you are wrong about that," I explained. "I'm not trying to fight you with my writing. I've no political ambitions. You must believe that. I'm trying to depict Negro life."

"Have you finished writing about Ross?"

"No," I said. "I dropped the idea. Our Party members were suspicious of me and were afraid to talk." He laughed.

"Dick," he began, "we're short of forces. We're facing a grave crisis."

"The Party's always facing a crisis," I said.

His smile left and he stared at me.

"You're not cynical, are you, Dick?" he asked.

"No," I said. "But it's the truth. Each week, each month there's a crisis."

"You're a funny guy," he said, laughing, snorting again. "But we've a job to do. We're altering our work. Fascism's the danger, the danger now to all people."

"I understand," I said.

"We've got to defeat the Fascists," he said, snorting from asthma. "We've discussed you and know your abilities. We want you to work with us. We've got to crash out of our narrow way of working and get our message to the church people, students, club people, professionals, middle class."

"I've been called names," I said softly. "Is that crashing out of the narrow way?"

"Forget that," he said.

He had not denied the name-calling. That meant that, if I did not obey him, the name-calling would begin again.

"I don't know if I fit into things," I said openly.

"We want to trust you with an important assignment," he said.

"What do you want me to do?"

"We want you to organize a committee against the high cost of living."

"The high cost of living?" I exclaimed. "What do I know about such things?"

"It's easy. You can learn," he said.

I was in the midst of writing a novel and he was calling me from it to tabulate the price of groceries. "He doesn't think much of what I'm trying to do," I thought.

"Comrade Nealson," I said, "a writer who hasn't written anything worth-while is a most doubtful person. Now, I'm in that category. Yet I think I can write. I don't want to ask for special favors, but I'm in the midst of a book which I hope to complete in six months or so. Let me convince myself that I'm wrong about my hankering to write and then I'll be with you all the way."

"Dick," he said, turning in his chair and waving his hand as though to brush away an insect that was annoying him, "you've got to get to the masses of people."

"You've seen some of my work," I said. "Isn't it just barely good enough to warrant my being given a chance?"

"The Party can't deal with your feelings," he said.

"Maybe I don't belong in the Party," I stated it in full.

"Oh, no! Don't say that," he said, snorting. He looked at me. "You're blunt."

"I put things the way I feel them," I said. "I want to start in right with you. I've had too damn much crazy trouble in the Party."

He laughed and lit a cigarette.

"Dick," he said, shaking his head, "the trouble with you is that you've been around with those white artists on the North Side too much. You even talk like 'em. You've got to know your own people."

"I think I know them," I said, realizing that I could never really talk with him. "I've been inside of three-fourths of the Negroes' homes on the South Side."

"But you've got to work with 'em," he said.

"I was working with Ross until I was suspected of being a spy," I said.

"Dick," he spoke seriously now, "the Party has decided that you are to accept this task."

I was silent. I knew the meaning of what he had said. A decision was the highest injunction that a Communist could receive from his Party, and to break a decision was to break the effectiveness of the Party's ability to act. In principle I heartily agreed with this, for I knew that it was impossible for working people to forge instruments of political power until they had achieved unity of action. Oppressed for centuries, divided, hopeless, corrupted, misled, they were cynical—as I had once been—and the Communist method of unity had been found historically to be the only means of achieving discipline. In short, Nealson had asked me directly if I were a Communist or not. I wanted to be a Communist, but my kind of Communist. I wanted to shape people's feeling, awaken their hearts. But I could not tell Nealson that; he would only have snorted.

"I'll organize the committee and turn it over to someone else," I suggested.

"You don't want to do this, do you?" he asked.

"No," I said firmly.

"What would you like to do on the South Side, then?"

"I'd like to organize Negro artists," I said.

"But the Party doesn't need that now," he said.

I rose, knowing that he had no intention of letting me go after I had organized the committee. I wanted to tell him that I was through, but I was not ready to bring matters to a head. I went out, angry with myself, angry with him, angry with the Party. Well, I had not broken the decision, but neither had I accepted it wholly. I had dodged, trying to save time for writing, time to think.

★

My task consisted in attending meetings until the late hours of the night, taking part in discussions, or lending myself generally along with other Communists in leading the people of the South Side. We debated the housing situation, the best means of forcing the city to authorize open hearings on conditions among Negroes. I gritted my teeth as the daily value of pork chops was tabulated, longing to be at home with my writing.

Nealson was cleverer than I and he confronted me before I had a chance to confront him. I was summoned one night to meet Nealson and a "friend." When I arrived at a South Side hotel, I was introduced to a short, yellow man who carried himself like Napoleon. He wore glasses, kept his full lips pursed as though he were engaged in perpetual thought. He swaggered when he walked. He spoke slowly, precisely, trying to charge each of his words with more meaning than the words were able to carry. He talked of trivial things in lofty tones. He said that his name was (Smith,) that he was from Washington, that he planned to launch a national organization among Negroes to federalize all existing Negro institutions so as to achieve a broad unity of action. The three of us sat at a table facing one another. I knew that another and last offer was about to be made to me, and if I did not accept it, there would be open warfare.

"Wright, how would you like to go to Switzerland?" Smith asked with dramatic suddenness.

"I'd like it," I said. "But I'm tied up with work now."

"You can drop that," Nealson said. "This is important."

"What would I do in Switzerland?" I asked.

"You'll go as a youth delegate," Smith said. "From there you can go to the Soviet Union."

"Much as I'd like to, I'm afraid I can't make it," I said honestly. "I simply cannot drop the writing I'm doing now."

We sat looking at one another, smoking silently.

"Has Nealson told you how I feel?" I asked Smith.

Smith did not answer. He stared at me a long time, then spat: "Wright, you're a fool!"

I rose. Smith turned away from me. A breath more of anger and I should have driven my fist into his face. Nealson laughed sheepishly, snorting.

"Was that necessary?" I asked, trembling.

I stood recalling how, in my boyhood, I would have fought until blood ran had anyone said anything like that to me. But I was a man now and master of my rage, able to control the surging emotions. I put on my hat and walked to the door. "Keep cool," I said to myself. "Don't let this get out of hand."

"This is goodbye," I said.

I attended the next unit meeting and asked for a place on the agenda, which was readily granted. Nealson was there. Evans was there. Ed Green was there. When my time came to speak, I said:

"Comrades, for the past two years I've worked daily with most of you. Despite this, I have for some time found myself in a difficult position in the Party. What caused this difficulty is a long story which I do not care to recite now; it would serve no purpose. But I tell you honestly that I think I've found a solution of my difficulty. I am proposing here tonight that my membership be dropped from the Party rolls. No ideological differences impel me to say this. I simply do not wish to be bound any longer by the Party's decisions. I should like to retain my membership in those organizations in which the Party has influence, and I shall comply with the Party's program in those organizations. I hope that my words will be accepted in the spirit in which they are said. Perhaps sometime in the future I can meet and talk with the leaders of the Party as to what tasks I can best perform."

I sat down amid a profound silence. The Negro secretary of the meeting looked frightened, glancing at Nealson, Evans, and Ed Green.

"Is there any discussion on Comrade Wright's statement?" the secretary asked finally.

"I move that discussion on Wright's statement be deferred," Nealson said.

A quick vote confirmed Nealson's motion. I looked about the silent room, then reached for my hat and rose.

"I should like to go now," I said.

No one said anything. I walked to the door and out into the night and a heavy burden seemed to lift from my shoulders. I was free. And I had done it in a decent and forthright manner. I had not been bitter. I had not raked up a single recrimination. I had attacked no one. I had disavowed nothing.

The next night two Negro Communists called at my home. They pretended to be ignorant of what had happened at the unit meeting. Patiently, I explained what had occurred.

"Your story does not agree with what Nealson says," they said, revealing the motive of their visit.

"And what does Nealson say?" I asked.

"He says that you are in league with a Trotskyite group,

and that you made an appeal for other Party members to follow you in leaving the Party."

"What?" I gasped. "That's not true. I asked that my membership be dropped. I raised no political issues." What did this mean? I sat pondering. "Look, maybe I ought to make my break with the Party clean. If Nealson's going to act this way, I'll resign."

"You can't resign," they told me.

"What do you mean?" I demanded.

"No one can resign from the Communist Party."

[margin note: what it this, slavery?]

I looked at them and laughed.

"You're talking crazy," I said.

"Nealson would expel you publicly, cut the ground from under your feet if you resigned," they said. "People would think that something was wrong if someone like you quit here on the South Side."

I was angry. Was the Party so weak and uncertain of itself that it could not accept what I had said at the unit meeting? Who thought up such tactics? Then, suddenly, I understood. These were the secret, underground tactics of the political movement of the Communists under the czars of Old Russia!

[margin note: connecting to Russia]

The Communist Party felt that it had to assassinate me morally merely because I did not want to be bound by its decisions. I saw now that my comrades were acting out a fantasy that had no relation whatever to the reality of their environment.

"Tell Nealson that if he fights me, then, by God, I'll fight him," I said. "If he leaves this damn thing where it is, then all right. If he thinks I won't fight him publicly, he's crazy!"

I was not able to know if my statement reached Nealson. There was no public outcry against me, but in the ranks of the Party itself a storm broke loose and I was branded a traitor, an unstable personality, and one whose faith had failed.

My comrades had known me, my family, my friends; they, God knows, had known my aching poverty. But they had never been able to conquer their fear of the individual way in which I acted and lived, an individuality which life had seared into my bones.

★

I was transferred by the relief authorities from the South Side Boys' Club to the Federal Negro Theater to work as a publicity agent. There were days when I was acutely hungry for the incessant analyses that went on among the comrades, but whenever I heard news of the Party's inner life, it was of charges and countercharges, reprisals and counter-reprisals.

The Federal Negro Theater, for which I was doing publicity, had run a series of ordinary plays, all of which had been revamped to "Negro style," with jungle scenes, spirituals, and all. For example, the skinny white woman who directed it, an elderly missionary type, would take a play whose characters were white, whose theme dealt with the Middle Ages, and recast it in terms of Southern Negro life with overtones of African backgrounds. Contemporary plays dealing realistically with Negro life were spurned as being controversial. There were about forty Negro actors and actresses in the theater, lolling about, yearning, disgruntled.

What a waste of talent, I thought. Here was an opportunity for the production of a worth-while Negro drama and no one was aware of it. I studied the situation, then laid the matter before white friends of mine who held influential positions in the Works Progress Administration. I asked them to replace the white woman—including her quaint aesthetic notions—with someone who knew the Negro and the theater. They promised me that they would act.

Within a month the white woman director had been transferred. We moved from the South Side to the Loop and were housed in a first-rate theater. I successfully recommended Charles DeSheim, a talented Jew, as director. DeSheim and I held long talks during which I outlined what I thought could be accomplished. I urged that our first offering should be a bill of three one-act plays, including Paul Green's *Hymn to the Rising Sun,* a grim, poetical, powerful one-acter dealing with chain-gang conditions in the South.

I was happy. At last I was in a position to make suggestions and have them acted upon. I was convinced that we had a rare chance to build a genuine Negro theater. I convoked a meeting and introduced DeSheim to the Negro company, telling them that he was a man who knew the theater, who would lead them toward serious dramatics. DeSheim made a speech wherein he said that he was not at the theater to direct it, but to help the Negroes to direct it. He spoke so simply and eloquently that they rose and applauded him.

I then proudly passed out copies of Paul Green's *Hymn to the Rising Sun* to all members of the company. DeSheim assigned reading parts. I sat down to enjoy adult Negro dramatics. But something went wrong. The Negroes stammered and faltered in their lines. Finally they stopped reading altogether. DeSheim looked frightened. One of the Negro actors rose.

"Mr. DeSheim," he began, "we think this play is indecent. We don't want to act in a play like this before the American public. I don't think any such conditions exist in the South. I lived in the South and I never saw any chain gangs. Mr. DeSheim, we want a play that will make the public love us."

"What kind of play do you want?" DeSheim asked them.

They did not know. I went to the office and looked up their records and found that most of them had spent their lives playing cheap vaudeville because the legitimate theater was barred to them, and now it turned out they wanted none of the legitimate theater, that they were scared spitless at the prospects of appearing in a play that the public might not like, even though they did not understand that public and had no way of determining its likes or dislikes.

I felt—but only temporarily—that perhaps the whites were right, that Negroes were children and would never grow up. DeSheim informed the company that he would produce any play they liked, and they sat like frightened mice, possessing no words to make known their vague desires.

When I arrived at the theater a few mornings later, I was horrified to find that the company had drawn up a petition demanding the ousting of DeSheim. I was asked to sign the petition and I refused.

"Don't you know your friends?" I asked them.

They glared at me. I called DeSheim to the theater and we went into a frantic conference.

"What must I do?" he asked.

"Take them into your confidence," I said. "Let them know that it is their right to petition for a redress of their grievances."

DeSheim thought my advice sound and, accordingly, he assembled the company and told them that they had a right to petition against him if they wanted to, but that he thought any misunderstandings that existed could be settled smoothly.

"Who told you that we were getting up a petition?" a black man demanded.

DeSheim looked at me and stammered wordlessly.

"There's an Uncle Tom in the theater!" a black girl yelled.

After the meeting a delegation of Negro men came to my office and took out their pocketknives and flashed them in my face.

"You get the hell off this job before we cut your bellybutton out!" they said.

I telephoned my white friends in the Works Progress Administration: "Transfer me at once to another job, or I'll be murdered."

Within twenty-four hours DeSheim and I were given our papers. We shook hands and went our separate ways.

I was transferred to a white experimental theatrical company as a publicity agent and I resolved to keep my ideas to myself, or, better, to write them down and not attempt to translate them into reality.

★

One evening a group of Negro Communists called at my home and asked to speak to me in strict secrecy. I took them into my room and locked the door.

"Dick," they began abruptly, "the Party wants you to attend a meeting Sunday."

"Why?" I asked. "I'm no longer a member."

"That's all right. They want you to be present," they said.

"Communists don't speak to me on the street," I said. "Now, why do you want me at a meeting?"

They hedged. They did not want to tell me.

"If you can't tell me, then I can't come," I said.

They whispered among themselves and finally decided to take me into their confidence.

"Dick, Ross is going to be tried," they said.

"For what?"

They recited a long list of political offenses of which they alleged that he was guilty.

"But what has that got to do with me?"

"If you come, you'll find out," they said.

"I'm not that naïve," I said. I was suspicious now. Were they trying to lure me to a trial and expel me? "This trial might turn out to be mine."

They swore that they had no intention of placing me on trial, that the Party merely wanted me to observe Ross's trial so that I might learn what happened to "enemies of the working class."

As they talked, my old love of witnessing something new came over me. I wanted to see this trial, but I did not want to risk being placed on trial myself.

"Listen," I told them. "I'm not guilty of Nealson's charges. If I showed up at this trial, it would seem that I am."

"No, it won't. Please come."

"All right. But, listen. If I'm tricked, I'll fight. You hear? I don't trust Nealson. I'm not a politician and I cannot anticipate all the funny moves of a man who spends his waking hours plotting."

Ross's trial took place that following Sunday afternoon. Comrades stood inconspicuously on guard about the meeting hall, at the doors, down the street, and along the hallways. When I appeared, I was ushered in quickly. I was tense. It was a rule that once you had entered a meeting of this kind you could not leave until the meeting was over; it was feared that you might go to the police and denounce them all.

Ross, the accused, sat alone at a table in the front of the hall, his face distraught. I felt sorry for him; yet I could not escape feeling that he enjoyed this. For him, this was perhaps the highlight of an otherwise bleak existence.

In trying to grasp why Communists hated intellectuals, my mind was led back again to the accounts I had read of the Russian Revolution. There had existed in Old Russia millions of poor, ignorant people who were exploited by a few educated, arrogant noblemen, and it became natural for the Russian Communists to associate betrayal with intellectualism. But there existed in the Western world an element that baffled and frightened the Communist Party: the prevalence of self-achieved literacy. Even a Negro, entrapped by ignorance and exploitation—as I had been—could, if he had the will and the love for it, learn to read and understand the world in which he lived. And it was these people that the Communists could not understand.

The trial began in a quiet, informal manner. The comrades acted like a group of neighbors sitting in judgment upon one of their kind who had stolen a chicken. Anybody could ask and get the floor. There was absolute freedom of speech. Yet the meeting had an amazingly formal structure of its own, a structure that went as deep as the desire of men to live together.

A member of the Central Committee of the Communist Party rose and gave a description of the world situation. He spoke without emotion and piled up hard facts. He painted a horrible but masterful picture of Fascism's aggression in Germany, Italy, and Japan.

I accepted the reason why the trial began in this manner. It was imperative that here be postulated against what or whom Ross's crimes had been committed. Therefore there had to be established in the minds of all present a vivid picture of mankind under oppression. And it was a true picture. Perhaps no organization on earth, save the Communist Party, possesses so detailed a knowledge of how workers lived, for its sources of information stemmed directly from the workers themselves.

The next speaker discussed the role of the Soviet Union as the world's lone workers' state—how the Soviet Union was hemmed in by enemies, how the Soviet Union was trying to industrialize itself, what sacrifices it was making to help workers of the world to steer a path toward peace through the idea of collective security.

The facts presented so far were as true as any facts could be in this uncertain world. Yet not one word had been said of the accused, who sat listening like any other member. The time had not yet come to include him and his crimes in this picture of global struggle. An absolute had first to be established in the minds of the comrades so that they could measure the success or failure of their deeds by it.

Finally a speaker came forward and spoke of Chicago's South Side, its Negro population, their suffering and handicaps, linking all that also to the world struggle. Then still another speaker followed and described the tasks of the Communist Party of the South Side. At last, the world, the national, and the local pictures had been fused into one overwhelming drama of moral struggle in which everybody in the hall was participating. This presentation had lasted for more than three hours, but it had enthroned a new sense of reality in the hearts of those present, a sense of man on earth. With the exception of the church and its myths and legends, there was no agency in the world so capable of making men feel the earth and the people upon it as the Communist Party.

Toward evening the direct charges against Ross were made,

not by the leaders of the Party, but by Ross's friends, those who knew him best! It was crushing. Ross wilted. His emotions could not withstand the weight of the moral pressure. No one was terrorized into giving information against him. They gave it willingly, citing dates, conversations, scenes. The black mass of Ross's wrongdoing emerged slowly and irrefutably.

The moment came for Ross to defend himself. I had been told that he had arranged for friends to testify in his behalf, but he called upon no one. He stood, trembling; he tried to talk and his words would not come. The hall was as still as death. Guilt was written in every pore of his black skin. His hands shook. He held on to the edge of the table to keep on his feet. His personality, his sense of himself, had been obliterated. Yet he could not have been so humbled unless he had shared and accepted the vision that had crushed him, the common vision that bound us all together.

"Comrades," he said in a low, charged voice, "I'm guilty of all the charges, all of them."

His voice broke in a sob. No one prodded him. No one tortured him. No one threatened him. He was free to go out of the hall and never see another Communist. But he did not want to. He could not. The vision of a communal world had sunk down into his soul and it would never leave him until life left him. He talked on, outlining how he had erred, how he would reform.

I knew, as I sat there, that there were many people who thought they knew life who had been skeptical of the Moscow trials. But they could not have been skeptical had they witnessed this astonishing trial. Ross had not been doped; he had been awakened. It was not a fear of the Communist Party that had made him confess, but a fear of the punishment that he would exact of himself that made him tell of his wrongdoings. The Communists had talked to him until they had given him new eyes with which to see his own crime. And then they sat back and listened to him tell how he had erred.

He was one with all the members there, regardless of race or color; his heart was theirs and their hearts were his; and when a man reaches that state of kinship with others, that degree of oneness, or when a trial has made him kin after he has been sundered from them by wrongdoing, then he must rise and say, out of a sense of the deepest morality in the world: "I'm guilty. Forgive me."

This, to me, was a spectacle of glory; and yet, because it had condemned me, because it was blind and ignorant, I felt that it was a spectacle of horror. The blindness of their limited lives—lives truncated and impoverished by the oppression they had suffered long before they had ever heard of Communism—made them think that I was with their enemies. American life had so corrupted their consciousness that they were unable to recognize their friends when they saw them. I knew that if they had held state power I should have been declared guilty of treason and my execution would have followed. And I knew that they felt, with all the strength of their black blindness, that they were right.

I could not stay until the end. I was anxious to get out of the hall and into the streets and shake free from the gigantic tension that had hold of me. I rose and went to the door; a comrade shook his head, warning me that I could not leave until the trial had ended.

"You can't leave now," he said.

"I'm going out of here," I said, my anger making my voice louder than I intended.

We glared at each other. Another comrade came running up. I stepped forward. The comrade who had rushed up gave the signal for me to be allowed to leave. They did not want violence, and neither did I. They stepped aside.

I went into the dark Chicago streets and walked home through the cold, filled with a sense of sadness. Once again I told myself that I must learn to stand alone. I did not feel so wounded by their rejection of me that I wanted to spend my days bleating about what they had done. Perhaps what I had already learned to feel in my childhood saved me from that futile path. I lay in bed that night and said to myself: "I'll be for them, even though they are not for me."

★

From the Federal Experimental Theater I was transferred to the Federal Writers' Project, and I tried to earn my bread by writing guidebooks. Many of the writers on the project were members of the Communist Party and they kept their revolutionary vows that restrained them from speaking to "traitors of the working class." I sat beside them in the office, ate next to them in restaurants, and rode up and down in the elevators with them, but they always looked straight ahead, wordlessly.

After working on the project for a few months, I was made acting supervisor of essays and straightway I ran into political difficulties. One morning the administrator of the project called me into his office.

"Wright, who are your friends on this project?" he asked.

"I don't know," I said. "Why?"

"Well, you ought to find out soon," he said.

"What do you mean?"

"Some people are asking for your removal on the ground that you are incompetent," he said.

"Who are they?"

He named several of my erstwhile comrades. Yes, it had come to that. They were trying to take the bread out of my mouth.

"What do you propose to do about their complaints?" I asked.

"Nothing," he said, laughing. "I think I understand what's happening here. I'm not going to let them drive you off this job."

I thanked him and rose to go to the door. Something in his words had not sounded right. I turned and faced him.

"*This* job?" I repeated. "What do you mean?"

"You mean to say that you don't know?" he asked.

"Know what? What are you talking about?"

"Why did you leave the Federal Negro Theater?"

"I had trouble there. They drove me off the job, the Negroes did."

"And you don't think that they had any encouragement?" he asked me ironically.

I sat again. This was deadly. I gaped at him.

"You needn't fear here," he said. "You work, write."

"It's hard to believe that," I murmured.

"Forget it," he said.

But the worst was yet to come. One day at noon I closed my desk and went down in the elevator. When I reached the first floor of the building, I saw a picket line moving to and fro in the streets. Many of the men and women carrying placards were old friends of mine, and they were chanting for higher wages for Works Progress Administration artists and writers. It was not the kind of picket line that one was not supposed to cross, and as I started away from the door I heard my name shouted:

"There's Wright, that goddamn Trotskyite!"

"We know you, you—!"

"Wright's a traitor!"

For a moment it seemed that I ceased to live. I had now reached that point where I was cursed aloud in the busy streets of America's second-largest city. It shook me as nothing else had.

Days passed. I continued on my job, where I functioned as the shop chairman of the union which I had helped to organize, though my election as shop chairman had been bitterly opposed by the Party. In their efforts to nullify my influence in the union, my old comrades were willing to kill the union itself.

As May Day of 1936 approached, it was voted by the union membership that we should march in the public procession. On the morning of May Day I received printed instructions as to the time and place where our union contingent would assemble to join the parade. At noon, I hurried to the spot and found that the parade was already in progress. In vain I searched for the banners of my union local. Where were they? I went up and down the streets, asking for the location of my local.

"Oh, that local's gone fifteen minutes ago," a Negro told me. "If you're going to march, you'd better fall in somewhere."

I thanked him and walked through the milling crowds. Suddenly I heard my name called. I turned. To my left was the Communist Party's South Side section, lined up and ready to march.

"Come here!" an old Party friend called to me.

I walked over to him.

"Aren't you marching today?" he asked me.

"I missed my union local," I told him.

"What the hell," he said. "March with us."

"I don't know," I said, remembering my last visit to the headquarters of the Party, and my status as an "enemy."

"This is May Day," he said. "Get into the ranks."

"You know the trouble I've had," I said.

"That's nothing," he said. "Everybody's marching today."

"I don't think I'd better," I said, shaking my head.

"Are you scared?" he asked. "This is *May Day*."

He caught my right arm and pulled me into line beside him. I stood talking to him, asking about his work, about common friends.

"Get out of our ranks!" a voice barked.

I turned. A white Communist, a leader of the district of the Communist Party, Cy Perry, a slender, close-cropped fellow, stood glaring at me.

"I—It's May Day and I want to march," I said.

"Get out!" he shouted.

"I was invited here," I said.

I turned to the Negro Communist who had invited me into the ranks. I did not want public violence. I looked at my friend. He turned his eyes away. He was afraid. I did not know what to do.

"You asked me to march here," I said to him.

He did not answer.

"Tell him that you did invite me," I said, pulling his sleeve.

"I'm asking you for the last time to get out of our ranks!" Cy Perry shouted.

I did not move. I had intended to, but I was beset by so many impulses that I could not act. Another white Communist came to assist Perry. Perry caught hold of my collar and pulled at me. I resisted. They held me fast. I struggled to free myself.

"Turn me loose!" I said.

Hands lifted me bodily from the sidewalk; I felt myself being pitched headlong through the air. I saved myself from landing on my head by clutching a curbstone with my hands. Slowly I rose and stood. Perry and his assistant were glaring at me. The rows of white and black Communists were looking at me with cold eyes of nonrecognition. I could not quite believe what had happened, even though my hands were smarting and bleeding. I had suffered a public, physical assault by two white Communists with black Communists looking on. I could not move from the spot. I was empty of any idea about what to do. But I did not feel belligerent. I had outgrown my childhood.

Suddenly, the vast ranks of the Communist Party began to move. Scarlet banners with the hammer and sickle emblem of world revolution were lifted, and they fluttered in the May breeze. Drums beat. Voices were chanting. The tramp of many feet shook the earth. A long line of set-faced men and women, white and black, flowed past me.

I followed the procession to the Loop and went into Grant Park Plaza and sat upon a bench. I was not thinking; I could not think. But an objectivity of vision was being born within me. A surging sweep of many odds and ends came together and formed an attitude, a perspective. "They're blind," I said to myself. "Their enemies have blinded them with too much oppression." I lit a cigarette and I heard a song floating over the sunlit air:

Arise, you pris'ners of starvation!

I remembered the stories I had written, the stories in which I had assigned a role of honor and glory to the Communist Party, and I was glad that they were down in black and white, were finished. For I knew in my heart that I should never be able to write that way again, should never be able to feel with that simple sharpness about life, should never again express such passionate hope, should never again make so total a commitment of faith.

A better world's in birth. . . .

The procession still passed. Banners still floated. Voices of hope still chanted.

★

I headed toward home alone, really alone now, telling myself that in all the sprawling immensity of our mighty continent the least-known factor of living was the human heart, the least-sought goal of being was a way to live a human life. Perhaps, I thought, out of my tortured feelings I could fling a spark into this darkness. I would try, not because I wanted to, but because I felt that I had to if I were to live at all.

I would hurl words into this darkness and wait for an echo; and if an echo sounded, no matter how faintly, I would send other words to tell, to march, to fight, to create a sense of the hunger for life that gnaws in us all, to keep alive in our hearts a sense of the inexpressibly human.

again, "faith"

Worshipers from Afar

André Gide

Foreword *by Enid Starkie*

BIOGRAPHICAL NOTE: *Enid Starkie was born in Killiney, Co. Dublin, Ireland, daughter of the late Right Honorable W. J. M. Starkie, Greek scholar and last High Commissioner of Education under British rule in Ireland. She was educated at Alexandra College, Dublin, and Somerville College, Oxford, where she held scholarships, and at the Sorbonne in Paris. She specializes in French literature and obtained a First Class Honors Degree at Oxford, the Doctorate of Paris University, the D.Litt. of Oxford, and was awarded the Légion d'Honneur for her contribution to French literature.*

Her works include studies, in English and French, of Rimbaud, Baudelaire, and other French writers—one of which was couronné *by the French Academy. She now holds the post of Reader in French literature at the University of Oxford and is a Fellow of Somerville College, Oxford.*

In the nineteen-twenties an immense change came over André Gide. From the tormented introvert whom we knew in the early works, he was transformed into the serene philosopher whom we know today. He cast aside self-torture and hair-splitting about motive and guilt to become what he thought was finally himself. "I allow all contradictions free play in me," he said. With his liberation from personal conflict he was freed from obsession with self and had energy to spare

165

for objective considerations—not merely for the problem of guilt and personal liberty. In July, 1925, after he had finished *Les faux monnayeurs,* he set out on the African expedition from which he was to return only a year later. In the French equatorial possessions he was horrified to see the exploitation of the natives by their white masters and, when he came home, he said, "Henceforth an immense lamentation abides in me." Then he wrote to his friend Charles du Bos, "I would like not only to attain happiness myself but to make others reach it as well. I consider that it consists in the surrender of self. That is why to feel happy is nothing; happiness consists in making others happy." He now became the champion of victims and underdogs—criminal offenders for whom he demanded more sympathetic treatment; women for whom he asked equality— particularly spiritual equality—colonial natives whose cause he pleaded in the two travel books which he wrote on his return from Africa—*Voyage au Congo* and *Le retour du Tchad* —finally, the socially underprivileged. It was then that he took up Communism and went to Russia. He declared that he had always been a Communist at heart, without knowing it, even when he had been most Christian. What he admired in Russia, he said in his *Journal,* was the abolition of the abominable formula, "Thou shalt earn MY bread in the sweat of THY brow!"

There emerges now a new shade in Gide's conception of personal liberty. In 1931, he wrote in a preface to *Vol de nuit,* of Antoine de Saint Exupéry, "I am particularly grateful to him for throwing light on a paradoxical truth which is of considerable psychological importance to me, namely, that the happiness of man does not consist in liberty but in the acceptance of a duty." This is a marked difference from the completely individualistic and personal sense of liberty expressed thirty years before in *Les nourritures terrestres.* He calls it now *la liberté serviable mais non servile.* In his play *Œdipe,* of 1931, he shows in the hero the final and utter destruction which comes on the individual when he accepts nothing greater than himself and values personal liberty above all else. Oedipus starts out with all the advantages which Gide thinks essential for the free individual, and he is proud and happy to be unencumbered by any attachment of family or tradition, for he can then be himself alone. Nevertheless, he is finally defeated because he tries to be entirely self-sufficient. After this bankruptcy, Gide is forced to the realization that man without God is doomed to defeat and despair, unless he substitutes some other idea for God. Oedipus, at the end, rejects God for man, and Gide looked towards Communism. He now thought that liberty was not sufficient in itself, that it destroys itself if it is not linked to some ideal beyond egoism and self-expression—to some duty even. Looking then for some sense of obligation and responsibility, he thought that he would find it in Communism. He thought that he would find there, with its ideal of service, its discipline, the completest expression of the individual and the sanest and total form of liberty. "The triumph of the individual," he said, "is in the renouncing of individualism." Later he was to say in *Les nouvelles nourritures terrestres*, of 1935, "Each human being who has only himself for aim suffers from a horrible void."

His interest in Russia was not, however, a new departure. He had been working on Dostoevsky even before the War and in 1922 he gave a course of lectures on him on the occasion of his centenary. He imagined then that he saw, shining through the darkness which had enveloped Russia since the Revolution, a bright ray of hope. He saw her as offering herself in sacrifice for the salvation of the world and of humanity. He thought now, ten years later, that salvation might already have been achieved. Hitherto he had had the reputation of being someone who would not commit himself and who would not choose. Now he committed himself uncompromisingly to the Communist solution for the ills of the world, and it was a kind of religious conversion—a conversion more sentimental than intellectual—and he said in his *Journal*, "I feel myself the brother only of those who have come to Communism through love." In 1931 he wrote again, "I would like to cry aloud my sympathy for the Soviet Union and hope that my cry might be heard and have effect. I would like to live long enough to witness the triumph of that tremendous effort which I hope from the bottom of my heart will succeed and for which I would like to work." Although he was ready to sacrifice some of the sanctity of his individuality, he did not think that this should be necessary, and in 1932 he said that there was no reason why there should be a clash between individualism and Communism. "I remain a convinced individualist," he said, "but I consider a grave error the contrast which some people try to establish between Communism and the individual. To believe firmly that one can be—indeed must be— at the same time a Communist and an individualist, does not prevent one from condemning privileges, the favoritism of inheritance and the whole procession of errors of capitalism to which our Western world is still attached and which are dragging it headlong to its ruin. Why do I long for Communism? Because I believe it to be equitable and because I suffer on account of the injustices which I feel more strongly than ever when it is I myself who am favored. Because the regime under which we live does not seem to me to protect men from the most grievous abuses. Because amongst conservatives I see only dead or dying things. Because it seems to me absurd to cling to things which have had their day. Because I believe in progress; because I prefer what is to be to what has ceased to exist. Why do I long for Communism? Because I believe that through it we shall be able to reach the highest culture and because it is Communism which can— indeed must—promote a new and better form of civilization." Communism properly understood, he thought, needs to encourage individual values in order to get the best out of everyone.

In 1935 he sent a message to the Communists at the Congress of Soviet Writers, in which he said,

On the high road of history on which each country, each nation, must sooner or later travel, the Soviet Union has taken the lead in a glorious manner. She gives us today an example of the new society of which we dreamed but for which we no longer dared hope. In the realm of intellect it is important that the Soviet Union should give a good example; she owes it to herself to prove to us that the Communist ideal is not—as her enemies are always pleased to claim—an anthill Utopia. Her duty today is to inaugurate in art and literature a Communist individualism—if I may be permitted to link together these two words which are usually quite wrongly contrasted. No doubt a period of mass affirmation was necessary, but the Soviet Union has now passed beyond that stage and Communism can prevail only by taking into account the particular idiosyncrasies of each individual. A society in which each resembled all is not to be desired—I would say that it was impossible to achieve—how much more so a literature. Each artist is of necessity an individualist—however strong may be his Communist convictions and his attachment to the Party. It is only thus that he can do valuable work and serve society. I consider foolish and dangerous that fear which only the impotent experience, of being absorbed in the mass. Communism has need of strong personalities, in the same way as these find in Communism their justification and strength.

During a meeting in Paris in 1935 of l'Union pour la Vérité, when he was asked to defend his opinions, he said,

I consider that on account of its compromises Christianity is bankrupt. I have written, and I believe firmly, that if Christianity had really prevailed and if it had really fulfilled the teaching of Christ, there would today be no question of Communism—there would indeed be no social problem at all.

He added later, during the discussion on Communism,

If I have felt no contradiction between the community and the individualist position, it is precisely because that contradiction is only theoretic and artificial. I have become

certain of that. It is not Marx who brought me to Communism—I have made strenuous efforts to read him, but in
vain; I persevere, but it is certainly not his theory which
won me over. What brought me to Communism with my
whole heart was the fact of the privileged position which
I personally enjoy—that seemed to me preposterous and
intolerable. I once had occasion to talk with one of the
shipwrecked survivors of *La Bourgogne* and he told me that
he had been lucky enough to get into a lifeboat in which a
number of men had got away; if more had been taken in,
the boat would have capsized and sunk. The men in safety
on board, armed with jack-knives and hatchets, had hacked
off the hands of those who, clinging to the sides of the boat,
were endeavoring to scramble in out of the sea. The knowledge of being one of those in the lifeboat, of being safe,
whilst others round me are drowning, that feeling became
intolerable to me. People argue with me but I am not sufficiently expert to answer them subtly, I only cling tena-
ciously to the one fact that I cannot accept a place in a
lifeboat in which only a limited number of people are saved.
If I could feel, at least, assured that it was the best who were
saved, it might not be so bad, but what makes me most
indignant is when somebody says to me "What are you
grumbling at? You must admit that it is very comfortable
in the lifeboat."

Gide then became ashamed of being a man of independent
means, of not having been obliged ever to work with his hands,
of never having been forced to earn his living in the sweat of
his brow; all that now gave him a feeling of inferiority.

He went to Russia hoping that the Soviet Union would be
able to produce the finest flowers of civilization without en-
slaving the mind, or without reducing to serfdom a single
class, or without denying the benefits of civilization to anyone. He went to Russia realizing that the new world might
entail sacrifice of much that was good in itself—he knew that
moral and artistic standards might have to go for a time, for
the sake of temporary social and material gain. He agreed

that perhaps man could not be improved morally and intellectually before the social abuses had been removed, before
the social system had been altered. He who had hitherto
fought shy of all orthodoxies, was ready now, for a time, to
accept the Marxist one—albeit fully realizing that it might be,
if adhered to too long and too earnestly, as dangerous as any
other. He even agreed that, if it could be proved that the
Marxist doctrine was useful—perhaps even indispensable—to
assure the establishment of the new social order, then he considered that it might be worth-while. "It is perhaps right," he
said, "for achieving that end to sacrifice even a few works of
art." He was eventually to consider that the price was too
heavy. In 1937 he could discover no distinction between what
he saw in huge letters on the walls in Italy and what he had
earlier observed in Russia. There were the same slogans—
"Believe, obey and fight"—identical in both creeds. "These
Italian inscriptions," he said then in his *Journal*, "would have
been equally in place on the walls of Moscow. The Communist spirit has ceased being in opposition to the Fascist
spirit, or even differentiating itself from it." He thought later
that the Soviet dream of a totalitarian state was an oppressive
Utopia where enslaved minorities were no longer heard, where
—what was worse—everyone thought alike. "There can be
no question of harmony when the whole choir sings in unison,"
he said.

After the War a further development in his conception of
individuality and liberty became apparent—a departure from
the total and irresponsible liberty of his youth but also from
the *liberté serviable* of his middle years. He now believed
that absolute liberty destroys the individual and also society
unless it be closely linked to tradition and discipline. He no
longer asked for radical changes. During the War he wrote
in *Interviews imaginaires* that if civilization depended solely
on those who initiated revolutionary theories, then it would
perish, since culture needs for its survival a continuous and
developing tradition. In his most recent work, *Thésée*, of 1946,

he shows how a strong, purposeful and courageous individual is able to return safely from the Maze, but only because he had clung tightly to the thread which linked him with the past. It is interesting to notice the change which has taken place in the conception of this book since Gide first conceived it thirty years before. At first he saw the thread which bound Theseus to Ariadne as dragging him back to his past, to the place whence he had come, to women who will always be a brake on man's urge for progress; later he imagined him entering the Maze assured only by the thread of an inner fidelity; and finally he showed how Theseus could return only because he had clung tightly to the thread which bound him to his past, to the thread of tradition. Daedalus said to him as he set forth, "Go back to her"—that is Ariadne symbolizing tradition —"or all the rest, and the best with it, will be lost. This thread will be your link with the past. Go back to it. Go back to yourself. For nothing can begin from nothing, and it is from your past, and from what you are today, that what you are going to be must spring."

Gide returned to the same conception in the Bryce Memorial Lecture which he delivered in Oxford in June, 1947. He took then as his text the lines from Vergil where Aeneas is described as fleeing from burning Troy with his old father on his back. Gide said that these lines should be interpreted symbolically, that Aeneas was not merely bearing his father on his shoulders, but the whole weight of his past. In the same way we were fleeing from the burning city of our civilization with the burden of our Christian past heavy on us, our Christian civilization based on the sanctity of each individual human soul, and it was incumbent on us to see that it did not perish. He realized, he said, that civilizations rose up and eventually died, but he did not believe that ours was of necessity doomed if we accepted the responsibility of the sacred charge laid on us by our traditions and our past. Though the city of European culture be burning, we could still preserve its most precious essence. He said that he remained an unrepentent individualist and protested with all his might against the submersion of individual responsibility in organized authority, in that escape from freedom which is characteristic of our age. He repudiated the fashionable catchwords, the theory of *la littérature engagée* to whatever creed or ideology, all the various "isms" which would eventually vanish—as they had always disappeared—leaving only the outstanding individuals.

This was in 1947; but, fifteen years before, when he was favoring Communism, he said in his *Journal,*

> My conversion is like a faith. My whole being is bent towards one single goal, all my thoughts—even involuntary —lead me back to it. In the deplorable state of distress of the modern world, the plan of the Soviet Union seems to me to point to salvation. Everything persuades me of this. The wretched arguments of my opponents, far from convincing me, make me indignant. And if my life were necessary to assure the success of the Soviet Union, I would gladly give it immediately. I write this with a cool and calm head, in full sincerity, through great need to leave at least this testimony, in case death should intervene before I have time to express myself better.

He went to Russia in June, 1936, full of high hopes which were soon disappointed, and he said on his return,

> There was in my Soviet adventure something tragic. I had arrived there a convinced and enthusiastic follower in order to admire a new world, and they offered me, to tempt me and win me, all the prerogatives and privileges which I abhorred in the old world.

It was not through Marx, but through the Gospels, that Gide had reached Communism, and he found little of that spirit in Russia itself. He was fêted everywhere, for he was a wonderful gain to the cause—the greatest living European writer and a man known for his integrity and honesty of mind. He was given all the privileges of a decadent civilization, but he did not need incense and it was not for material gain that he had gone to the Soviet Union. He saw everywhere the same gulf which separates the privileged from the underprivileged, the same enslavement of the mind, against which he had protested elsewhere in Europe. The books which he wrote on his return—*Retour de l'U.R.S.S.* and *Retouches à mon retour de l'U.R.S.S.*—show the measure of his disappointment and disillusionment. In them he expressed admiration and affection for the Russian people themselves; he was charmed by the smiling faces, the happy children, the recreation centers, the zest for learning and the atmosphere of hope. He was distressed by the inequalities he saw, the poor return the masses of the people received for their patience and endurance; he was depressed by the drabness and ugliness of the clothes, the poor quality of the goods displayed in the shops and for which the people stood long hours in queues; and he was appalled by the lack of criticism and the absence of liberty of opinion and thought. It is from these two books, with the help and approval of André Gide himself, that the following narrative has been composed.

André Gide

BIOGRAPHICAL NOTE: *André Gide was born in Paris in November, 1869; educated privately and at the Ecole Alsacienne in Paris. He is a man of independent means who has never been obliged to earn his living by a profession and this has helped him to become the kind of author he is today. In his twenties he first published* Les nourritures terrestres, *the work which was to exercise so much influence on the postwar generation of the First World War. His works include* La Porte étroite, La symphonie pastorale, Les faux monnayeurs, Œdipe, Thésée. *But it is his* Journal *which is probably his greatest work and the one most suited to his particular genius. In it he appears as a moralist in the great classical tradition, whose nobility of thought and purity of style place him on equality with the great masters of French literature. He was awarded an Honorary D.Litt. by the University of Oxford in June, 1947—the first honor he had ever received although he was then seventy-eight—and the Nobel Prize for literature at the end of the year.*

Although never actually a member of the Communist Party he was much interested in the Communist experiment in Russia and thought that thence the only salvation for humanity would come. On an invitation from the Soviet Society of Authors he visited Russia in June, 1936, and came back utterly disillusioned. He returned then to his individualistic and liberal philosophy of life. He has published nothing new since Thésée *of 1946, but has been occupied in bringing out his collected works and in writing his* Journal.

Homer relates how the great goddess Demeter, in her wanderings in search of her daughter, came to the court of Celeus. No one recognized her in the disguise of a nurse, and a newborn child—the boy Demophoön—was entrusted to her care. At night, with the doors closed and while the household slept, Demeter used to lift Demophoön from his warm soft cradle and, with seeming cruelty—though in reality inspired by great love and the desire to transform the child into a God—she would lay him naked on a bed of glowing coals, and bend lovingly over her bonny nursling, as if over the incarnation of future mankind. He endured the heat of the embers and this ordeal by fire made him strong and glorious beyond all dreams and hopes. Demeter, however, was not permitted to complete her daring endeavor. Metaneira, the mother—so the legend relates—anxious for the safety of her child, burst one night into the room, and, thrusting aside the goddess, scattered the embers with all the superhuman virtues which were being wrought and, in order to save the child, sacrificed the God.

Some years ago I wrote of my love and admiration for the Soviet Union, where an unprecedented experiment was being attempted, the thought of which inflamed my heart with expectation and from which I hoped a tremendous advance, an impulse capable of sweeping along the whole of humanity. It was certainly worth-while to be alive at such a moment to be able to witness this rebirth and to give one's whole life to further it. In my heart I bound myself resolutely, in the name of future culture, to the fortunes of the Soviet Union.

Four days after my arrival in Russia I declared, at the funeral of Gorky, in the Red Square at Moscow, that the fate of culture was linked, in my mind, with the future of the Soviet Union. "Culture," I said, "had long remained the prerogative of a privileged class, and leisure was necessary for its development. One whole section of society had toiled in order to allow a small number of people to enjoy life, while the garden of culture, literature and art had long remained a private enclosed property to which only the most intelligent could ever hope to have access—those who from childhood had been sheltered from need. It is of course true that ability does not necessarily accompany wealth and in French literature Molière, Diderot and Rousseau had risen from the people, but their readers had been men of leisure. When the October Revolution stirred up the deep masses of the Russian people, it was said in the West, oft repeated and universally believed, that this tidal wave would swamp all art. As soon as literature ceased being the privilege of one class would it not—it was asked—then constitute a danger? It was to answer that accusation that writers from all countries grouped themselves together with the firm conviction of accomplishing an urgent duty. It is true that culture was menaced—but the peril did not come from the revolutionary and liberating forces; it came, on the contrary, from the parties which were trying to subjugate these forces and to break them. It is War which most threatens culture, war toward which national forces inspired by hate and envy drive us. It is the great international and revolutionary forces on which the duty is laid to protect culture and to make it illustrious. Its fate is bound up, in my mind, with the fate of the Soviet Union and it shall be defended."

This speech belonged to the early part of my visit, to the time when I still believed—still had the naïveté to believe—that one could seriously discuss questions of culture with the Russians. I wish that I could still believe it. If I was mistaken at first, it is only right that I should recognize my error as soon as possible, because I am responsible for those at home whom my opinions might lead astray. No personal pride must hinder me—I have little in any case—there are matters far more important than myself and my personal pride, more important than the Soviet Union. The future of humanity and the fate of its culture are at stake.

As long as my tour in Russia was conducted everything seemed to me wonderful. In direct contact with the working people, in their workshops, in their factories, in their recreation centers, I was able to enjoy moments of deep joy. Nowhere are human relationships as easily formed as in the Soviet Union, nor as warm or deep. Friendships are quickly made—often a mere glance suffices—and strong bonds of sympathy are instantly forged. I verily believe that nowhere as much as in the Soviet Union does one enjoy so deep a feeling of humanity, an immediate up-surge of brotherly love. My heart swelled and tears came into my eyes through excess of joy—tears of love and affection. The children whom I saw in the camps were well-fed, well-cared-for, cherished and happy. Their eyes were clear and full of confidence and hope. This expression of illumined happiness I saw also on the faces of workers in the recreation centers, where they assembled, in the evening, when their work was done. Each town in the Soviet Union has now its recreation center and its kindergarten. Like many other visitors, I saw model factories, clubs, pleasure grounds, at which I marveled. I asked for nothing better than to be carried away with admiration and to convert others as well. And so, as it is very pleasant to be enraptured and to persuade others, if I protest against all this enchantment, I must have serious grounds for doing so. I only began to see clearly when, abandoning the government transport, I traveled alone through the country in order to be able to get into direct contact with the people. I had read too much Marxist literature to feel a fish out of water in Russia, but I had also read too many accounts of idyllic trips and too many enthusiastic apologies. My mistake, at first, was to believe all the praise that I heard, and everything which might have enlightened me was always said in a spiteful tone of voice. It happens too often that the friends of the Soviet Union refuse to see anything bad there—or at least to recognize it—so it happens that truth is spoken with hatred and falsehood with love. My mind is constituted in such a way that my greatest severity is directed especially toward those of whom I would like always to approve, and I do not think that it is the best way to express one's love to be content with praise alone. I think that I do more service to the cause which the Soviet Union represents by speaking without pretense and without too much circumspection and consideration. I certainly had personally nothing to complain of in the course of my trip, in spite of all the spiteful explanations which were invented subsequently to invalidate my criticism, which was too often interpreted as the result and expression of personal pique and disappointment—that is most absurd of all. For never have I traveled in greater or more luxurious ease—I had the most comfortable cars everywhere, a private coach on the train, the best rooms and meals in all the hotels—always the best was offered me and what a reception I received everywhere! I was acclaimed and fêted. Nothing was considered too good for me. I could not fail to carry away with me a most wonderful memory of the welcome I had received, but nevertheless all these favors reminded me constantly of the privileges and differences where I had hoped to find equality. When I escaped from officials and went amongst the workers, I discovered that most of them lived in the direst poverty, while I was offered a ceremonial banquet every evening, at which the variety, richness and quantity of the hors d'oeuvres alone were sufficient to sate the appetite before the main part of the meal had even begun—a dinner of six courses which lasted four hours. Never having had to settle a bill while I was in Russia, I cannot form an estimate of the cost of such a feast, but one of my friends who knows the range of prices in the Soviet Union, told me that it would cost two or three hundred roubles a head, and the workers whom I had seen earned only five roubles a day and had to be content with black bread and dried fish. During our stay in Russia we were not exactly the guests of the government, but of the wealthy Society of Soviet Authors. When I think of all they spent on us—and there were six of us, with our guides, and often as many hosts as guests! Of course they had counted on a different return for their money, and I think that part of the resentment of *Pravda* came from the fact that

I was so poor an investment. Certainly it seemed to me quite natural that they should want to receive a guest as well as possible and to show him the best of everything, but nevertheless it surprised me to find so great a difference between the best and the common lot, such excessive privileges beside such depths of poverty. It is on account of my admiration for the Soviet Union and the marvels she has already accomplished by herself, that my criticism is going to be severe: because of what we expect from her and what she gave us reason to hope from her. I trusted her and so, in Russia, what distressed me most was not what was not yet perfect, but rather to find there everything from which I had always fled at home—the privileges which I had hoped abolished forever.

Who can ever say what the Soviet Union had been for me? Far more than the country of my choice, an example and an inspiration, it represented what I had always dreamed of but no longer dared hope—it was something toward which all my longing was directed—it was a land where I imagined Utopia was in process of becoming reality. The Soviet Union is, however, at an early stage of construction—that needs to be remembered constantly—and we are present at the parturition of the future. There are both good and bad points—I should say both the best and the worst; one moves from the brightest to the darkest with alarming and disconcerting suddenness. Much has already been accomplished which has filled our hearts with joy and this, doubtless, made me exacting. It seemed at first to me as if the most difficult had already been achieved, and I was ready to throw myself with all my heart into the contract, as it were, into which I had entered with the Soviet Union in the name of all suffering mankind. I felt myself so much committed that failure was not to be contemplated.

I admired particularly in Russia the extraordinary impulse toward education and culture. But the sad thing is that the education the people receive only informs them on what leads them to flatter themselves on the present state of affairs and to believe in the Soviet Union *Ave Spes Unica.* Culture is directed toward one aim only, the glorification of the Soviet Union; it is not disinterested, and critical discrimination is entirely lacking. I know well that they make a parade of self-criticism and, at first, I believed and hoped in that, thinking that it might lead to great results if it was applied with integrity; but I soon discovered that criticism consists solely in inquiring whether such or such a work is in agreement with the Party line. It is not the Party line which is discussed or criticized, but only the question whether a certain theory tallies or not with this sacred line. No state of mind is more dangerous than this, nor more likely to imperil real culture. Soviet citizens remain in the most complete ignorance of everything outside their own country and—what is worse—have been persuaded that everything abroad is vastly inferior to everything at home. On the other hand, although they are not interested in what prevails outside their country, they are very much interested in what foreigners think of them. What they are very anxious to know is whether they are sufficiently admired abroad; what they fear above all else is that foreigners may not be sufficiently well-informed concerning their merits; what they want from them is praise and not information.

I happened to visit a model collective—it is one of the finest and most prosperous in the Soviet Union—and I went into several of the houses. I wish that I could give some conception of the uniformly depressing impression which is communicated by each of the dwellings, that of a total absence of individuality. In each there are the same ugly pieces of furniture, the same picture of Stalin and absolutely nothing else—not the smallest vestige of ornament or personal belonging. Any house could be exchanged for any other without the tenant being aware of the alteration. Of course the members of a collective take all their pleasures in common, and their homes are only, as it were, lairs to sleep in; the whole interest of their lives is centered in the club. Doubtless the happiness of all can most easily be achieved by the sacrifice of the individuality of each, through conformity. But can it be called progress, this loss of individuality, this uniformity, toward which everything in Russia is now tending? I cannot believe that it is. In the Soviet Union it is accepted once and for all that on every subject—whatever may be the issue—there can only be one opinion, the right one. And each morning *Pravda* tells the people what they need to know, and must believe and think. When I was in the Soviet Union, I was astonished to see no mention in the papers of the Civil War in Spain which, at the time, was causing much troubled anxiety in democratic circles. I expressed my pained surprise to my interpreter and noticed some embarrassment on his part, but he thanked me for my observations and said that he would transmit them to the correct quarter. That evening, at the usual ceremonial dinner, there were many speeches and toasts according to the usual custom. When the health of all the guests and hosts had been drunk, one of my party, Jef Last, rose to his feet and, in Russian, proposed a toast to the triumph of the Red cause on the Spanish Front. The company applauded with some embarrassment and lack of cordiality, I thought, and replied immediately with a toast to Stalin. When my turn came, I lifted my glass to the political prisoners in Germany. This time the toast was vociferously applauded and with no halfhearted enthusiasm—answered again by another toast to Stalin. All present knew what to think about the victims of Fascism in Germany and what attitude to adopt. But on the Spanish question *Pravda* had not yet made any official pronouncement and they did not dare risk approval without getting a lead and knowing what they were expected to think. It was only a few days later, when we had arrived at Sebastopol, that an immense wave of sympathy unfurled from the Red Square in Moscow and, through *Pravda* swept across the whole country. By now the minds of the people are so well-trained in conformity that compliance has become natural and easy for them—I do not believe that it is hypocrisy—so that each time you speak with one Russian it is as if you had spoken with all.

The disappearance of capitalism has not brought freedom to the Soviet workers—it is essential that the proletariat abroad should realize this fully. It is of course true that they are no longer exploited by shareholding capitalists, but nevertheless they are exploited, and in so devious, subtle and twisted a manner that they do not know any more whom to blame. The largest number of them live below the poverty line, and it is their starvation wages which permit the swollen pay-packets of the privileged workers—the pliant yes-men. One cannot fail to be shocked by the indifference shown by those in power toward their inferiors, and the servility and obsequiousness on the part of the latter—I almost said the poor. Granted that there are no longer any classes nor class distinctions in the Soviet Union; but the poor are still with them—and there are far too many of them. I had hoped to find none —or more exactly, it was precisely in order to find none that I went to the Soviet Union. But poverty there is frowned upon —one might imagine that it was indelicate and criminal—it does not arouse pity or charity, only contempt. Those who parade themselves so proudly are those whose prosperity has been bought at the price of this infinite poverty. It is not that I object to inequality of wages—I agree that it is a necessary and inevitable measure—but there ought to be some way of relieving the most grievous disparities. I am afraid that all this means a return to a form of working-class bourgeoisie, gratified and hence conservative—too like the petty bourgeoisie at home for my taste. I see the symptoms already. There is no doubt that all the bourgeois vices and failings still lie dormant, in spite of the Revolution, in many. Man cannot be reformed from the outside—a change of heart is necessary—and I feel anxious when I observe all the bourgeois instincts flattered and encouraged in the Soviet Union, and all the old layers of society forming again—if not precisely social classes, at least a new kind of aristocracy, and not an aristocracy of intellect or ability, but an aristocracy of right-thinkers and conformists. In the next generation it may well be an aristocracy of money. Are my fears exaggerated? I sincerely hope so.

When I visited Sotchi I marveled at the number of sanatoria and rest-houses that are being erected for the workers. These hostels are most pleasant, with beautiful gardens and private bathing beaches. It is praiseworthy that all this semi-luxury should be provided for the use of the workers; nevertheless those who enjoy this comfort are all too often the new privileged class. It is true that those in need of rest or treatment are given priority—but always provided that they agree with the Party line. And it is lamentable to see near by, the men employed in building these very rest-houses so badly paid and parked in such sordid encampments.

If I am full of admiration for the rest-houses at Sotchi, what can I say about the hotel at Sinop, near Soukhoum, where I stayed, so vastly superior to anything else that it can be compared only to the most comfortable and luxurious hotels abroad. Each room has its own bathroom, its private balcony, the furnishings are of the finest and the cooking equal to first class anywhere. Near the hotel is a model farm to supply it with produce, comprising model stables, cowsheds, pigsties and an enormous hencote provided with the latest contrivances. But, if you cross the stream which marks the boundary of the farm, you come across a row of mean hovels in which each small room of six square feet houses four people at a rent of two roubles a month per person.

Although the long-heralded Dictatorship of the Proletariat has not materialized, there is nevertheless dictatorship of one kind—dictatorship of the Soviet bureaucracy. It is essential to recognize this and not to allow oneself to be bamboozled. This is not what was hoped for—one might almost say that it is precisely the last thing in the world that was hoped. The workers have no longer even the liberty of electing their own representatives to defend their threatened interests. Free ballot—open or secret—is a derision and a sham; the voters have merely the right of electing those who have been chosen for them beforehand. The workers are cheated, muzzled and bound hand and foot, so that resistance has become well-nigh impossible. The game has been well played by Stalin, and Communists the whole world over applaud him, believing that in the Soviet Union at least they have gained a glorious victory, and they call all those who do not agree with them public enemies and traitors. But in Russia this has led to treachery of a new sort. An excellent way of earning promotion is to become an informer, that puts you on good terms with the dangerous police which protect you while using you. Once you have started on that easy, slippery slope, no question of friendship or loyalty can intervene to hold you back; on every occasion you are forced to advance, sliding further into the abyss of shame. The result is that everyone is suspicious of everyone else and the most innocent remarks—even of children—can bring destruction, so that everyone is on his guard and no one lets himself go.

During my tour I was taken to see the model town of Bolchevo, which is unique of its kind since all its inhabitants are convicts—housebreakers, pickpockets and murderers. It started as a small penal settlement founded in the belief that criminals are only invalids or neurotic misfits whom proper treatment, sympathetic kindness and a normal life would cure and turn into valuable, contented citizens, but it has grown into a large and flourishing town in which not only factories are found, but also libraries, rest-centers and clubs. When I visited it, it seemed to me one of the noblest and most successful experiments in the Soviet Union and a great achievement. It was only later that I discovered, what I did not know at first, that only informers—those who had betrayed their fellow-convicts to the authorities—were granted the privilege of living in this model settlement. Could moral cynicism sink lower than this?

The unfortunate Soviet worker is tied to his factory—just as the agricultural worker is tied to his collective—like Ixion to his wheel. If the worker for some personal reason—either because he imagines, or hopes, that he will elsewhere be better off, or less badly off, or merely because he would welcome a change—thinks of leaving his job, then, classified and regimented as he is, he runs the risk of obtaining no employment anywhere. And even if, whilst remaining in the same town, he leaves his factory, he is deprived of the living quarters, to which his work gave him the right—hard to find elsewhere—and for which moreover he had been paying rent. He also discovers that he forfeits, on leaving, a considerable part of his wages and loses the whole of the accumulated profits from his collective work. On the other hand, if his transfer is considered necessary by the authorities, he cannot refuse to leave. He is free neither to go when he wishes nor to stay where his affections and personal interests are centered. Then, if he does not belong to the Party, those who do outstrip him in promotion. Yet all who desire cannot become Party members, and moreover everyone does not possess the requisite qualities of flattery, obsequiousness and submission. If, on the other hand, he is lucky enough to be a Party member, he cannot resign without losing all the advantages his employment gave him, and he is also liable to suspicion and reprisals. Why, it is asked, should anyone want to leave a Party which grants such substantial rewards in return for mere acquiescence and obedience? Why, besides, should anyone want to think for himself since it is universally agreed that everything is for the best in the best of all possible worlds? To think for oneself is to run the risk of being accused of being counter-revolutionary, and then—if one is a Party member—one is expelled and there follows the probability of Siberia. This impoverishment of the human stock is all the more tragic since it passes unobserved and those who disappear—or are made to disappear—are amongst the bravest and most independent of those who distinguish themselves from the masses and hinder uniformity and mediocrity. These deportees—thousands of them—who have been unable to be humble or to bend the knee—it seems to me that I hear them in the darkness around me: it is the cries of these countless victims which rouse me in the long watches of the night; it is their unwilling silence which urges me to speech today; it is thinking of these martyrs that I now pen these lines; and recognition from them—if my words could ever reach them—would be more sweet and precious to me than all the incense from *Pravda*. No one intervenes on their behalf, and those who are responsible for justice and liberty are silent, while the masses of the people are blinded. When I raise my voice in their favor I am told—again in the name of Marx—that these deportations, the poverty of the workers and the abolition of suffrage, all these are only provisional measures and are the necessary price to pay for the gains of 1917. It is, however, terrifying to see abandoned, one after the other, all the benefits gained at the price of so much suffering. It is time that eyes should be opened to this tragic failure in which all our hopes have foundered. One might perhaps have accepted the absence of personal and intellectual freedom in Russia today, if at least there had been evidence that the material progress of the masses was being gradually, if slowly, achieved, but this is far from being the case and, on the contrary, it is evident that all the worst and most reprehensible features of capitalist society are being re-established. That petty-bourgeois mentality, to which I have previously referred, which I greatly fear is on the increase, is, in my opinion, profoundly and fundamentally counter-revolutionary. Yet what they call counter-revolutionary is precisely that revolutionary spirit, that surging torrent, which, at first, tore through the rotting and crumbling dikes of the Czarist world. One would like to be able to believe that love still filled their hearts to overflowing—or at least a passionate need for justice—but once the Revolution was accomplished, it all vanished and the generous ardor which had inspired the first revolutionaries became, as it were, the rusting debris of tools whose utility is done. Now that the Revolution has become established, it parleys with iniquity; and those in whom the rebel spirit still burns, those for whom all these successive concessions are compromises, these are disregarded or liquidated. Would it not then be better to cease quibbling and to recognize that the inspiration of the Revolution no longer prevails, since what is expected is submission and conformity? What is demanded is approbation of everything done by the government. The slightest opposition and the merest criticism exposes its agent to the severest penalties and is, moreover, instantly suppressed. From top to bottom of the reformed social ladder, those with the best references are the most servile, and those who stand out independently are mown down or deported. Soon, in that heroic race which has deserved so well of our love and admiration, there will be left only the profiteers, the executioners and the victims. The small, independent worker has become a hunted animal, starved, broken and finally eliminated. I doubt whether in any country in the world—not even in Hitler's Germany— have the mind and spirit ever been less free, more bent, more terrorized over—and indeed vassalized—than in the Soviet Union. Yet the suppression of the opposition in a country—or even the curtailing of its expression—is a very dangerous thing, an invitation to terrorism. If all the citizens in a state thought alike, it would no doubt spare the government much trouble, but, faced with such a prospect, can one then talk of culture? Real wisdom consists in listening to opposition views—in fostering them even whilst preventing them from harming the common weal.

Humanity is complex and not all of a piece—that must be accepted—and every attempt at simplification and regimentation, every effort from the outside to reduce everything and everyone to the same common denominator, will always be reprehensible, pernicious and dangerous.

With artists it is still more sinister than with the ordinary citizen. I believe that the real value of an author consists in his revolutionary force, or more exactly—for I am not foolish enough to credit the Left alone with intellectual and artistic powers—in his quality of opposition. A great artist is of necessity a "nonconformist" and he must swim against the current of his day. But what will eventually happen in the Soviet Union when the transformed state has removed from the artist all need for opposition? What will happen to the artist when there will be no longer any possibility even of opposition? Will the only course left to him then be to drift with the current? Doubtless, as long as the struggle persists and victory has not been wholly achieved, he will be able to lead the revolution and, by fighting himself, assure its victory. But what is to happen then? It is precisely this which makes me look with so much anxiety toward the Soviet Union; that was the vital question which I had been asking myself before I went to Russia and to which I found no satisfactory answer. Furthermore, what is to happen to the subtle and truly original artist? One painter whom I met in Russia told me that subtlety and originality were no longer what the country wanted, not what was now needed. He said that an opera was no use to the workers if, on leaving the theater, there were no tunes that they could whistle. What was now needed, he insisted, were works which could be immediately apprehended and understood. I protested that the greatest works—and even those which later became popular—were never appreciated when they were first heard—or were only appreciated by a small and select public. He admitted that even Beethoven would have found it impossible, in the Soviet Union, to make a come-back after an initial failure. "You see," he said, "an artist here must first and foremost be in the Party line—otherwise even the highest works will be considered examples of mere 'formalism.'" That is the expression now used in Russia to designate everything which they do not care to see or hear. "We intend," he went on, "to create a new art worthy of the great people that we have now become." I answered that this would oblige all the artists to be "conformists" and that the best and most original would never consent to debase their art and to bow to such a *diktat*; they would therefore be reduced to silence. Then the very culture which the leaders were anxious to further, illustrate and glorify would spurn them and despise them. He said that I was only talking as a bourgeois and that he, for his part, was convinced that Marxism, which in so many other fields had achieved great things, would also produce great works of art. He claimed that the only thing which prevented their emergence was the excessive importance still attributed by artists to outworn forms of art. He was speaking in an ever rising voice and seemed to be delivering a lecture or else to be reciting a lesson by rote. I could not listen any longer in patience and left him without answering. Some time later, however, he came to my room and admitted that, at heart, he agreed with me but that, in the lounge downstairs, he was being overheard, that he was opening a one-man show in the near future and needed official support and approval.

When I arrived in the Soviet Union, the general public had not yet resolved the thorny controversy about "formalism." I tried to understand what was meant by the expression and discovered that the works which were accused of "formalism" were those by artists who had laid more emphasis on form than on content. I might, however, add that only one content was considered worthy of consideration—or indeed tolerated —the right one, and every work was held to be "formalist" which did not point in that one direction. It is enough to make one weep to realize that this is the spirit which inspires all criticism in the Soviet Union. Such sectarianism may once have been politically useful, but one certainly cannot describe it as culture. Culture will always be in peril where criticism cannot be freely practised. In Russia a work which is not in the Party line is condemned, and beauty is considered a bourgeois aberration. However great may be the talent of an artist, if he does not follow the Party line he labors unknown and unrecognized—if he is allowed to labor at all—but if he conforms, he receives recompense and praise. It is easy to see what advantage can accrue to a government from singling out for reward an artist who can sing the praises of the regime. Conversely, it is easy to see the advantages which accrue to the artist himself if he is prepared to sing the praises of the government which gives him so goodly a heritage.

Amongst all workers and artisans in the Soviet Union it is the writer who is most favored and indulged. The immense privileges that I was offered amazed and terrified me and I was afraid of being seduced and corrupted. I did not go to the Soviet Union for the sake of benefits, and those that I saw were glaring; but that did not prevent my criticism, since the most favored position enjoyed by writers in Russia—better than in any other country in the world—was granted only to the right-thinking. That was a danger signal to me and I was immediately on my guard. The price exacted is the total surrender of all opposition, and opposition in the Soviet Union is merely the exercise of free criticism. I discovered that a certain distinguished member of the Academy of Sciences had just been released from prison, whose sole crime had been independence of judgment, and when foreign scientists tried to get in touch with him, they were always told that he was indisposed. Another was dismissed from his professorship and denied laboratory facilities for having expressed scientific opinions which did not tally with current Soviet doctrine, and he was obliged to write a public letter of recantation to avoid deportation. It is a characteristic trait of despotism to be unable to suffer independence and to tolerate only servility. However just his brief, woe betide the Soviet lawyer who rises to defend an accused whom the authorities wish to see convicted. Stalin allows only praise and approbation, and soon he will be surrounded only by those who cannot put him in the wrong since they have no opinions whatsoever. His portrait is seen everywhere, his name is on everyone's lips and praise of him occurs in every public speech. Is all this the result of worship, love or fear? Who can say? I remember, on the way to Tiflis, as we went through Gori, the little village where he was born, I thought it would be a kind and courteous attention to send him a personal message as an expression of gratitude for the warm welcome we had received in the Soviet Union, where we had been treated everywhere with lavish hospitality. I thought that no better opportunity would occur again, so I had the car stopped at the post office and I handed in a telegram which began: "Passing through Gori on our wonderful trip I feel the impulse to send you—" But here the translator paused and said that he could not transmit such a message, that "you," when addressed to Stalin, was not sufficient. It was not decent, he declared, and something must be added. He suggested "You leader of the workers" or else "You Lord of the people." It seemed to me absurd and I said that Stalin must surely be above such flattery, but all in vain. Nothing would budge him, and he would not transmit the telegram unless I agreed to the emendation. I reflected sadly that such formalities contribute to erect an insuperable barrier between Stalin and his subjects. I was also frequently obliged to make additions or alterations in the speeches I delivered in the course of my visit. They explained to me that a word like "destiny" must always be preceded by the epithet "glorious" when it referred to the destiny of the Soviet Union; on the other hand they requested me to delete the adjective "great" when it qualified a king, since a monarch can never be "great"! At Leningrad I was invited to address a society of students and writers and I submitted my script beforehand to the committee, but I was informed that what I had intended to say would be considered unseemly since it was not in the Party line. The ensuing difficulties were so many and so tortuous, that I eventually abandoned the project of the address, which ran as follows:

I have often been invited to give my views on Contemporary Soviet Literature, and I would like to explain why I have hitherto refused to express an opinion. This will permit me to clarify and amplify certain statements which I made in the Red Square in Moscow on the occasion of Gorky's funeral. I spoke then of the new problems which the very success of the Revolution had provoked, and I said it would be to the eternal credit of the Soviet Union to have resuscitated them for our consideration. As the future of civilization is closely linked with whatever solution is found for them in Russia, it seems to me profitable to raise them again here. The majority, even when it comprises the best elements, never appreciates what is new or difficult in a work of art, but only what can readily be recognized—that is to say, what is most commonplace. It must be remembered that there are revolutionary as well as bourgeois commonplaces and clichés. It is also essential to realize that what gives quality to a work of art and brings it immortality, is never what comes from the revolution nor what reflects its doctrine, however noble it may be. A work of art will survive only by what is truly original in it, by the new questions it asks or anticipates, and by the answers that it gives to questions which have not yet been formulated. I greatly fear that many of the works of art impregnated with the purest Marxist doctrine—to which indeed they owe their contemporary success—will, for posterity, smack only of the laboratory. The only works of art which will survive oblivion are those which have risen superior to contemporary preoccupations. Now that the Revolution is triumphant, art runs a grave risk—as grave as any under the most calamitous oppressions—the danger of becoming an orthodoxy. What triumphant revolution needs to grant, above all else, to the artist, is freedom. Without complete freedom, art loses all its significance and worth. And, since the applause of the majority means success, reward and fame will go to those works which the public can grasp and understand at the first attempt. I often ask myself anxiously whether a Keats, a Baudelaire or a Rimbaud may not languish unknown today in the Soviet Union who, by reason of their originality and power, have not yet been heard. It is they who interest me most, those who, at first, were despised and neglected—the Baudelaires, the Rimbauds and the Keatses—those whom posterity will single out for immortality. You may argue perhaps that we do not need nowadays a Keats, a Baudelaire or a Rimbaud, that they are significant only insofar as they reflect the decadent and dying society of which they were the sorry products; you may say that if they cannot prevail, so much the worse for them and so much the better for us, since we have nothing further to learn from their like, and the writers who can teach us something today are those who, in the new society, feel perfectly at home—in other words, those who approve and flatter the regime. But I personally believe that it is precisely the works which flatter and approve which are of poor educational worth, and that a culture, if it is to progress, must ignore them. As for the literature which confines itself to reflecting society, I have already said what I think of it. To remain in constant self-contemplation and self-admiration may be one stage in the development of a young society, but it would indeed be regrettable and tragic if this first stage were to remain the final and only one.

As long as man is oppressed and downtrodden, as long as the compulsion of social injustice keeps him in subjection, we are at liberty to hope much from what has not yet had opportunity to burgeon, from all the latent fertility in the fallow classes. Just as we hope much from children who may eventually grow up into quite commonplace people, in the same way we often have the illusion that the masses are composed of men of a finer clay than the rest of disappointing humanity. I think that they are merely less corrupt and less decadent than the others, that is all. I see already a new bourgeoisie developing in the Soviet Union from these untried masses, with exactly the same faults and vices as ours. No sooner have they risen above the poverty line, than they despise the poor and become jealous and possessive of the belongings of which they were so long deprived; they know how to acquire them now and how to keep them. Are these really the people who made the Revolution? No! They are merely those who have turned it to their own selfish advantage. They may well still be members of the Communist Party, but they are no longer Communist at heart. I blame the Soviet Union not for having failed to achieve more—I see now that nothing better could have been accomplished in that time, the country had started from too low—what I complain of is the extent of their bluff, that they boasted that the situation in the Soviet Union was desirable and enviable—this from the country of my hopes and trust was painful to me.

I blame the Communists in France—and elsewhere too— and I do not mean those who were duped in all good faith, but those who knew—or ought to have known—better, and yet lied to the workers abroad while all the time seeking political aims. It is time that the workers outside the Soviet Union should realize that they have been bamboozled and led astray by the Communist Party, just as the Russian workers were duped before them.

Deplorable and unsatisfactory as the state of affairs in the Soviet Union is, I would have remained silent if I could have been assured of any faint progress toward something better. It is because I have reached the firm conviction that the Soviet Union is sliding down the slope that I had hoped to see it ascend, and because it has abandoned, one after another— and always for the most specious reasons—the liberties gained by the great Revolution after so much hardship and blood-shed. It is because I see it dragging in its wake to irreparable chaos the Communist Parties of other countries, that I consider it my duty to speak openly.

No question of Party loyalty can restrain me from speaking frankly for I place truth above the Party. I know well that in Marxist doctrine there is no such thing as truth—at least not in any absolute sense—there is only relative truth. I believe, however, that in so serious a matter it is criminal to lead others astray, and urgent to see matters as they are, not as we would wish them to be or had hoped that they might be. The Soviet Union has deceived our fondest hopes and shown us tragically in what treacherous quicksand an honest revolution can founder. The same old capitalist society has been re-established, a new and terrible despotism crushing and exploiting man, with all the abject and servile mentality of serfdom. Russia, like Demophoön, has failed to become a God and she will never now arise from the fires of the Soviet ordeal.

Louis Fischer

BIOGRAPHICAL NOTE: *Louis Fischer was born on February 29, 1896, in Philadelphia. After a few years as a schoolteacher, he found his vocation as a journalist, when he was sent to Berlin in 1921 by the New York* Post. *He spent most of the next twenty-five years on roving assignments in Europe and Asia.*

Though he never joined any political party, he became a champion of Soviet Russia and, later, of Republican Spain, which he covered during the Civil War.

Among his books are The Soviets in World Affairs, Men and Politics, The Great Challenge, Gandhi and Stalin, *and* Thirteen Who Fled. *He is now at work on a full-length biography of Gandhi.*

The adventure literature of my boyhood included tales of brave rebels who cheated death by escaping from Siberian salt mines. My parents, born in the small town of Shpola, near Kiev, told me of bloody pogroms perpetrated by vodka-filled muzhiks. Prince Peter Kropotkin, page to the Czar, became an anarchist; his *Memoirs of a Revolutionist* thrilled me with its idealism and humane protest. I read novels by Tolstoy, Turgenev, and Dostoyevsky, and short stories by Gorky and Gogol. I had never been in Russia; my mental picture of it was confused. Russia seemed crude and Eastern, civilized yet uncivilized, literary yet illiterate; bright dots of culture, imperial glamour, and tasteless wealth stood out against a vast darkness.

The entire world outside America remained hazy to me until the beginning of the military conflict with the Kaiser's Germany, and then the war and my personal involvement in it apparently shut out even such tremendous events, crucial to the war itself, as the Czar's abdication in favor of the Provisional Government in March, 1917, and the birth of the Soviet regime in November, 1917. Neither of these revolutions left a memorable impression on me when they occurred, and if they had, I certainly would not have understood why the Provisional or "Kerensky" Government, which, in Lenin's phrase, made Russia "the freest country in the world," should nevertheless have been overthrown by the Bolsheviks in favor of an avowed dictatorship.

Home in Philadelphia again in 1920, after overseas military service, I had a strong curiosity about the origins of the First World War and studied volumes of research by scholars of several nationalities. They differed in their conclusions, but all distributed the war-guilt widely; in a scale of culpability Czarist Russia or Austria-Hungary would have ranked first or second, Germany next, followed by France and England. All these great powers had, by secret treaties, agreed to carve up and share small, helpless nations. This expansionist urge of one set of countries ultimately brought them into conflict with another set of expanding countries, and then came war. Liberal New York weekly magazines now charged that the Versailles Peace Conference had worked on the same evil, imperialistic principle. Despite occasional lofty admonitions from President Woodrow Wilson, the statesmen showed more interest in immediate territorial and financial gains than in solutions guaranteeing a solid peace.

My new attitude toward the War and the peace made me receptive to Bolshevik criticism of the West. Moscow denounced annexations and reparations, and warned that they were the seeds of another war. A University of Pennsylvania engineering student who spoke Russian acquainted me with the contents of barbed, bitterly sarcastic notes in which Soviet Foreign Commissar Chicherin taunted bourgeois governments for their unwarranted intervention in the Russian civil war on the side of "White" reactionaries and Czarists. The Bolsheviks, fighting against heavy odds, defiantly challenged the old world which refused to allow a new one to be born. Russia was the underdog battling forces that had made the World War but could not make the peace.

I felt a compulsion to know the Europe that had so recently spawned a great war and a revolution. I saved part of my income from odd jobs, and in December, 1921, I went abroad as a free-lance correspondent.

Europe was a mess. Able-bodied war heroes turned beggars wandered through the streets of British cities playing harmonicas, singing in quartets, or selling pencils. Rows of seats in London theaters were filled solidly by women without men, women who had lost their men in the trenches or who had never had men and now would never have men because the men who might have been theirs lay under poppy fields in France and Flanders. . . . Maxim Gorky appealed to the world to send food quickly for twenty-five million starving Soviet Russians. . . . From Poland in January, 1922, I wrote about the "crisis which spares nobody" and the "strong strain of chauvinistic nationalism." Beset by myriad domestic problems, Poland nevertheless maintained a "resource-draining army" and insisted on annexing Vilna. . . . I spent part of the next month in Austria. "Vienna," I reported to the *New York Post* of March 1, 1922, "grows gruesome as evening falls. There is a strange dullness and absence of motion. The streets are only dimly lighted. But in the section of rich cafés, near the opera, expensive theatres, and fashionable hotels, there are light and life, taxis, dancing, music, much wine, fine clothes." Large plate-glass windows in banks, stores, restaurants, and hotels had been broken during recent popular riots against speculators.

Germany, whose size, natural endowments and central position had enabled her at various periods to contaminate, frighten and conquer, or invigorate, stimulate and strengthen large areas of Europe, was experiencing a perpetual nightmare of monarchistic-republican strife and inflation. At the International Conference in Genoa in April, 1922, the Western victors, unable to forget, forgive, or unite, pushed Russia, the revolutionary pariah, and Germany, the war pariah, into a diplomatic-commercial entente; the outcasts agreed to arm one another illegally.

Dazed, and still dripping with blood from the First World War, Europe was already blundering toward a second, while, at best, citizens and politicians wrung their hands in helpless despair.

Meantime, I kept hearing and reading about Soviet Russia. The Bolsheviks glorified the common man and offered him land, bread, peace, a job, a house, security, education, health, art, and happiness. They championed international brotherhood. They would abolish racial discrimination, exploitation, inequality, the power of wealth, the rights of kings, the lust for territory. They proudly liberated Poland, Finland and the Baltic countries from Russia's rule. They renounced the Czar's special privileges in China and his spheres of influence—with its oil concession—in Persia. The oppressed of the world, and the friends of the oppressed, accordingly saw Soviet Russia as the herald of a new era.

A state covering one-sixth of the surface of the globe had joined the Sunday afternoon soapbox orator and was talking his language. For the first time, a government undertook to fulfill the dreams of the reformers, iconoclasts, and pioneers of all ages. A thrill shot through humanity. Fear shook the upholders of privilege, tradition, militarism, empire, white supremacy, and the status quo; their fear spurred others' hope.

The unique appeal of the Bolshevik Revolution was its universality. It did not propose merely to introduce drastic change in Russia. It envisaged the world-wide abolition of war, poverty, and suffering. In all countries, therefore, the little man, the laborer, and the intellectual felt that something important had taken place in their lives when revolution took root in Russia. Actually, this general sympathy stemmed more from discontent with conditions in their own countries than from knowledge of conditions inside Russia. Most people did not quite know what had happened or was happening under the Bolshevik regime, but everybody talked about it with heat. The partisans leaned on promises and "objective" difficulties; the detractors cited the absence of achievement. This unending, passionate debate stimulated my desire for first-hand information.

I went to Moscow from Berlin in September, 1922, equipped with not a word of Russian, little understanding of the Soviet System, and some sympathy for its aspirations, but knowing that conditions were terrible. I was not traveling to Utopia or Mecca.

Peasant revolts, starvation, and moribund production had compelled the Soviet government, in the spring of 1921, to introduce the New Economic Policy, or NEP, which legalized domestic capitalism and concessions to foreign capitalists. The weak Bolshevik regime was pulled back into the past. Lenin admitted the retreat; he never masked setbacks. Petty street hawkers of underwear, socks, rubber heels, corsets, silverware, and other ancient objects appeared like a rash over the face of Moscow, Leningrad, Kiev, etc. The countryside buzzed with hopeful get-rich-quick "Nepmen." The government operated huge gambling casinos, luxury restaurants and cabarets full of foods unavailable to the average citizens.

None of this suggested Communism or a new way of life. The capitalist instinct was apparently a very powerful one and sprang to life on the first touch of NEP. I wondered whether the Revolution was petering out. Communists said, No. Material things gave little evidence of Bolshevism; but the spirit of the Communists did.

The Communist Party was Soviet Russia's most remarkable

institution. In the requirements of austerity and dedication imposed on members, it resembled a monastic order. Its tradition of automatic obedience, secrecy, and strict discipline made it kin to a military caste. It served as dynamo, watchdog, and inspiration of the regime. It originated policy and was the sole source of political power, yet it did not directly exercise power. That was the function of the government bureaucracy. The Party instructed, prodded, and supervised the government. This division of tasks was designed to prevent the corrupting effect of high office and power on individual Communists. Most government officials were Party members, but thousands of leading Communists (Stalin, Zinoviev, Bukharin, for instance) did not hold government jobs.

Communists addressed one another as "comrade" and the majority received a uniform low salary which conduced to spartan living and puritanism. The Communist's duties outnumbered his privileges. The Party expected him to be a model of antireligious zeal, ideological loyalty, personal morality, and political devotion. Lapses were severely punished.

Russia throbbed with dynamic energy. The cities seemed to be filled with people fresh from the forests and wheat fields. Young persons dominated every scene. Lenin was 52 in 1922, Trotsky 43, Stalin 43, Zinoviev 39, Kamenev 39, Bukharin 34, Radek 37.

The Revolution was a churning process which ground the former ruling castes into dust and brought new vital forces to the surface. Grateful for the opportunity, they were ready to accept discipline, hard work, and sacrifices. Famine still gripped wide expanses of the country; a meal cost billions of roubles; Russia's inflation was even worse than Germany's; the inherited poverty, aggravated by world war, civil war, and revolutionary ravages, staggered me; yet the regime and its supporters manifested neither pessimism nor fatigue.

The enthusiasm was infectious. Why should foreign governments, and foreign diplomats and correspondents in Moscow, obstruct and deride the efforts of a great nation to pull itself out of the mire? Born and bred in poverty, I instinctively welcomed any endeavor to eradicate it. The Bolsheviks' confiscation of private capital and nationalization of land did not prejudice me against them. The Revolution broke completely with the past. That was its chief attraction. The past was black. Now the Soviets were groping in an unmapped area toward something never previously seen or sketched. I admired their courage. No one could doubt their sincerity.

At the top of a list of Communist virtues stood internationalism. National frontiers are often the consequence of robbery and aggression. Nationalism, the breeder of wars, economic rivalries, and hatreds, is a variety of racism. But the Bolsheviks regarded all races as equal though different. Over a hundred ethnic populations inhabited the Soviet Union; the more advanced discriminated in favor of those wronged by the chances of history and geography. Abroad Bolshevism recognized national divisions but fostered an international Communist society to supersede them and thereby create permanent world peace.

Almost all nations had been hostile, prejudiced, and unfair to the new Russia. The collection of dead debts, the restitution of nationalized properties, and the venting of ideological animosities seemed more urgent to capitalist diplomacy than the establishment of normal political and economic contacts which would have hastened real peace and recovery.

Talking with Soviet friends, one would condemn Bolshevik stupidities and crudities, but on trips to Europe and America I found people arrayed in two opposing camps, one pro-Soviet, the other anti-Soviet, and I just could not join the latter. Russia's basic aspirations became more attractive to me after a look at the dull "normalcy" of the Harding-Coolidge era in the U.S.A. and the aimlessness of Europe. Vacillating democracy in Italy had already succumbed to Mussolini Fascism. The German Socialists had muffed a unique postwar opportunity to immunize their country's past and potential warmakers: the Junkers, militarists, and monopoly industrialists.

This historic blunder of moderation closed my mind to the fierce moderate-socialistic criticism of the Bolsheviks who did liquidate Russia's political and economic royalists. It also kept me from regarding democratic reform-socialism as an alternative to capitalism.

Before long, I realized that my choice was made. A choice depends on the available alternative to it. I preferred fresh sweeping winds to stale stagnant air, and well-intentioned pioneers to proved failures. I liked the Soviets because they were an experiment in the interest of the downtrodden majority, because they destroyed the privileges of the powerful few, because they were weak, and because the world's conservatives and reactionaries opposed them. All these preferences and likes arose from a temperamental predisposition which, almost imperceptibly, soon made me a partisan of the Soviet Union.

One's general alignment with a cause is more compelling than all but the most shocking facts about it. Just as religious conviction is impervious to logical argument and, indeed, does not result from logical processes, just as nationalist devotion or personal affection defies a mountain of evidence, so my pro-Soviet attitude attained complete independence from day-to-day events. Developments which seemed detrimental to Russia were regarded as ephemeral, dishonestly interpreted, or canceled out by more significant and countervailing developments. I studied conditions carefully and reported them faithfully. Sometimes they were no credit to Bolshevism, but that did not weaken my admiration of the Soviet System or my belief in its bright future.

The New York *Nation* of March 4, 1925, published my article on "Political Prisoners Under Bolshevism," in which I referred to Emma Goldman and Alexander Berkman, two well-known anarchists who visited Soviet Russia in 1920-21. In those years, I said,

> More political prisoners crowded the jails than today and they were worse treated. Berkman and Goldman knew

these things, for they enjoyed freedom of movement and the company of many anti-Bolsheviks who kept them informed. Nevertheless they found it possible to support the Communists and to lend themselves to winning anarchist converts to the Bolshevik cause. In other words, when you are pro-Soviet, political prisoners and imprisonment are a blot on the fair escutcheon which you regret; when you grow disillusioned, they become a weapon for an open struggle against Russia.

Alexander Berkman criticized my statement. From Berlin he wrote,

Entirely well-disposed toward the Bolsheviki, as I was during the first year of my stay in Russia, and anxious to aid in constructive revolutionary work, I sought every opportunity to convince the Communist leaders that a policy of revolutionary tolerance and an ethical attitude toward their political opponents from the Left would serve the revolution far better than persecution. Even after my final and open break with the Bolsheviki, after the Kronstadt blood bath, I still strove to help change their policy toward the imprisoned revolutionaries.

Berkman only confirmed my thesis. He was pro-Soviet while abominating the inhuman Bolshevik treatment of political prisoners. Later the draconic Soviet suppression of the sailors' revolt on the Island of Kronstadt near Petrograd embittered him against the entire Soviet regime. This "Kronstadt blood bath" transformed the Bolshevik treatment of prisoners from a subject of private protest to a reason for public attack. Moscow's cruelty toward political prisoners lessened Berkman's immunity to the shock of Kronstadt, but it was only after Kronstadt that Berkman became an avowed enemy. What counts decisively is the "Kronstadt." Until its advent, one may waver emotionally or doubt intellectually or even reject the cause altogether in one's mind and yet refuse to attack it.

I had no "Kronstadt" for many years.

Throughout, I consciously and subconsciously weighed the Soviet regime in the balance. My reading of the scales, of course, depended on what I put into them. On the one hand, it was obvious to me in 1924 that the Soviet State "has disregarded the wishes of the human unit. Liberty is not as sacred an ikon as it is in the West. To give economic freedom to the mass is a nobler aim. Thus the Communists would explain and justify (but in my opinion this does not justify) the absence of a free press and the activities of the GPU." I condemned Bolshevik suppression of personal freedom, which has always meant more to me than practically anything else. On the other hand, I noted in the same article that "the aim of the Bolsheviks was a new society"—and this new society without exploitation outweighed the absence of a free press and the presence of the secret police.

The Soviet promise stimulated my imagination. The Soviet government's promissory notes and its postdated checks, even when postdated a whole decade, were more valuable evidence than the inefficiency and insufficiency of current industrial production. Russia's ugly past and her plans for the beautiful future shaped every judgment of the present. The future was Bolshevik capital. The Bolsheviks offered to sell everybody a share in it. They presented each new Five Year Plan as a hard but necessary step in the ascent to the new world. How could you complain about the scarcity of potatoes when you were building Socialism? Wouldn't you forego butter for Dnieperstroy and Magnitogorsk, which meant more water power, more steel, and ultimately more butter?

The Soviets knew the hypnotic effect of the great dream, and as the promised future faded into the past they strove to keep alive the trust in delayed benefits. Among other things, they ordered all writers, in the middle of the 1930's, to treat the present as though it did not exist and the future as if it had already arrived. This literary device became known as "Socialist realism."

Vsevolod Ivanov, a well-known Soviet novelist, was writing

a novel about life at the new gigantic automobile factory in Gorky. For better acquaintance with his subject he went to stay at the plant, and while there he read parts of his manuscript to meetings of working people. He read them a chapter dealing with the difficulties encountered by the workers in traveling great distances in poor buses over bad roads. Communists at the meetings took him to task.

"How long before you finish the novel?" they asked.

"Six months," Ivanov estimated.

"Then the censoring will require a few months, and printing a few more. Your book won't appear until a year from now and in a year we will have good roads, new buses, and new apartment houses near the plant. So why not describe these roads, buses and homes as already existing?"

Once I was ill in Moscow for several weeks. After a time, when friends telephoned to inquire about me, Markoosha, my wife, would reply, "He's much better but he doesn't know it yet." That was a domestic version of "Socialist realism," intended, since it was said in my hearing, to serve as a kind of Couéistic propaganda.

"Socialist realism" is the Soviet device for distorting the truth about the present. The opposite to "Socialist realism" is "formalism," usually condemned as "bourgeois formalism" because of its excessive loyalty to facts instead of hopes.

"Pie by and by" sustains young ambitious men and their parents. It sustained those who expected the new Soviet society to break ground for mankind's betterment. They looked on every inch of progress as an earnest of miles of further advance.

Probably because it supports my innate faith in progress, construction excites me, and the Soviet construction of huge factories, hydro-electric power stations, and towns excited me the more since I looked at it through the magnifying glass of hope. This was but the initial installment of a grandiose program which would change the face and raise the living standards of an unfortunate country, and thereby demonstrate that governments of the people could work effectively and exclusively for the people.

Statistics of industrial growth now commenced to fill the Soviet press. They were the music of Socialism, the overture to the new society. I was present at the birth of the mammoth tractor factory in Kharkov when the ground was being cleared, and I visited the construction site once a year. Later I toured the plant annually. I felt related to it.

Similarly, the Dnieperstroy Dam. With the chief Soviet engineer I climbed over the boulders on the river-bed when the water was first pumped away, and five years later I drove in a car over the mighty concrete wall, more than a hundred feet high and a third of a mile long, which rested on those boulders. The Soviets had built a Niagara to bring light, heat, and consumers' goods to millions. When the Nazis blew up a section of that dam, it hurt me.

Abroad, numerous power stations and factories stood silent. The 1929 Wall Street crash and the depression threw millions into bread lines and despair. This too weighed in the scales and tipped the balance toward the Soviet side. Capitalist economists and intellectuals came to study Soviet planning and wondered whether it could be applied at home.

Parallel with industrialization in the Soviet Union, the government spurred the collectivization of agriculture. One of these tasks would have strained the capacities of any regime. The Bolsheviks took on both simultaneously. In 1929, the authorities started a process whereby the small farms of at least a hundred million private-capitalistic peasants would be merged into collectives.

Collectivization was the first revolution in the organization of agriculture since the land-chained serfs of Europe became free, land-owning peasants. Collectives promised rational, large-scale production. As the urban factory replaced the artisan of the Middle Ages so the *kolhoz* would replace the small individual farmer. Collectivization looked like a turning point in human events. With the drastic dramatism that characterizes them, the Bolsheviks squeezed this whole chapter of sociological development into a few quick years. The foreign observer congratulated himself; history was being made under his eyes.

Yet collectivization was the "Kronstadt" of many foreign sympathizers and, incidentally, of innumerable Soviet citizens who realized before I did that the collectives were an ingenious, twentieth-century form of wholesale serfdom which forced the peasant to work under the eyes and prods of picked village Communists and made him dependent on the state for seed, tools, work animals, and most of his income.

This nationalization of agriculture naturally encountered fierce, far-flung peasant resistance and we saw how the government responded. It banished hundreds of thousands of kulaks, or prosperous farmers, to slave-labor camps. Even these mass deportations did not break the village's opposition. Poorer peasants refused to take their animals into the collectives and either sold or ate them before they yielded to the pressure and accepted membership. The consequent shortage of livestock and horses plagues Russia to this day. The authorities employed force to drive the peasants into collectives. Red Army units frequently appeared in a village and went from hut to hut ordering the inhabitants to form a *kolhoz*. Peasants were threatened with exile to Siberia and Turkestan as kulaks if they persisted in individual farming.

By such methods the vast majority of Russia's peasants were corralled into collectives. But once in, many sulked or sabotaged the co-operative effort; they still hoped the government would abandon the collectives as failures. In the Ukraine these circumstances produced the famine of 1931-32, which killed several million people. Whole villages died. The price of Bolshevik haste and dogmatism was enormous.

I visited scores of collectives in the Ukraine, Crimea, the Caucasus, and Northern Russia between 1932 and 1936. They were far superior to the tiny strip farms of earlier years. Fences and dividing ruts had disappeared. Machinery had

been introduced. Childrens' crèches and kindergartens had
been established. Officials said the yield per unit of land had
risen. Seed experiments, artificial cattle insemination, deep
electric plowing, and other scientific innovations beyond the
private peasant's wildest fancy were now available to the
collectives.

Did the pros equal the cons? Did the promise equal the
cost?

My own attitude began to bother me. Was I not glorifying
steel and kilowatts and forgetting the human being? All the
shoes, schools, books, tractors, electric light, and subways
in the world would not add up to the world of my dreams
if the system that produced them was immoral and inhuman.

Black squares appeared in the weave of my Soviet impressions. The Bolsheviks staged the first of their big Moscow
trials in June, 1928: the Shakhti trial. About fifty important
Soviet engineers were charged with sabotage and espionage.
I sat through the proceedings in the famous Hall of Columns.
I did not know how much to believe. I believed part. I
wondered about the remainder. My doubts grew when a
GPU soldier with bayoneted rifle led a person named Mukhin
to the witness stand. To this day I remember his name, his
brown suit, and his pasty, fleshy, sallow, round face. He gave
evidence against Defendant Rabinovitch, a man past seventy
who, fighting brilliantly for his life, had all but worsted the
terrifying, theretofore-invincible Prosecutor Krylenko in brain-
to-brain combat. Mukhin was brought in to clinch the case
for the government. He had been in prison for several months
on a charge unrelated to the current Shakhti trial. Mukhin
declared under oath that he handed Rabinovitch a bribe for
himself and further bribes for distribution among other de-
fendants.

Rabinovitch walked over to within two feet of Mukhin and,
peering straight into his eyes, said, "Tell me, please, about
whom are you speaking, about me or somebody else?"

"I am talking about you," Mukhin replied.

"Why do you lie, eh?" Rabinovitch exclaimed. "Who told you to lie? You know you gave me no money."

Mukhin, pastier and paler than before, repeated his story like a tutored automaton. The GPU soldier marched him out of the courtroom. Krylenko looked crestfallen. Clearly, Mukhin had merely enacted a part invented for him in the cellar of the GPU. I shared my interpretation of the scene with a key official of the Foreign Affairs Commissariat. He knew me well and did not dissent.

The Mukhin act in isolation might not have been very significant. But it could not stand alone because the GPU, which directed it, had been gaining power and new functions and, therefore, a new arbitrariness. In January, 1928, Leon Trotsky was arrested and banished to Central Asia. His crime consisted in doctrinal and political differences with Stalin. Before the Revolution and under Lenin's leadership such controversies were resolved by Communist Party debates and ballots. Now the revolver of the GPU became the supreme argument.

Irrespective of the merits of Trotsky's or Stalin's position—and on rereading my reports I find that I aligned myself with neither—the use of the secret police to end a dispute on policy was the Communist Party's Waterloo. Thereafter, those who had force would think they had wisdom. Dissenters preferred security to self-expression. Cynicism accordingly triumphed over honesty.

I noted these phenomena but did not understand that they were the beginning of a decadence that has produced today's great lie and great silence. Inevitably, too, they contributed to the emergence of The Great Leader.

Everything in me rebelled against the fawning adulation and saccharine glorification of Joseph Stalin. The official propaganda, for which he himself was responsible, portrayed him as the infallible, kind, omniscient author of everything that was good in the Soviet Union. From him all blessings flowed. Necessarily, of course, blunders, mass suffering, and setbacks were the handiwork of "wreckers," "Trotskyites," and "enemies of the people."

I vented my repugnance for Stalin-idolatry in an article written in Moscow and published in New York in 1930. I placed the responsibility at Stalin's door and called it the worst of all names: "anti-Bolshevik." Actually, I see now, it was Bolshevik, the inescapable end-effect of dictatorship. Mussolini and Hitler conducted similar symphonies of self-praise. At the time, I did not realize that Stalin's bad taste and the GPU's bad behavior were deadly germs. I thought they were sores on a healthy body which was building new cities and creating new values. I thought the favorable was fundamental and the unfavorable ephemeral. Hope distorted judgment. Seeing did not interfere with believing.

Perhaps disenchantment was slowly maturing. But no conscious "Kronstadt" threatened, and if it had, Hitler's advent in 1933 would have prevented me from rejecting the Soviet regime. The Nazis loudly avowed their cult: the axe ("Heads will roll," Hitler said), the Führer, an expanded Germany, antisemitism, and anti-Communism. If they won, the world would sink into barbarism and blood. The German Communists had helped Hitler come to power; they thought the destruction of the democratic center would facilitate their struggle with the Nazi extreme. This is an incurable Communist miscalculation. But once the Fascists took over in Germany, German and other Communists led the anti-Nazi fight, and, after at least a year of hesitation, the Soviet government joined that fight. Capitalist nations recognized the Hitler menace much later.

Soviet Foreign Commissar Litvinov now launched a dynamic drive for an anti-Fascist coalition to check the descent to war. In Geneva he mercilessly flayed the appeasers of Hitler, Mussolini, and Japan. His success among journalists and pacifists was no compensation for his failure to alter the policies of conservative and opportunist bourgeois governments. Yet Litvinov's name became a symbol, and as such it still stands to mock those who contend that only the Fascist aggressors made the Second World War. Hitler had many active and passive democratic collaborators.

It seemed better strategy to combat Hitler than to combat the Soviet government, which was urging a world mobilization against Fascism and war. Veteran critics of Moscow on the Left half of the political semicircle moderated their attacks and, here and there, closed ranks to form the Liberal-Socialist-Communist Popular Front. Even old "Kronstadters" subsided into silence; few new recruits joined their flag in the first two or three years after the establishment of the Hitler regime.

In Russia, living conditions improved measurably, though by foreign standards meagerly, during 1935. At the same time, Communist morality and idealism were disintegrating. The GPU's intervention in Stalin's ideological assaults on the Left and Right oppositions reduced the Communist Party to an obedient rubber stamp of the personal dictator. Its bureaucracy merged with the greater bureaucracy of the government and both bred sycophants, cynics and cowards. In the highest rank as well as in the lowest, fear rather than thought, self-interest rather than public welfare was the father of every word and deed. Anybody who had uttered a dissenting view in the past or whose independence and originality might some day nurture unorthodoxy received a two A.M. visit from the secret police and soon joined the involuntary "builders of Socialism" in Siberia and the Arctic wastes.

The cautious, calculating, submissive, nervous time-servers in the apparatus of the government, Party, and trade unions, watched their step, looked over their shoulders, loudly professed loyalty, monotonously repeated the official propaganda, and, for solace, tried to eat, drink, dance and, in general, live as luxuriously as the relaxed material standards permitted. The Kremlin decreed equality "a bourgeois virtue." It certainly was not a Soviet virtue. The spread between richest and poorest reached super-capitalist dimensions. Piece work for labor was now universal and the trade unions became paper organizations, while the directors of factories and offices became "sole commanders" who hired, fired, and fixed wages.

In December, 1934, a young man named Nikolaiev shot and killed Sergei Kirov, the Communist boss of Leningrad, Number Four Bolshevik of the Soviet Union. Forthwith, the GPU executed 103 persons who were in jail and had been in jail for many months before Kirov's death. Then Lenin's co-worker Zinoviev was exiled for the same deed. Then the heads of the GPU in Leningrad were punished for it. I was sick at heart. The Soviet State, doomed by theory to "wither away," had expanded into a cruel, overgrown Frankenstein. Abroad, to be sure, this same Bolshevik government continued its efforts to mold a collective-security bloc against Fascist aggression. But I felt that this was not enough. "I believe," I wrote in an article in the New York *Nation*, "that the democratization of the Soviet Union would weaken the enemies of peace."

One evening in Moscow I read this sentence from my manuscript to Constantine Oumansky, chief of the Foreign Office Press Department, and to his assistant, Boris Mironov. Mironov agreed. Oumansky, the rigid official, said it wasn't relevant. Subsequently, in connection with one of the trials, Mironov was shot. Oumansky became ambassador at Washington and Mexico; within a decade he too succumbed in a mysterious airplane accident.

Democracy inside Russia would have been very relevant to the policy of collaboration for peace with the Western democracies against Hitler. A democratic Russia would have helped anti-Fascist forces in England and France unseat their Neville Chamberlains and Daladiers. A democratic Russia would have avoided the Stalin purge and the Moscow trials, which weakened Russia economically and militarily. A democratic Russia would not have signed the 1939 pact with Hitler. A democratic Russia, in other words, might have prevented the war which the totalitarian Soviets helped to precipitate.

Except for the compulsions to folly inherent in his own system, Stalin is wise, and there are indications that he was aware of the internal crisis caused by waxing oppression and waning faith. The Bolsheviks had spent the spiritual heritage of the Revolution. To be sure, by 1935 there was more bread, but man does not live by bread alone, especially when its supply is precarious. The regime needed new popular incentives. It accentuated the already inaugurated policy of granting ever-growing special privileges and emoluments to the army, the GPU, the engineers, the aristocracy of the proletariat, and the upper reaches of the state bureaucracy, who, together, constituted the mercenary praetorian guard of the Soviet System. But the only new and untried incentives available to the Bolshevik regime were nationalism and freedom. Stalin tried nationalism.

Having destroyed the vision of the future, the dictatorship had no choice but to turn its back on the future and embrace the past. That was the essence of the nationalist "line" adopted by the Kremlin in 1934. The Nazi revolution began with the glorification of Germany's past. The Bolshevik Revolution ended when it glorified Russia's past.

Russia had a great past and its heroes were anti-Czarist rebels. This new phase, however, celebrated not the rebels but the Czars. Ivan the Terrible, Peter the Great, Catherine the Great, Czarist princes, anti-revolutionary Czarist generals like Suvorov, and monks of the Middle Ages were lifted out of cobwebs, dusted off, refurbished as national saints, and presented for worship to a startled people who had earlier been taught to abhor them. These antics merely intensified the crisis of faith that commenced when the nation was told that Trotsky and other fathers of the Revolution were Fascists. If Trotsky was a Fascist and Ivan the Terrible a Soviet hero, all fixed standards of judgment vanished and nobody knew what to believe. Tonight, the angels of this morning might be declared devils. The resulting mental confusion conduced to hypocrisy and automatic, unthinking acceptance of the unpredictable revelations from the heights of the Kremlin. Therein lay at least a minimum of personal security.

The new nationalism was Russian nationalism. Goose-stepping scholars rewrote history to prove that Czarist Russia had not been a "prison of nations" as Communists used to contend. The study of the Russian language was made obligatory for all national minorities. The outward trappings of Czarism, formerly reviled by the Bolsheviks as relics of the ugly past, were restored; titles for army officers and epaulets reappeared. This was the inception of the new dogma of *Russia über alles*, of the strident exclusive nationalism which, a few years later, led to the scrapping of the "Internationale" in favor of an anthem dedicated to Russia, to the employment of the church as an instrument of the Soviet government at home and abroad, to the emergence of bemedaled marshals looking like Göring, to the rise of Soviet imperialism (the child of nationalism), and to official propaganda for Pan-Slavism, a teaching as pregnant with evil as Pan-Germanism. Inevitably, these deep and reactionary changes have provoked interracial frictions in the Soviet Union.

The Bolshevik regime represented a revolt against the ugly material, cultural, and psychological heritage of Czarism. But Czarism proved very resistant, and the outside world did not help the new to defeat the old.

The fact that Bolshevism would want to drink at the mouldy wells of Czarism shocked and repelled me. My strongest bond with the Soviet System had been its internationalism and its forward look.

Suddenly, in 1935, whispers about a new democratic constitution were heard, and in 1936 it became official. The "Stalin Constitution." I clutched at it. I wanted to believe. I did not want to forswear a cause in which I had made such a large spiritual investment. Maybe Stalin understood that the people thirsted for freedom. They had had it, as Lenin said, in the brief Kerensky interlude. Indeed, they had had more of it under Nicholas the Second than under the Bolsheviks. Now that all the hostile classes in the Soviet Union had been liquidated beyond recall, Stalin could, without danger to the regime, grant a new charter of liberty which would release new enthusiasm, recapture some of the old élan, and thereby facilitate the tasks of the government both in administration and production. I wanted to believe that a dictatorship born of noble motives could abdicate.

I recognized the Constitution's deficiency. It enunciates an inspiring bill of rights but describes no executive machinery to implement it and no judiciary to safeguard it. I discussed this with Karl Radek on the eve of the publication of the Constitution.

Radek was a Soviet writer, friend of Lenin, member of the inner party circle, co-worker of Stalin, and brilliant conversationalist. He knew all the answers. He would put a question, and before one could formulate a reply he gave it himself. On this occasion, I said to him, "The question of the Constitution is a question of the GPU."

He was dumbfounded and silent for fully two minutes, walking up and down the length of his room. "You are right," he finally declared.

Stalin was having trouble with the GPU. Under Yagoda, later executed for his ambitions, the GPU attempted to make itself the head as well as the arm of the dictatorship. It aspired to be a state within a state. Stalin was purging it. Would he also curb, restrain, and dismantle it, and thus convert the Constitution into an encouraging reality? If not, the charter that bore his name would remain a blunt arrow in the quiver of the professional Soviet agitator, and a device to mislead foreign and domestic innocents.

While I was assiduously collecting indications to nurture my hopes, they were completely blasted. The GPU was neither curbed nor restrained nor dismantled. It was merely reshuffled and then clothed with more rights at the expense of the bill of rights.

The noisy Moscow trials of 1936, 1937, and 1938 were already in preparation. In their course, the public would be shown only a tiny fraction of those many thousands whose death, without trial, from a shot in the back of the neck in GPU cellars, beat a shrill discord to the official hosannahs for the new "Stalin Constitution."

The black plague cast its shadows before, and by the middle of 1936, with the trials still to be announced, I sensed the on-coming night and knew that I no longer wished to live in the Soviet Union.

I could still wax enthusiastic about the potential achievements of new factories and new agricultural methods. I loved the Soviet people. I hoped they would some day have more shoes, homes, electric light. They were having more schools, medical treatment, and vacation facilities. But when I first came to Soviet Russia, practical attainments of the Revolution were negligible; the spirit, however, was strong. It was a spirit of idealistic dedication and courageous protest. Communism stood for revolt and change. Now, nineteen years after the fiery birth of the Bolshevik regime, ubiquitous fear, amply justified by the terror, had killed revolt, silenced protest, and destroyed civil courage. In place of idealism, cynical safety-first. In place of dedication, pursuit of personal aggrandizement. In place of living spirit, dead conformism, bureaucratic formalism, and the parroting of false clichés.

These thoughts, neither clear nor complete, coursed through my mind. Officials who were friends of mine dropped occasional hints but no longer talked from the heart. Journalistic work in Moscow had lost all its excitement and inner compensation. Why should I live in such a country?

At this very juncture—July, 1936—civil war erupted in Spain. General Francisco Franco, aided by other reactionary militarists, the Fascist Falange, the monarchists, the rich aristocracy, and the big landlords, had launched an insurrection against the liberal, enlightened, legally-elected government.

The Spanish people had won my heart during visits in 1934 and the spring of 1936. They are cultured even when illiterate and starving. They have temperament and a penchant for dramatic pose which would be repulsive if it were not so profoundly dignified. Form is important to them. It was a Spanish woman who said, "We would rather die on our feet than live on our knees." And they had been living for centuries on their knees, held down in poverty and oppression by a thin, backward-looking upper stratum which kept out the French Revolution and, in 1936, undertook to keep out the twentieth century. That was the purpose of Franco's insurrection. Therefore, it immediately received military supplies and personnel from Hitler and Mussolini.

Spain now became the front line against Fascism. I gladly left Russia to be near the battle. Death stalked Russia in the cellar. Death came to Spain in open combat in the sun. Spain was sad but noble.

The Spanish Civil War postponed my "Kronstadt." It held my attention and absorbed my energy. But the Soviet Union always remained in the back of my mind. I could reflect on it at a distance that lent perspective.

The Republic's struggle against Fascism in Spain was probably the zenith of political idealism in the first half of the twentieth century. Even in the best years, the outside sympathy for Soviet Russia was political and cerebral. Bolshevism inspired vehement passions in its foreign adherents but little of the tenderness and intimacy which Loyalist Spain evoked. The pro-Loyalists loved the Spanish people and participated painfully in their ordeal by bullet, bomb, and hunger. The Soviet System elicited intellectual approval, the Spanish struggle aroused emotional identification. Loyalist Spain was always the weaker side, the loser, and its friends felt a constant, tense concern lest its strength end. Only those who lived with Spain through the thirty-three tragic months from July, 1936, to March, 1939, can fully understand the joy of victory and the more frequent pang of defeat which the ups and downs of the Civil War brought to its millions of distant participants.

After observing the situation for several months, I decided that writing about a struggle so crucial to the future of freedom and world peace was not enough. I therefore enlisted in the International Brigade, the first American to do so. André Marty, French Communist leader and the chief commissar of the Brigade, appointed me quartermaster. But he loved power and abused it, in the GPU way, through nocturnal arrests and similar outrages. Soon, the presence of an independent, non-Communist began to irk him, and my efforts were transferred to other fields. They continued till the collapse of the republic.

We were all convinced that the Spanish contest was the first battle of the approaching Second World War. Germany and Italy treated it as such. They used it to test their weapons and train their men and, above all, to entrench an ally in the strategic peninsula. But England, France, and the United States, with rare myopia and a pathological urge for self-punishment, did almost everything in their power to destroy the democratic republic which would have been their eager and valuable associate in an anti-Fascist war.

Mexico, and among the great powers only Soviet Russia, gave arms and experts to the Loyalist government. Moscow's assistance could not have sufficed for victory. It was predicated on the ultimate abandonment by Prime Minister Chamberlain and Premier Daladier of their pro-Franco, pro-Nazi, pro-Fascist appeasement policy. That consummation might have prevented the Second World War or won for the democracies an invaluable fortress in Spain from which to wage it. But when they failed to save, and indeed dismembered, Czechoslovakia at Munich in September, 1938, it was clear that they would not save the Loyalists. Thereafter, the Spanish Republic was doomed, and Soviet aid abated.

At the front, on airfields, in hospitals, staff headquarters, and private apartments I met many of the Soviet Russians who had been sent to do their best for the Loyalists. In all the Spanish War, there were no more tireless workers, valiant fighters, and devoted partisans. They seemed to pour into the Spanish struggle the pent-up revolutionary passion which no longer found application in Russia. Innumerable persons in the Soviet Union felt the same way and hoped that Spain would be a spiritual blood transfusion for the prostrate élan of Bolshevism. But on trips in 1937 and 1938 to see my wife and two sons in Moscow, I found the funereal atmosphere blacker than ever. Stalin and his new GPU chief, Yezhov, had conducted and were conducting a mass massacre of top leaders, lower-rank Communists, government officials, engineers, military men, artists, intellectuals, foreign Communists, trade unionists, and functionaries in collectives. The Bolshevik regime was burying its brains. People talked in whispers; none felt secure from spiteful denunciations ending in imprisonment or worse; everybody suspected everybody of being a spy. Even fawning automatons were not safe.

But if I announced my "Kronstadt," I would lose my contacts with the wonderful Russians in Spain and my chance of working with the Loyalists. By this time, the Spanish Communists had gained great strength in the Republican camp, and a critic of Soviet Russia would not have been welcome in it. I therefore limited myself to talking to Loyalist Prime Minister Negrin and a few of his close collaborators about the true horror of Russia and warning them against a dictatorship in Spain.

While deploring Soviet domestic policy, I approved of Soviet foreign policy. Russia's help to the Loyalists was in sharp contrast with the stupid, scandalous pro-Franco behavior of the democracies—"Non-Intervention" they called it. I realized that in the end the atrocities within Russia and the perversion of Bolshevism through nationalism would corrupt Soviet relations with the outside world. For the moment, however, the Moscow government's role in Spain mellowed my emotional, if not my intellectual, antagonism to it, and I hesitated to attack.

The scales in which I weighed the pros and cons of Sovietism were precariously balanced. A feather would tip them against Russia. Now a ton was dropped on to the anti-Soviet scale.

Even before Franco's victory over the Spanish people in March, 1939, Loyalist officials had been collecting proof of Soviet measures against the Russians who worked in Spain. From time to time, one or more of these self-sacrificing, self-effacing aides of the Loyalists would be recalled to the Soviet Union and disappear. Ultimately, the heads of the Loyalist government were convinced, on the basis of substantiated facts, that almost all the important military and civilian Soviet citizens who served so well in Spain were executed or exiled on their return home.

General Goriev, who directed the defense of Madrid, was executed. General Grishin, the first Soviet chief of staff in Spain, was arrested. Stashevsky, the Soviet trade representative in Spain in 1937-38, an old Polish revolutionist, a valued economic adviser of Negrin, was banished. Marcel Rosenberg, first Soviet ambassador to Loyalist Spain, Gaikis, his counselor, and Antonov-Avseenko, the Soviet representative in Catalonia who in November, 1917, stormed the Czar's Winter Palace and took it for the Revolution, were executed. General Uritsky, in charge of Soviet arms shipments to the Loyalists, and Michael Koltsov, *Pravda* correspondent who reported on Spain direct to Stalin and Voroshilov, were likewise shot. This is only a partial list of those who have not been seen or heard of since they were in Spain. Perhaps they were simply caught in the big net of the big Stalin-Yezhov purge. Perhaps they knew too much about conditions abroad.

I have been criticized for not announcing my "Kronstadt" at this point or earlier. Maybe I should have. I had no doubts about what had happened and why, and I was even fairly certain that an improvement in Soviet policy was unlikely. But since it was possible, I waited and remained silent.

Then came the Soviet-Nazi Pact of August 23, 1939, which committed the Soviet government to the course it has pursued from that day to this. The pact produced my "Kronstadt." The pact was an agreement not to gain time but to gain territory. In secret protocols, now published, it provided for a spheres-of-influence division of the areas accessible to Soviet-Nazi aggression. Therewith commenced Russia's planned aggression which gave her today's creaking empire and made her mankind's worst problem.

The Communists and their fellow-travelers had denounced anybody who predicted a Soviet-Nazi agreement; they said it was inconceivable. On the very eve of its signing, they heatedly refused to believe it. When it became official, they defended it. They defended it because they automatically defend everything Moscow does. On all other grounds, the pact was indefensible.

The Soviet-Nazi Pact was the gravestone of Bolshevik internationalism and the cornerstone of Bolshevik imperialism. It was possible because Bolshevik Russia had become the cemetery of Bolsheviks. Czarist expansion was longitudinal and latitudinal. It conquered territory instead of concentrating on the improvement of the lot of the people. In this respect too, Stalin was now copying the crowned Romanovs.

On the backs of the nationalized proletariat and the nationalized peasantry, with the cowed, kowtowing bureaucracy and intelligentsia crying "Bravo," Stalin has built a supernationalistic, imperialistic, state-capitalistic, militaristic system in which he is, and his successor will be, the Supreme Slave Master.

Why should, how can, anyone interested in the welfare of people and the peace and progress of humanity support such a system? Because there is rottenness in the democratic world? We can fight the rottenness. What can Soviet citizens do about Stalinism?

But since many persons did not understand why I postponed my "Kronstadt" so long after they had seen the darkness in Russia, I am tolerant of those who are still in the pre-"Kronstadt" phase. The Pact was "Kronstadt" for me. Others did not "leave the train" to stop at "Kronstadt" until Russia invaded Finland in December, 1939. Finland was their ideological melting point. But a well-known British radical did not strain at the Pact or at Finland. He persisted until the Nazi attack on Norway in April, 1940, when he forsook the Communist line of sabotaging the anti-Hitler war effort and enlisted in the defense of England. He had thought that the Soviet Union was Socialist and therefore could not sin. But countries which call themselves Socialist are as prone to sin as countries which call themselves Christian.

The timing of one's "Kronstadt" depends on a variety of objective and temperamental factors. Some are so obsessed with the crimes of the capitalist world that they remain blind to the crimes and bankruptcy of Bolshevism. Not a few use the defects of the West to divert attention from the hideous horrors of Moscow. My own prescription is: Double Rejection. A free spirit, unfettered by economic bonds or intellectual bias, can turn his back on the evils of both worlds and strive, by improving his own, to create a condition of peace, prosperity, and morality in which dictatorships on both sides of the Iron Curtain would suffocate and perish.

This raises the decisive question: Where does each year's new levy of disenchanted go from "Kronstadt"? "Kronstadt" is not a dead end. It should be a stop on the road to a better terminus than dictatorship.

Among the ex-Communists and among those Soviet supporters who, like myself, were never Communists, there is a type that might be called the authoritarian by inner compulsion. A changed outlook or bitter experience may wean him from Stalinism. But he still has the shortcomings which drove him into the Bolshevik camp in the first place. He abandons Communism intellectually, yet he needs an emotional substitute for it. Weak within himself, requiring security, a comforting dogma, and a big battalion, he gravitates to a new pole of infallibility, absolutism and doctrinal certainty. He clings to something outwardly united and strong. Often he deserts Communism because it is not secure enough, because it zigzags and flipflops and thus deprives him of the stability he craves. When he finds a new totalitarianism, he fights Communism with Communist-like violence and intolerance. He is an anti-Communist "Communist."

Doriot, a French Communist leader, member of the Third International's ruling executive committee, became a Fascist and crusaded fiercely against Communism. Laval, former Communist, former French Premier, was later pro-Nazi and reactionary. Similarly, since the war, many Italian, Rumanian, Hungarian, and Polish Fascists and German Nazis, many thousands of them, have joined the nationalistic, totalitarian Communist Party of their countries. Totalitarians of all feathers understand one another.

The authoritarian by inner compulsion does not forsake Stalin for his antithesis Gandhi. When the Generalissimo ceases to command his complete devotion, he embraces the General. When Storm Troopers butcher millions of his people, he does not abjure terror; he takes up terror himself; his only reaction to dictatorship is the desire to be the dictator rather than the dictator's victim.

Dissatisfied, disillusioned commissar types are drawn from "Kronstadt" toward new and apparently more heroic forms of regimentation, toward new and apparently less brutal absolutes, or toward a more successful totalitarianism. Their "Kronstadt" is a shift of loyalty, not a change of heart and mind.

A "Kronstadt" is creative and socially valuable only when it represents a complete rejection of the methods of dictatorship and a conversion to the ideas of democracy.

No dictatorship is a democracy and none contains the seeds of liberty. This I did not understand in the years when I was pro-Soviet. I believed that a temporary suspension of freedom would enable the Soviet regime to make rapid economic strides and then restore the freedom. It has not happened. The Soviet dictatorship has been barren of groceries because it has been barren of liberties. There can be no material security or economic democracy without political democracy. The millions in Soviet concentration camps and prisons thirty years after the Revolution mock every claim of political or economic democracy.

Nor is there the slightest sign that the police state is withering away. On the contrary, every purge alienates new groups and necessitates another purge, thus making the lawless purge a permanent weapon of the dictator against the people.

There is no freedom in a dictatorship because there are no inalienable rights. The dictator has so much power, and the individual so little, that the dictator can take away any right which he gives. The right to work, for instance, may today mean the right to work in a factory for pay and tomorrow the grim necessity to work in a concentration camp for starvation rations. And the citizen has no redress, for the dictator is the legislator, the executive, and the judge. The hard-working, talented Soviet peoples deserve better and know better, for it is easy to love freedom; but they cannot help themselves, and each year the terror increases.

My pro-Sovietism led me into the further error of thinking that a system founded on the principle of "the end justifies the means" could ever create a better world or a better human being.

Immoral means produce immoral ends—and immoral persons—under Bolshevism and under capitalism.

Ends like money, promotion, and successes are in themselves means to an end which constantly retreats. For individuals, therefore, most of life consists of means. And any way of life which reduces the pleasure and purity in means for the sake of a supernatural or natural future transforms life into a cold, unclean, unhappy corridor.

Dictatorship rests on a sea of blood, an ocean of tears, and a world of suffering—the results of its cruel means. How then can it bring joy or freedom or inner or outer peace? How can fear, force, lies, and misery make a better man?

My years of pro-Sovietism have taught me that no one who loves people and peace should favor a dictatorship. The fact that a system of society proclaims liberty yet limits it is no good reason for embracing a system which completely crushes liberty. It is a good reason for abolishing the numerous limitations on personal, political, and economic liberty in all democracies and enriching democracy with Gandhian morality, which consists, above all, in respect for means, man, and truth.

In retrospect I see that I turned to Soviet Russia because I thought it had the solution of the problem of power. Science places ever-growing power at the disposal of man and he does not know what to do with it. The twentieth century's biggest problem is the control of personal, group, and national power. My acceptance of Soviet Russia was, I suspect, a by-product of my protest against the power over human beings which accumulated wealth and property give to their owners. In my youth I read *Progress and Poverty* by Henry George. I imbibed the trust-busting spirit of the Theodore Roosevelt Era and the liberalism and populism that were part of every poor American's heritage. Then Soviet Russia emerged, promising to break forever the power of landlords, trusts, big business exploiters, and private capital generally.

I have not changed my attitude to the dangers of excessive power. But I now realize that Bolshevism is not the way out because it is itself the world's biggest agglomeration of power over man. I boil at the injustices perpetrated on the unfortunate residents of company towns in the coal regions of my native state of Pennsylvania, where the mining company owns the workers' homes and runs the only stores. But all of the Soviet Union is one gigantic company town in which the government controls all the jobs, owns all the homes, and runs all the stores, schools, newspapers, etc., and from which there is no escape, as there is for some from a Pennsylvania company town. Stalin's Russia is condemned as a "police state." That is a fraction of the evil. The Kremlin holds its citizens in subjugation not only by police-and-prison power but also by the greater power inherent in the ownership and operation of every economic enterprise in the nation. Capitalism's trusts and cartels and monopolies are pygmies compared to the one mammoth political-economic monopoly which is the Soviet State. There is no appeal from its might because there is no power in the Soviet Union which does not belong to the government dictatorship.

Russia, therefore, taught me that the transfer of property from private hands to government hands does not alone conduce to freedom or improved living. If all property is transferred to the government, and if in the process the middle class, a decisive factor in modern industrial civilization, is ruined, nothing is gained; much, indeed, is lost.

What the world needs is a balance of economic and political power so that no party, no class, no government, no assembly of private interests is omnipotent and beyond challenge. Soviet Russia lacks balance. This is the essence of dictatorship, and this explains the Soviet government's arbitrary acts abroad and at home in relation to workers, peasants, officials, Communists, musicians, artists, etc. Russia cannot solve the problem of power because it is the ugliest manifestation of the problem.

After "Kronstadt," the ex-friend of a dictatorship should work for a democracy in which power is so divided that it can never be monopolized even by a government with majority support nor, of course, by a private group. A wise leader exercises restraint in the accumulation of power as well as in its use.

After "Kronstadt," the ex-Communist or ex-apologist for Soviet Russia should enlist in a crusade for full liberty to dissenters and to those of contrasting religions, races, appearances, names, etc. The highest mark of culture is the ability to live in peace with persons who are different from ourselves. The alternatives are dullness and dictatorship. Moreover, the ex-Communist and ex-sympathizer of Russia should be tolerant of Communists and sympathizers. They too will awaken from their dreams. Every Communist is a potential anti-Communist and should be wooed.

After "Kronstadt," the former supporters of Soviet Russia

should support an internationalism which excludes national-ism. In theory, and perhaps in practice, some day, nationalism need not conflict with internationalism. But the myth of an isolated country as a citadel of security or of capitalism or of socialism, or as a paragon of virtue, does actually prevent the growth of internationalist sentiment. When the tongue preaches world government while the heart leaps to the mili-tary exploits and material successes of one's own nation, the tongue might as well be still. The racist, the isolationist, the hater of a foreign people, be it enemy, ex-enemy, or possible enemy, is not an internationalist and only a paper advocate of world government. Ultimately, no nation can enjoy successes that are not shared. There is no real peace or happiness while your neighbor down the street or ten thousand miles away is suffering.

After "Kronstadt," above all, the "Double Rejector" of the evil of dictatorship and the evil in democracy should mind the human being. All goals—national independence, interna-tionalism, economic and scientific progress, national security, the preservation of capitalism, the establishment of Socialism, etc., etc.—are nothing in the abstract. They only have meaning in relation to the interests of living men, women, and children who are the means through which everything on earth is achieved. In one's zeal for a cause, it is possible to forget them, or to suppose that they can wait or to imagine that they don't mind. In one's absorption in an ideal, it is possible to imagine that one generation can be sacrificed for the sake of its de-scendants. But sacrificing people may become a habit unto the second and third generation. I thought, in my Soviet phase, that I was serving humanity. But it is only since then that I have really discovered the human being.

Stephen Spender

BIOGRAPHICAL NOTE: *Stephen Spender was born in 1909 of the well-known Liberal writer, Edward Harold Spender. He was educated partly in Switzerland and partly at University College, Oxford. At Oxford, together with Day Lewis and Auden, he began to write poetry.*

Caught up in the political movement of the thirties, he published Forward from Liberalism *in 1937 and, shortly afterward, joined the Communist Party for a brief period.*

In 1946 he studied the impact of Nazism on German intellectuals for the Political Intelligence Branch of the Foreign Office.

His first Poems *were published in 1933; his book of literary criticism,* The Destructive Element, *in 1935; and* European Witness *in 1946. He is now assembling his* Collected Poetry.

I was a member of the British Communist Party for a few weeks during the winter of 1936-37. My membership lapsed soon after I had joined. I was never invited to join the cell in Hammersmith, where I then lived, nor did I pay any dues after my initial payment.

Shortly before I joined, I had published *Forward from Liberalism,* which was chosen by the Left Book Club as book of the month. I argued in this book that there was a flaw in the liberal conception of the freedom of the individual. Sometimes liberals spoke and wrote as though they believed in the unrestricted freedom of the individual to exploit other individuals; at other times, the freedom of all among equals. I argued that in the Nineteenth Century, during the period of expansion of British trade, liberals could reconcile the aim of free competition of the employers with that of reform for the workers, without the contradiction in their position becoming apparent. But in the 1930's, in a postwar world of depression, tariffs and unemployment, where there were growing Fascist movements in Europe, liberals could not support unrestricted freedom for both employers and workers. They must base their conception of freedom on social justice restricting exploitation. I suggested that liberals must support the workers, accept the necessity of fighting Fascism, and at the same time defend individual freedom of self-expression, by which I meant free speech and habeas corpus.

The task of liberals was to attach individual freedom to the interests opposed to Fascism; and at the same time face the methods which might be necessary to achieve power. In short, they must put the cause of freedom on the side of social justice. They must transplant individual freedom from the capitalist to the workers' interest.

My book was much discussed. Amongst those who wrote to me was Mr. Harry Pollitt. He invited me to come and see him. So I went one afternoon to the dingy offices of the Communist Party near the Charing Cross Road. Mr. Pollitt had a warm, reassuring, frank manner. He was small, with a ruddy complexion and brown eyes under raised thick eyebrows which reminded me of George Robey's. He grasped my hand and said at once: "I was interested in your book. What struck me about it was the difference between your approach to Communism and mine. Yours is purely intellectual. I became a Communist because I witnessed in my own home the crimes of capitalism. I had to see my mother go out and work in a mill, and be killed by the conditions in which she worked."

Another difference between us, he said, was that I showed

no hatred. He believed that hatred of capitalism was the emotional driving force of the working-class movement.

He objected to my criticizing in my book the Moscow trials of Bukharin and the others. I said that I wasn't convinced that the accused were guilty of anything except opposing Stalin. He disagreed vehemently and seemed to think them lucky to have had any trial. Then he pointed out that although we might disagree about the Moscow trials, nevertheless we agreed on action which the Communists were taking in support of the Spanish Republic. He had a suggestion to make. This was that we should agree to disagree, but that nevertheless I should join the Communists in order to support them over Spain. I could write an article in the *Daily Worker* criticizing the Communists at the same time as I joined the Party.

I accepted this offer. I received a Party card, and my article appeared. The article infuriated the Communists in Scotland and the North of England and my membership in the Party was quickly forgotten.

Although Pollitt had been right in observing that my reasons for becoming a Communist were not those of a worker, nevertheless a whole chain of events had led to my attempt to compromise with the Party.

These go back to my childhood. What had impressed me most in the gospels was that all men are equals in the eyes of God, and that the riches of the few are an injustice to the many. My sense of the equality of men was based not so much on an awareness of the masses as on loneliness. I can remember lying awake at night thinking of this human condition in which everyone living, without the asking, is thrust upon the earth, where he is enclosed within himself, a stranger to the rest of humanity, needing love and facing his own death. Since to be born is to be a Robinson Crusoe cast up by elemental powers upon an island, how unjust it seems that all men are not free to share what nature offers here; that there should be men and women who are not permitted to explore the world into which they are born, but who are throughout their lives sealed into leaden slums as into living tombs. It seemed to me—as it still seems—that the unique condition of each person within life outweighs the considerations which justify class and privilege.

However, I did not associate these ideas with being a revolutionary. They were Christian and really to act according to them I would have had to give all I had to the poor and live as simply as a peasant in India or China. The Communists were to me terrible people like cannibals or wolves, who wanted to destroy all the towns of the world and rampage among the ruins. I had absorbed the opinions of my family and their friends who regarded revolutions as disasters like earthquakes. The Socialists were only a little less dangerous than the Communists. I learned to exclude certain points of view by thinking of people who held them as mad or subhuman.

When I was sixteen, at the London day school to which I went, I came in contact with a master and one or two boys who were Socialists. The master had been in the war, belonged to the 1917 Club, and read the *Daily Herald*. According to him, Socialism was not a reign of terror and unreason. It meant nationalizing industries so that they produced goods and wealth which belonged to all the people in a country, instead of to a· few, removing the competitive system based on profit which led to international rivalry in trade and hence to war, and giving all children of all classes equal opportunity. This corresponded to my primitive idea of social justice. A boy with whom I was friendly at school was Maurice Cornforth, who read the plays of Bernard Shaw and wrote plays which seemed to me quite as good as Shaw's. Cornforth had the kind of mind which can explain things by arranging them into a system of ideas. He rescued me from Anglo-Catholicism only to plunge me into Buddhism. He was a vegetarian, and he went for walks of thirty or forty miles a day in Metroland at week ends. He was tousle-headed and had a tousle-haired dog. He dominated school debates and covered reams of paper with his plays, poems and letters.

To Cornforth and me Socialism was only one of several interests. Others were modern post-impressionist painting, the theater, the ballet and poetry. In fact, Socialism was a variety of modernist behavior which went with red ties and Shaw's beard. Thus when I was at Oxford I easily accepted the view held there by most of my friends, that art had nothing to do with politics. I subtracted politics from my other "advanced" views and was left with art for art's sake. The years 1928, 1929, and even 1930 today seem remote and peaceful, and at Oxford it was possible to forget human injustices or at least to think that they were not the business of "the poet." I remained a Socialist in the way in which certain people who never go to church remain Catholics. A kind of orthodoxy has frozen in their minds. They know that it is there and that it may one day melt and engulf them in a flooding struggle, but, for the time being, it seems to bear little relation to their activities.

After I had left Oxford I went to live in Germany. There the sense of humanity as social struggle re-awakened in me. Nearly every young German I met was poor, living from hand to mouth on little money. The barriers between classes had broken down. All classes were conscious of a fate of defeat and inflation and recovery in which all after the War had been involved. Much music, painting and literature of the Weimar Republic expressed either revolutionary spirit or pity for the poor. The eyes of the victims of the postwar world might be said to stare through German expressionist art.

I was a foreigner and my first reaction to this misery was an intense pity for the victims of the crisis which began in 1930. But although I felt deeply moved by the unemployed whose eyes stared from the edges of pavements, I did not, at first, feel that I could do more than pity them. This was partly because, as a foreigner, I felt outside Germany. Only when the crisis spread to Great Britain and other countries did I begin to realize that it was a disease of capitalism throughout the world. Gradually I became convinced that the only cure for unemployment, other than war, was an international society in which the resources of the world were exploited in the interests of all the people of the world.

A friend, whom Isherwood in his autobiographical sketch *Lions and Shadows* calls Chalmers, came to Berlin and one day Christopher invited me to meet him. Chalmers, who had recently joined the Communist Party, had been on an Intourist tour of Russia, lasting a few days, and was visiting Berlin on his return from Moscow. He was a small, dark young man with a keen miniature-like beauty. He looked at objects steadily with the concentration of a bird-watcher, often fixing one intently with his eyes while he was talking or listening. He gave the impression of combining humor with high moral seriousness. When I asked him what the Russian landscape was like, he stared in front of him and said with an effect of mysticism mixed with irony: "The most beautiful in the world." In another age he would probably have been a country parson who discovered poetic inspiration in paradoxes of orthodoxy symbolized by flowers concealed amongst the hedgerows of an English lane.

One afternoon Chalmers and I went for a walk in Berlin. It was not long before we discussed Communism. Chalmers had a simple and clear point of view. Unemployment, war and nearly all the evils of the time, including sexual jealousy and the problems of writers, were due to the capitalist system. The cure was to abolish capitalism and establish Communism. Within society, one must cooperate with the class-conscious workers, within oneself one must make "an act of the will." Chalmers agreed that there were people within the present form of society who did not like unemployment and war. They might even sincerely renounce their own interests in the effort to remove such evils. But as long as they accepted the context of bourgeois society, their efforts were vain. For capitalism inevitably meant competition between classes and nations. To work against the direction of such a system whilst accepting it, was at most to produce a little backwater of one's own clear conscience within a rushing stream. The only action one could take "on the side of history" was to change the direction of the stream altogether.

To do this was a prodigious task, and in doing it one did not have to consider, except from the point of view of their effectiveness, the means which were used nor the fate of individuals. History did not care about those who were not on its side. "History" to Chalmers was, of course, the workers' revolution, the Dictatorship of the Proletariat and the establishment of Communism, which would abolish all the evils of the present and finally establish a free world. Chalmers had a sincere vision of that world, and he decidedly wished for the happiness of mankind. But he was impervious to the injustices and cruelties which "history" produced on its way. I think it is not unjust to say that these even rather appealed to his ironic literary sensibility. He had made up his mind on a course of revolutionary action, and having done so, he viewed the concrete results of that action as it were from a distance. His mind was so entirely fixed on the future that what happened in the present was, I believe, a matter of as complete indifference to him, as the fate of the people who perished in the Lisbon earthquake two hundred years ago. He lived in the future, and for him the present belonged to a grim pre-revolutionary past. What Chalmers demanded of himself and of others who put themselves "on the side of history" was that they should identify all their thoughts and actions with the processes which would produce the classless society. He wished to submit the present absolutely to a course of action dictated by the future.

I felt very unsure of myself with Chalmers as I confessed to my dislike of violence, my attachment to freedom of self-expression, my wish nevertheless for revolutionary changes which would produce a socially just international society without destroying the liberty of the individual. He took his pipe out of his mouth and said with friendly terseness: "Gandhi."

I had spoken of the League of Nations. Chalmers explained how idealism of the kind embodied in the League could do nothing to prevent war. The League was a society of imperialist powers determined to use it as a principle for protecting, if not extending, their own sovereignties. The nations which used the League were themselves the instruments of the armaments interests. The League was in effect an alliance directed against Russia. "Under the present system all talk about disarmament is nonsense."

Part of our discussion was about the novel. Chalmers, like a great many Communist writers, found that being a Communist cut the ground of his experience from under his feet, leaving him only with a theory of revolution. He was one of the bourgeoisie, envisaged in the "Communist Manifesto," who had "gone over" to the proletariat. Politically, this is a tenable position (most of the Russian revolutionary leaders were bourgeois), but for the creative artist it it difficult. His sensibility, which is decided for him in his childhood, is bourgeois. He can scarcely hope to acquire by an act of political will a working-class mentality. Even if he did do so, he would be confronted with the difficulty that, actually, the working class is in the main, and except for a few class-conscious workers, "until after the Revolution," more bourgeois than the bourgeoisie. The workers do not care for the "Proletarian novel." To write a revolutionary novel attacking capitalism also presents an artistic problem; political activists, thinking only of political necessity, are more concerned with activist propaganda than with art based on experience and observation, which inevitably must include discouraging as well as revolutionary features. Chalmers admitted these difficulties freely. And theorizing, he said: "I do not think the novel with a working-class hero and wicked capitalists is the best kind of Communist novel. A better kind might well be one in which the capitalist characters were sympathetic people of good will, and the Communists embittered and unsympathetic. But the novel would make the point that the unsympathetic Communists are right and the middle-class characters of good will wrong. Of course I admit that the Party would not welcome a book of this kind." Chalmers' idea for a novel with unsympathetic Communists who justify the cause of historic development against well-meaning but historically wrong capitalists, is a parable illustrating very exactly the position of the intellectual Communist. He puts his faith in an automatism of history which even if it is achieved by bad men by bad means will eventually make men good, just as the system of capitalism automatically turns all good aims into channels of war and destruction. To state the Communist faith so truthfully is not popular among the Communists. Mr. Harry Pollitt had told me that the best revolutionary novel, in his opinion, was Jack London's *The Iron Heel*.

Some years after this conversation, in 1937, I asked Chalmers what he thought about the latest series of Russian trials, involving Bukharin, Radek and others. He hesitated a moment, looked away at some object in the distance, blinked, and then said: "There are so many of these trials that I have given up thinking about them long ago." He had decided. He accepted present methods because his hope was fixed in the future, and that was that.

He combined a belief in the inexorable Marxist development of history with mystical confidence in the workers. He believed that the workers represented the future, and that given the opportunity, they would flower into a better civilization. Doubtless, if he ever had misgivings about Communist methods, he reflected that, in a workers' world, the classless proletarian society would grow in the soil ploughed over by the methods of the Dictatorship of the Proletariat.

It is obvious that there were elements of mysticism in this faith. Indeed, I think that this is an attraction of Communism for the intellectual. To believe in political action and economic forces which will release new energies in the world is a release of energy in oneself. One ceases to be inhibited by pity for the victims of revolution. Indeed one can regard pity as a projection of one's own revolutionary wish to evade the issue of revolution. One can retain one's faith in the ultimate goals of humanity and at the same time ignore the thousands of people in prison camps, the tens of thousands of slave workers. Do these exist? Whether or not they do, it is bourgeois propaganda to maintain so. Therefore one must deny that there are any slave camps in Russia. These lives have become abstractions in an argument in which the present is the struggle, and the future is Communism—a world where everyone will, eventually, be free. If one admits to oneself the existence of the prison camps, one can view them as inevitable sacrifices demanded by the good cause. It is "humanitarian" weakness to think too much about the victims. The point is to fix one's eyes on the goal, and then one is freed from the horror and anxiety—quite useless in any case—which inhibit the energies of the liberal mind. (Nevertheless, I was to learn that the secret of energy does not lie in shutting one's eyes.)

Moreover, if Communism produces victims, capitalism produces far more. What are the millions of unemployed in peacetime, the millions killed in wars, but the victims of capitalist competition? Capitalism is a system based on victimization, in which the number of victims increases all the time. Communism is a system in which, theoretically—when all are Communists in a classless society—there will be no victims. Its victims today are the victims not of Communism but of revolution. When the revolution has succeeded and when the Dictatorship of the Proletariat has "withered away," there will be a decreasing number of victims. For Communism does not need exploited classes of people. It needs only cooperation of all men to make a better world. During the early years of the 1930's I used to argue with myself in this way. My arguments were re-enforced by feelings of guilt and the suspicion that the side of me which pitied the victims of revolution secretly supported the ills of capitalism from which I myself benefited.

The seeds which Chalmers had planted in my mind were his condemnation of the League of Nations and the criticism he had implied in saying that I was a follower of Gandhi.

He left me to reflect during the coming months that almost all public actions and many private and personal ones were of two kinds: those for, and those against the Revolution. Subjective motives made no difference to the objective tendency of actions. Thus someone who works among the poor and sincerely wishes their lot to be bettered would be objectively against the workers if he made the people to whom he did good contented with capitalist society. In fact, the poor parson and the East End social worker are the agents of the rich.

A country, I saw now, might be governed by leaders genuinely believing themselves to be Socialists, yet unwilling to employ the ruthless methods of revolution. These Socialists might find themselves in a position where their Socialism was threatened by capitalists prepared even to destroy the credit of the country abroad, in the hope that by doing so they could destroy at the same time the credit of the Socialist government. In such a situation, the Socialist government would either have to fulfill the requirements of the capitalists or adopt ruthless methods to destroy capitalism.

Events of the 1930's showed that when faced by this choice, the Social Democrats, Braun and Severing in Prussia, Ramsay MacDonald in Britain, refused the challenge of revolution. They went over to the other side or resigned from power.

I submitted my own personality to the same searching analysis as I applied to the official Socialists. What did I really want? Did I merely enjoy as a luxury of my position in society a self-flattering pretense that I wished others to be as fortunate as I? Was I prepared to accept a Socialist world —on the condition that I suddenly woke up one day to find that it painlessly had happened? Or was I prepared to support the means which would accomplish this end? Could I accept a transitional state of society which would be uncomfortable indeed, worse even perhaps than capitalism, and for a long, hard time very unlike the goal which Socialists desired? And if I could not accept the means which would bring Socialism about, were my views anything but a self-deluded, self-pitying, self-justifying dream? Socialism today was not the World Federation of Socialist States. It was the means which would accomplish this end, however unpleasant these might be.

When I asked myself these questions, I had to admit that what I really wanted was that others should live as I did, not that I should "join the workers": a prospect which discomfited me. I could scarcely endure the thought of the loss of that independence which I owed to my position in bourgeois society. By a great effort of intellectual imagination I attained a state of mind where I could say to myself that I would support the Revolution even if it meant the loss of my own social independence, just as I would accept the same losses in the event of being called up in a war. Yet when I had attained this standpoint, I was still confronted with prospects which horrified me and which seemed to have nothing to do with my own self-interest. I could not accept that it was necessary to deny to others the freedom to say what they believed to be true, if this happened to be opposed to the somewhat arbitrary boundaries to freedom laid down by the Proletarian Dictatorship. I could not believe that it was politically reactionary to believe in God or to hold views about nature or humanity which were not "scientific" in the Marxist sense; which, as it seemed to me, bases a scientific method on denying the scientific spirit of free inquiry.

For the intellectual of good will, Communism is a struggle of conscience. To understand this, explains many things. Amongst others, that Communists, who act in ways which may seem to the non-Communist unscrupulous, may nevertheless be perfectly sincere. Such Communists are like ships doubly anchored fore and aft, amid crosscurrents which swing all other craft. The two anchors are: the fixed vision of the evils done by capitalism, and the equally fixed vision of the class-

less society of the future. Crosstides disturbing liberal consciences are scruples about the methods necessary to achieve
the ends of Communism and awareness of events such as the
suffering of thousands of people who do not happen to be
Communists.

This doubly secured Communist conscience also explains
the penitential, confessional attitude which non-Communists
may sometimes show towards orthodox Communists with their
consciences anchored—if not petrified—in historic materialism.
There is something overpowering about the fixed conscience.
There is a certain compulsion in the situation of the Communist with his faith reproving the liberal whose conscience
swings from example to example, misgiving to misgiving, supporting here the freedom of some writer outside the Writers'
Syndicate, some socially-conscienceless surrealist perhaps, here
a Catholic priest, here a liberal professor in jail. What power
there is in a conscience which reproaches us not only for vices
and weaknesses but also for virtues, such as pity for the oppressed, if they happen to be the wrong oppressed, or love
for a friend, if he is not a good Party member! A conscience
which tells us that by taking up a certain political position
today we can attain a massive, granite-like superiority over our
own whole past, without being humble or simple or guilty, but
simply by virtue of converting the whole of our personality
into raw material for the use of the Party machine! How easy
to affirm that liberal scruples, well-meaning though they may
be, ignore the ultimate social good of all; to argue that they
are really little outposts of the defense of the bourgeoisie, and
that the man of good will may be defending the forces which
have produced the worst calamities of the modern world.

I have already mentioned the almost mystical faith in the
workers as a class who will supersede the bourgeoisie, which
undoubtedly influenced Chalmers. The concept of "The Workers" also affects the struggle of conscience of the intellectual
Communist or fellow-traveler. For however great may be his
belief in intellectual freedom, he may well ask himself: "Why

should the workers care about my freedom?" What the millions of miners and industrial workers and peasants and colonial people want is not freedom to develop their individuality, but peace and bread and decent living conditions. If the sacrifice of intellectual freedom of a few thousand people is the price which must be paid for the bread of the millions, then perhaps one should sacrifice freedom. What value does the individuality of a young writer sitting at a table in the Café de Flore and talking about existentialism have to an Indian peasant or a Chinese coolie?

Although the intellectuals, as Harry Pollitt had pointed out to me, were not the workers, the debate, quite early, ceased to be one in which they played a purely theoretical role. Their own interests were vitally affected by Fascism. The victory of Hitler in 1933 was the defeat of intellectual liberty in Germany and a threat to freedom everywhere. It made the Jews and the intellectuals political forces, by the mere fact of their being Jews and intellectuals. Liberty of racial minorities, of the scientific workers to develop conclusions without having to consider political attitudes, of the poet and the painter to observe and create his most intimate experience, was threatened. At this time I saw Russian films such as *Earth, Potemkin, The Mother, Turksib, Ten Days That Shook the World, The Way into Life,* which seemed to rank amongst the most exciting creative works of art of the twentieth century. I read books and articles by Maurice Hindus, Louis Fischer and others, which emphasized the great social progress made in the Soviet Union. Criticism which I read of Russia, and at first believed, often was later revealed to be anti-Soviet propaganda. The publication of the Soviet Constitution seemed to extend hope of an era of greater freedom in Russia.

Today, when I write these lines, they have an ironic overtone, because the Stalinists now present the same threat to intellectual liberty as did the followers of Hitler in 1933. But at the time of which I am writing this was not obvious. Until the murder of Kirov it seemed probable that Russia was on the verge of attaining an increased intellectual liberty. Exciting experiments in the theater, the cinema and music were taking place. Although the visitors to Russia through Intourist schemes were guided and shepherded, Russia was not sealed off from the rest of the world. The fanatical propaganda directed by counter-revolutionaries on the whole helped Russia very much, by producing a dense fog of prejudice in which it became impossible for a detached observer to accept what was said against Russia. (In parenthesis, I suggest that anti-Communist propaganda has proved the most reliable and best propaganda, working in the long run in favor of Stalin, since the Revolution.)

So the Jews and intellectuals, the "clercs" whose intellectual training detached them from sectarian passions, were forced to look for allies. Disappointed by the leaders of the democracies, they turned to the Workers' Movement. They weighed the evils of mass unemployment, Fascism and war against the evils of Communism, and hoped that Communism at least offered an end to these things. Even a liberal like E. M. Forster wrote at this time that Communism was the only political creed which offered hope for the future, although he added that he himself would not be a Communist. Soon the intellectual life of the 1930's turned into a debate about Ends and Means.

From day to day, of course, the individuals involved in this agonizing debate did not see it in such terms. They felt shaken out of a sense of security, by the slump of the 1930's. Their assumption that they were living in a world where intolerance was decreasing was shattered by the triumph of Hitlerism. They were moved to pity and fury by the persecution of the Jews.

The climax of the 1930's was undoubtedly the Spanish Civil War. In Spain itself, among Spaniards, the issues of the war may well appear more complex than they did to those outside Spain. There may be some truth in the argument of Arthur Bryant that the Spaniards on either side hated the interventionists who rushed in to help them, even more than they hated their Spanish opponents. Nevertheless, for the rest of the world Spain became a theater where the drama of the struggle of Fascism and anti-Fascism was enacted. The intervention of Mussolini and Hitler, followed by that of Russia, and then by the enrollment of the International Brigade, made the Spanish War, for the time being, the center of the struggle for the soul of Europe. Spanish generals had revolted against a government elected by the Spanish people. When the rebels could not consolidate their rebellion, and outside forces intervened, the resistance of the Republic became the cause of democracy, and that of the rebels the cause of Fascism. Whatever a great many Spaniards on both sides may have been fighting for, this was the issue being fought out by Italy, Germany, Russia and the International Brigade on Spanish soil.

The European Fascist versus anti-Fascist struggle was dramatized in Spain as in a theater. The peculiar Spanish passion, idealism and violence of temperament, and even the Spanish landscape, colored the struggle and gave it intensity and a kind of poetic purity which it scarcely had before or afterward. Above all, this was a war in which the individual, with his passion and his comparative independence of mechanical methods, still counted. It was in part an anarchist's war, a poet's war. At least five of the best young English writers gave their lives as did the poets of other countries. This drew the intellectuals still deeper into the struggle. After the fall of the Republic the struggle of Fascism against democracy became one in which armies and machines and bureaucracies counted more than individuals.

Quite early in the Spanish War I traveled to Gibraltar, Oran and Tangier. Here I was amazed by the fervor of the common people who crowded to the meetings in support of the Spanish Republic. I have never seen any meeting to compare with one I attended at Tangier. Several hundred of the poorest people, amongst them the crippled and blind, listened with strained passionate faces to the speakers who defended the cause of the Republic. There was a devoutness, a sense of hope, which made me think of the crowds described in the New Testament.

Everywhere in these places where I came in touch with Communist groups, I was impressed by their confidence and their decency. In Oran, amidst the blatancy, the squalor, the drunkenness of the life of the port, the group of Communists who met at a little café where they had their headquarters seemed to belong to another world.

In contrast to the favorable impression which I gained of the Communists, I had a bad one of the officials and businessmen who represented the interests of the democratic countries. Nearly all those I met seemed to support Franco. I could give many examples. The most comprehensive is from Tangier. Tangier was governed by an international commission consisting of the ministers of several powers, Britain, Italy, Spain, Belgium and France. The Spanish Minister, Prieto del Rio, who represented the Spanish Republic, was isolated. When I took a taxi and asked the driver to take me to the Spanish Ministry, he, following an automatic procedure, drove me to the Central Post Office, General Franco's headquarters. At the residence of the British Minister, the guests at a cocktail party discussed how it could have happened that poor old Prieto, who was a good fellow, should have chosen the wrong side; this side being the legal government of his country, recognized by other governments. When I finally did visit Prieto del Rio, I found him with two members of his staff, cut off from the official life of Tangier, of whose government he was a member.

In Gibraltar a retired British official put the situation very neatly, with an irony which he by no means intended. "What the people at home don't realize," he said, "is that the Republicans aren't our kind of democrats. Why, if you go out into the streets here and ask the first ten Spanish workers you meet which side they support, they will all say the Republic. It isn't the British conception of democracy at all. It's what ninety per cent of the people want." The British officials in Gibraltar did not have connections with the Spanish people who wanted the Republic. They knew only the Spaniards who took part in the Calpe fox hunt. From these they learned stories of atrocities committed by the Republicans. They denied all knowledge of the savagery of the other side.

After going to Barcelona, Madrid and Valencia on a visit which followed this first one, I took part at home in the agitation on behalf of the Spanish Republic. I made speeches and served on committees. On one occasion, with some other writers, I walked down Oxford Street and Regent Street carrying sandwich boards which bore Republic slogans.

These were the days of the Popular Front. The emotion which gave life to this movement was a widespread revival of liberal feeling, yet there was no political party except the Communist to which this feeling could attach itself. The British Labor Party still had not recovered from the betrayal of Ramsay MacDonald. Accordingly, this resurgent liberalism in its anti-Fascist form was exploited by the Communists.

Amongst intellectuals and writers, men like Victor Gollancz, John Strachey, George Orwell, Arthur Koestler, E. M. Forster, were prepared to go as far as the Communists in their opposition to Fascism, their defense of freedom and social justice. Many people who were not Communists gave their energies to supporting the Spanish Republic, which they believed to be the cause of democracy.

If the Communists had entered into the Popular Front with the same good faith as the Socialists and Liberals, a democratic movement would have extended from the extreme Left to the Liberal Center, which would have had the fervor, generosity and imagination of the liberal revolutions of 1848. But the fatality of the Communists was to think only of forming united fronts in order then to seize control of them from within. The diversity of positive energies of many parties was thus inhibited by that party which most loudly and persistently proclaimed its desire for unity.

The slump of the 1930's, the catastrophe of the Weimar Republic, the fall of Socialist Vienna, all of them events which I witnessed more or less from the outside, had forced me to accept a theoretically Communist position. In poems, and in *Forward from Liberalism*, I had stated Communism as an intellectual and emotional necessity. Pollitt's appeal to me to help in Spain pushed me momentarily over into the Communist Party. Nevertheless, it was Spain which involved me in my first practical experience of working politically with other people. This action which had first made me a Party member also took me beyond and outside the Party. For I soon began to realize that even if the directing and organizing force behind the support for the Spanish Republic was Communist, the real energy of the Popular Front was provided by those who had a passion for liberal values. Even the Communists realized that what made Spain an action and a symbol in this century as important as 1848 in the last, was the very fact that the Republic was *not* Communist. Indeed, the Communists while trying to exploit the situation there were the very first to declare this and to deny indignantly that the Republic was Communist: but they did so because they thought that to do so was good propaganda, while at the same time in their actions they were doing their best to belie their propaganda and to gain control in Spain itself, and in the organizations which brought aid to Spain from abroad. The liberals, the men of good will, even while they supported the Popular Front, were forced by their Communist allies into a struggle of conscience which caused a deep division amongst the supporters of the Republic. For the Communists, the Spanish War was a phase in their struggle for power. Being single-minded and fanatical, they were the driving force in the Popular Front, especially in Spain. Even so, they were also the force which held back all the other forces, forces ultimately more vital than themselves, because more complex and caring more for freedom and variety of expression. Almost the whole literature of the Spanish War depicts the energy of a reviving liberalism rather than the Communist orthodoxy which produced an increasingly deadening effect on all discussion of ideas, all witnessing of the complexity of events. The best books of the War—those by Malraux, Hemingway, Koestler and Orwell—describe the Spanish tragedy from the liberal point of view, and they bear witness against the Communists.

During my second visit to Spain, I saw how the Communists had gained complete control of the International Brigade. It was recruited on the merits of the Popular Front of the Republic. The concentration into Communist hands of all the mixed democratic elements which made up the Brigade was, on a small scale, the model of the Communist method in Spain. Within the Republican Army this policy was to call upon the parties to form one army in which all the formations of the political groups were merged, and then, having taken the lead in this way, gain control of the Army.

In the International Brigade personal tragedies arose from the domination of the Communists. One of these comes to my mind. When I visited the front near Madrid I met an English Public School boy, L——, aged eighteen. L—— told me that he had come to Spain in the belief that the Brigade was as liberal as the Republic itself. He had lost faith in the Republican cause on finding that the Brigade was dominated by the Communists, with whom he had no sympathy. When I questioned him it was obvious that he had never thought about Communism before he came to Spain. I asked him whether I could attempt to obtain his recall from Spain. He said no; and, pointing to the crest of the hill above the valley where we were standing, said: "The rest of my life is to walk every morning up here until one day I am killed." He was killed six weeks later.

When I returned to England, I wrote an article, which was published in the *New Statesman*, protesting against the propaganda which enrolled young men in the International Brigade without it being explained to them that this was a Communist-controlled organization. This article did not please the Communists. A few weeks later, in Valencia, I met the correspondent of a Communist newspaper. He said that he had seen my article and that what I had written about Spain was true. He pointed out, though, that the important thing was to write that which would best serve the ends of winning the war and of Communism. He argued very amiably and with considerable charm, showing that kind of indifference to the misfortunes of the victims of a righteous cause which is even rather seductive in its ease.

Just as the pattern of Communist behavior in the Brigade was followed by the Communists within the Republic, so was the pattern of propaganda. Thus, there was an atrocity propaganda which attributed all murders to the Francoists and depicted Republicans as angels, denouncing as "Fascists" those who suggested that some atrocities had been committed by the Republicans. This picture of the Republic was repudiated in the novels of Malraux and Hemingway, the two outstanding books of the Spanish War. Another example of the crude propaganda was the use of the murder of Lorca. The fact that Lorca was not a Communist, but a Catholic who in fact fled to Franco territory at the beginning of the War, made his assassination by Fascists the more useful to the Communists. The Communists hate live heretics; but dead ones, so long as the Communists have not killed them themselves, can serve a useful purpose. Retrospectively, their heresies may be used to show how liberal the Communists really are and how illiberal their opponents. Thus, to say that Lorca was a Catholic, a conservative, even a reactionary did not displease them, since Franco was responsible for the murder. They would even get indignant if Lorca was spoken of as a Red. What was inexcusable, from their point of view, was to suggest that there was something unexplained, perhaps accidental, about the circumstances of his death. I noticed when I was in Spain that most of the Spanish poets felt a certain shame about the propaganda that had been made from Lorca's death.

More sinister, though, than the propaganda of heroics, was that of slanderous attack against groups within the Republic who were unfriendly to Communism. The liquidation of the Trotskyite organization, the POUM, leaps and the vilification of all its members as Fascists, was a stain on the Republic in the eyes of all who were not Communists.

After the war, a Spanish corps commander told me that he considered the Communist propaganda to have done the Republican cause more harm than good. "We had a good enough cause to have been able to afford to tell the truth." This remark contained wisdom. Propaganda which paints friends entirely white and enemies black persuades only those who are already convinced: to others it is humanly incredible. It paints human events as abstractions which only those who have no eyes can believe in. It dismays those who are sympathetic to the cause but also open-eyed.

On several occasions Communist-directed propaganda resulted in strong reactions against the Republic by people who had been deceived. In Valencia I met a man who provided a striking example of this disillusionment. He was an American journalist, writing for a great British newspaper, and certainly one of the most distinguished sympathizers with the Republicans. He would sit in the lounge of the Hotel Victoria, reading his paper with indignation, as he saw, day after day, that it printed the long reports of the correspondent who was with Franco, and cut his own almost to nothing. One day this journalist, who had that innocence which is sometimes a quality of intelligent Americans, asked me whether I considered that several murders which had been reported recently in Valencia and Barcelona were really committed by Republicans. I replied that it was only to be expected that violent acts should accompany a revolutionary war. "In that case, why do they deny what is going on?" he asked innocently, and went on: "Doesn't such an idea shake your confidence in the Republic?" "Not at all," I answered. "If I believed that such things really happened whilst they denied them, I would lose all faith in the Republican cause," he said.

A few weeks later he went to Barcelona at the time of the liquidation of the POUM. He repudiated the Communist-inspired version of the POUM activities, left Spain, and ceased to be a supporter of the Republic.

In July, 1937, I attended the International Congress of Writers which met in Valencia and Madrid. At this time André Gide had just published his book *Retour de l'U.R.S.S.* This book was a journal which, if it had been written about America, Britain, Italy or France, would have excited little comment and certainly no indignation. But, as it concerned Russia and as, while finding much to praise, Gide also noted the adulation of Stalin and an atmosphere of suspicion and fear which he found distasteful, a shriek went up from all the Communists all over the world as from the mother of a spoiled child whom a passer-by has rebuked roughly. From being the world's greatest writer who had gone to pay homage to the world's most advanced democracy, Gide became a Fascist, a decadent, a traitor, reviled by the Communist press in terms which seemed to me at the time almost unbelievable.

The Russian delegates at this congress were impressive only for their arrogance and mental torpidity. When they made speeches, they said little or nothing about literature. Instead, they snarled at Trotsky and Gide, praised Stalin and the Communists, and then sat down. Ilya Ehrenburg, Alexei Tolstoy, Koltsov and the others never said anything, in public or in private, which could stimulate discussion amongst the other delegates. They had no views of their own. Koltsov excelled in improvising parodies of Gide's book. However, this gift did not save him from disappearing entirely from the public view on his return to Russia.

At the Writers' Congress I remarked on the unwillingness of people to believe what they did not want to believe, to see what they do not want to see. I drove from Valencia to Barcelona, on our return, in a car in which there was also a Communist poet, a lady novelist and her friend, a poetess. I sat in front of the car with the Catalan driver, a genial, violent man, who boasted to me that during the incidents at the time of the liquidation of the POUM he had shot five people dead in cold blood on the streets of Barcelona.

When we were waiting on the frontier, the lady novelist, who had a correct, governessy manner—and whose way of explaining her every wish was to say: "I thought it would be less selfish, Comrade"—remarked that during the ten days of the Congress and our journey in Spain we had seen no evidence of behavior on the Republican side which was not perfectly nice. I could not resist repeating what the chauffeur had just told me. At this the ladies and the poet stared at me in stupe-fied indignation, looked at one another and then moved away without a word.

There was in Madrid an English writer, who had become a political commissar. Fat and fussy, he explained that his private's uniform was a typical example of the improvisation of the Republican side, as he ought, really, to be attired as a high-ranking officer. The writer-commissar used to give the lady writers, the poet and myself little talks explaining the background of the War, in our hotel bedroom. The theme of his talks was always the same: that the Communists stood for unity among the divided supporters of the government and in the army and the International Brigade; and that whenever they had persuaded the other parties to unite, they then led and controlled, if they could, the unified forces. If in some instances they held back before gaining control, this was for strategic reasons.

To protest, as I sometimes futilely did, that this kind of unity was no unity but betrayal of the other parties from within, produced a hopeless stare of reproach from the selfless lady novelist. Then perhaps the writer-commissar would ex-plain to me, for the hundredth time, my failure to think clearly. What I should have thought amounted to this: that "his-torically" there was no real position except the Communist one. Thus when Communists talk of unity they mean unifying various deviating groups and showing them the correct line of historic development. In order to achieve this, they emphasize that they are the party of democracy which wants all the forces of progress to unite. To say, though, that the Communists in doing this represent betrayal of the other parties from within is a "Fascist" argument. Communists themselves really think that they are forming a people's front and to think otherwise is simply to be a bad Communist. The writer-commissar's argument was an example of what George Orwell calls in his novel *1984* "double-thinking."

Another example of "double-thinking" was to say that Communists stood for freedom, democracy and the Popular Front, and at the same time to label Liberals, Socialists or members of the POUM who opposed them Fascists, and, in fact, to liquidate them, as the POUM was liquidated in Spain.

At this time I came to a conclusion which, although it may appear obvious, was important to the development of my thinking about politics. This was simply that nearly all human beings have an extremely intermittent grasp on reality. Only a few things, which illustrate their own interests and ideas, are real to them; other things, which are in fact equally real, appear to them as abstractions. Thus, when men have decided to pursue a course of action, everything which serves to support this seems vivid and real; everything which stands against it becomes abstraction. Your friends are allies and therefore real human beings with flesh and blood and sympathies like yourself. Your opponents are just tiresome, unreasonable, unnecessary theses, whose lives are so many false statements which you would like to strike out with a lead bullet as you would put the stroke of a lead pencil through a bungled paragraph.

Not to think in this way demands the most exceptional qualities of judicious-mindedness or of high imaginative understanding. During the Spanish War it dismayed me to notice that I thought like this myself. When I saw photographs of children murdered by the Fascists, I felt furious pity. When the supporters of Franco talked of Red atrocities, I merely felt indignant that people should tell such lies. In the first case I saw corpses, in the second only words. However, I never learned to be unself-critical, and thus I gradually acquired a certain horror of the way in which my own mind worked. It was clear to me that unless I cared about every murdered child impartially, I did not really care about children being murdered at all. I was performing an obscene mental act on certain corpses which became the fuel for propagandist passions, but I showed my fundamental indifference by not caring about those other corpses who were the victims of the Republicans.

If I am correct in thinking that human beings have a tendency to think abstractly, and without weighing the human realities which are operated on by their political passions, the mentality of Communists is not very difficult to explain. They have adopted a theory of society which encourages a human vice: to regard their own cause and their own supporters as real, and all other causes and their exponents as abstract examples of outmoded theoretical positions.

It may be maintained that the theory justifies the vice because Communism is bound ultimately to increase the quantity and quality of human happiness. During these years I gradually decided that I did not think so, for the reason that the self-righteousness of people who believe that their "line" is completely identifiable with the welfare of humanity and the course of history, so that everyone outside it exists only to be refuted or absorbed into the line, results in a dehumanization of the Communists themselves. Human history is made by people acting upon principles, not on principles regardless of the quality of the people. If the principles dehumanize men, then the society which these men make is dehumanized. Although I never have agreed with the view of such as Aldous Huxley that all power corrupts, I think that power is only saved from corruption if it is humanized with humility. Without humility, power is turned to persecutions and executions and public lies.

I could not help noticing with myself and my colleagues that the encouragement amongst us of the vice of thinking that there was only one human cause and one human side had a bad effect on our personalities. It taught us to exploit suffering for our own purposes, and to ignore it when it did not serve these. It encouraged us to form a partial and incomplete picture of conflicts, and discouraged us from correcting this picture in the light of immediate experience if this conflicted with our theoretical views.

With the Communist intellectuals I was always confronted by the fact that they had made a calculation when they became Communists which had changed the whole of reality for them into the crudest black and white. In day-to-day living every factor which they confronted could not affect the huge abstract calculation in their minds. The Revolution was the beginning and the end, the sum of all sums. Someday, somewhere, everything would add up to the happy total which was the Dictatorship of the Proletariat and a Communist society. This way of thinking canceled out all experiential objections.

Thus the intellectual Communists seemed extremely interested in theory, very little in evidence which might conflict with theory. For example, I never met any who had the slightest interest in any side of Russia which was not the Stalinist propagandist presentation. It does not surprise me that during the Kravchenko case in Paris, Communists and fellow-travelers should have volunteered to give evidence against the book *I Chose Freedom* though they had no pretensions to any knowledge of Russia. From their point of view all they had to know was that Kravchenko was opposed to the Soviet System. This proved he must be wrong.

The same disregard for scrupulousness in anything but theory applied to behavior. The ends, justified the means. Thus the correspondent of the Communist paper took a quite pedantic pleasure in telling me that it was necessary to lie. Thus the writer-commissar told me with pride how he had arranged for a soldier who was in some way unreliable to be sent to a part of the Spanish Front where he was certain to be shot. Thus Harry Pollitt, who published in 1939 a statement that the war was being waged for democracy against Fascism, promptly withdrew this statement when it did not suit the convenience of Russia, and agreed that it was a squabble between imperialist capitalists on both sides. Thus, when in 1946 I met a leader of the British Communist Party, he said to me accusingly: "Why do you fuss about the lives of a few thousand Poles, when the whole Soviet Union is at stake?" The argument of an abstract sum held in one's mind, which cancels out all lesser considerations, always holds. If the Party line changes and it is decided that what yesterday was democracy today is called Fascism, there is no inconsistency, because the Party line consists only of an attitude taken up by the Party towards non-Communists, all of whom are equally the objects of statements turning them into abstractions.

The emphasis of the Communists is thus always on the application of theory to reality. The happy Communist lives in a state of historical-materialist grace in which, instead of never seeing the wood for the trees, he never sees the trees for the wood.

As I was never in a state of grace, the extraordinary certainty of Communists about things of which they knew almost nothing, but to which they applied their theories, always mystified me. Another mystery was the way in which Communists who had known the answer to everything could and did sometimes cease to be Communists, producing then as reasons for their change those very objections which had previously existed for them only to be disregarded or explained away.

An interesting example of such a change was Mrs. Charlotte Haldane, the novelist, who was then the wife of Professor Haldane. When I knew her at the time of the Spanish Civil

War, Mrs. Haldane was a good example of the Communist in a state of grace. On one occasion, after a meeting, I remember driving with her along a London road where there were queues of people waiting in drizzling rain for trams. "Queues!" Mrs. Haldane exclaimed. "How disgraceful. Such things would not be tolerated in Russia!" "But surely there are queues in Russia," I protested, "I have read about them." Mrs. Haldane gave me the look of noble scorn coupled with lofty pity which is typical of derided Communist womanhood.

However, during the War, Mrs. Haldane went to Russia, as a strong Stalinist sympathizer. On her return, she parted company with both the Communist Party and her husband, Professor Haldane. Later she wrote an article for the press which is illuminating in one sense, mystifying in another. In this she wrote:

> Every word and every act of Soviet citizens, scientists as well as others, is permeated by the conscious awareness of unceasing Communist Party vigilance, spying and recording.
> Every word that is spoken, written, published, is subject to such totalitarian scrutiny, and at any time may be produced in evidence against the speaker or writer.

What mystifies about this is why Mrs. Haldane should have had to go to Russia to discover it. She could have deduced as much from a dozen books, of which she can hardly have failed to read one, Gide's *Retour de l'U.R.S.S.* If she did not believe that there was Communist persecution on Gide's evidence, she can scarcely have failed to notice the hysterical Communist persecution with which that book was received, which made perfectly clear the treatment which the Communists would give Gide if they had the opportunity. The only explanation of her change of heart is that what had seemed irrelevant to her before she went to Russia suddenly became relevant during her visit. She is certainly to be congratulated on the honesty with which she changed her views. In the same article she raises, with what may be a backward look at Professor Haldane, a question far more important than why writers should be Stalinists: why scientists should be. She essays to answer this:

> . . . They only see, as through a glass, darkly, or preferably through rose-colored spectacles, a "socialist" country in which fabulous sums are devoted by the State to scientific research, in which scientists are highly paid compared to the rest of the people, and are unimpeded in their work by the fear that their discoveries may be exploited for personal profit by big business men.

Perhaps some personal impressions of Professors J. B. S. Haldane and J. D. Bernal, whom I have observed at a distance over some years, will at least show that scientists are human like everyone else, and will underline what I have already suggested: that we cannot begin to trust our fellow beings, however intelligent they may be, unless we are sure that their principles are tempered by that sense of their limitations which I call humility.

Professor Haldane strikes me as a man of great qualities, of which perhaps humility is the least outstanding. When he was teaching at Cambridge University, he had the reputation of a rather eccentric professor who indulged in heroic self-display. Shortly before the War, when he was making experiments in the Haldane Air Raid Shelter, publicity was given to the fact that Professor Haldane insisted on sitting in one of the shelters whilst high explosives were dropped near by.

During the Spanish Civil War I was one evening at a Christmas party given by his sister, Naomi Mitchison, when Haldane appeared, having just returned from Spain. Haldane seemed quite unhappy until the children's charades were stopped and he could regale the guests with stories of his violent Spanish adventures. I have the impression of Haldane as a kind of schoolboy, with a delight in scientific adventure, underneath the professor. He seems to enjoy displays of violence. Mrs. Haldane has probably indicated another aspect of his character when she hints that scientists see in the Soviet Union a vast field where highly honored scientists are free to carry out scientific experiments.

I do not say all this to denigrate scientists such as Haldane and Bernal, but simply to indicate that it is wrong to think that scientists show the same qualities of detachment and considerateness in their social attitudes as they do in the laboratory. They are as liable as anyone else to be carried away by their emotions; and planned societies offer them special temptations.

Bernal makes a less bearish and schoolboyish impression than Haldane. Or rather, he is another type of boy, a genius no doubt in his scientific work, but inspired also with a social passion. He is excited by ideas of designing the perfect house for socialized human beings, which will be a machine of living to supersede all past architecture. He is fascinated also by every kind of planning for human beings. In his social thought, he shows a tendency to extravagant fantasies which he probably would not indulge in his scientific work.

In our society we give scientists credit for superhuman wisdom. In fact, it would perhaps be truer to say that, like other specialists and virtuosi, they are slightly inhuman. On the one hand, they show enthusiasm for schemes which tend to turn society into a vast field for scientific experiment. On the other hand, they have done little or nothing to protect society from the misuse of their discoveries. For the most part, when there is mention of their being responsible for destructive inventions, they take refuge in their position as pure scientists. They show extremely little sense of what a contemporary society owes to the cultural tradition of the past, or of what we would lose if, for example, most past architecture were destroyed and replaced by perfect machines for living.

In Hitler's Germany, the scientists lent themselves to schemes for sterilizing and destroying the mentally unfit, for exterminating whole populations, for using human beings as the subjects for experiments. A friend of mine, himself a scientist who went to Germany after the War to study the activities of German scientists, told me that what shocked him most was to discover that when human beings were made available to German scientists for experimental purposes, they used them with ruthless extravagance, often to make experiments which were completely unnecessary. I am not suggesting that scientists elsewhere would do the same thing. But it is necessary to point out that scientists can derive from science qua science no objections to such experiments as exterminating the mentally unfit. If they do object, they are acting upon non-scientific values. Modern science has produced no reason to prevent science from being directed by governments toward purposes of enormous destruction in every country. Science is simply an instrument, for good or for bad. For it to be directed toward good, whoever directs it must have some conception of humanity wider than that of a planned scientific society. There must be a purpose in society beyond good planning. Without such a purpose, to submit society to a dictatorship for the purpose of planned science is simply to lay down the lines for another misuse of science. For in Russia it is the politicians who plan the science.

Thus when people like Bernal, Haldane and Joliot-Curie become Communists, I am skeptical of their having any motive except a blind faith in the instrument of science. But this instrument has no moral purpose, and when scientists are in favor of its being put into the hands of politicians who imprison their political opponents, and who even go so far as to persecute scientists whose researches show a tendency to produce results inconsistent with the political views of the State, then we may say that these Communist scientists are victims of a kind of moral blindness which has long characterized science.

During the 1930's I observed my Communist colleagues. I admired their courage and I did not suspect them of self-interest. They had sacrificed a great deal, and were prepared to sacrifice more, for the sake of a cause in which they profoundly believed. But apart from this courage and sacrifice, it seemed often that their best qualities had been put to the service of their worst, and their personalities destroyed. They believed in making the poor militant, but not in loving their neighbors. Truth for them was a slave which waited on the convenience of a small inner circle of leaders. They accepted hatred as the mainspring of action. They distorted the meanings of epithets which they applied to nations, parties and individuals without the slightest realization that to misuse words produces confusion. "Peace" in their language could mean "War"; "War"—"Peace"; "Unity"—"betrayal from within"; "Fascism"—"Socialism."

Apart from the necessity of serving the Party, they were under no obligation to discipline vanity, malice, officiousness and treachery in themselves. Indeed, these things might well become virtues if they were useful to the Party.

Often I found that a human and sympathetic Communist was a bad Communist to the extent that he was human and sympathetic, and that he was well aware of this himself.

During these years I came to realize that Communists are divided, roughly, into four categories: (A) The theoreticians who know in an abstract and general way the methods they are using, but who think of these abstractly as "necessity." (B) Those who are completely and happily deluded about Russia and about the methods employed by their comrades. (C) The workers who have nothing to lose except their chains, who are fighting against capitalist exploitation and for whom bread is more important than freedom. (D) The police, political commissars, agents, spies, etc. These last are perhaps the only Communists who know, with any completeness, the facts about prison camps and trials.

When I joined the Communist Party, I expected that in doing so I would get to know what the Communists were doing; that I would be able to measure their means against the methods of capitalism; and that I would learn to accept the relationship of means to ends.

I had not expected to find that the actions of the Communists in Russia and in Spain were denied by the Communists amongst themselves. Or possibly, that they were completely ignorant of them.

I have already given the examples of Chalmers not being interested in the Russian trials, and of the refusal of my literary companions in Spain to listen to facts which complicated their simple picture of events. There came a time when I had collected two examples, which seemed to me irrefutable, of behavior for which Party members should accept responsibility. One of these was a story told to me by a famous American woman writer, whose husband was a Russian. One morning when they were in Moscow, the police had arrived at their apartment at 3 A.M. and taken her husband away. Since then, she had never seen him nor received any communication from him. She had no idea what he was supposed to have done. She herself had been a Communist. This was a case which was fairly well known, as American and British intellectuals had concerned themselves with the fate of this unfortunate man. They had written letters to the Secretariat of the Comintern. At first these letters had been acknowledged with a promise that inquiries would be made into the case. After this there was silence from the Secretariat, and further letters from the friends of the American woman were not answered.

The other story concerned a friend of mine, Y, who was in the International Brigade. Y was a nephew of an influential statesman, who at the request of Y's mother had asked the heads of the Brigade that Y should not be sent into battle.

Through an indiscretion, when I was in Spain, I mentioned to Y that his uncle had done this. Y, who was brave, was furious. He deserted from the Brigade, and allowed himself to be retaken, asking that as a punishment he should fight. In this, he succeeded. He fought in the battle of Morata. During the few days when he was in prison, he was confined with several other prisoners in a very small cell. "But that was nothing," he told me. "Other prisoners came into our cell who regarded it as the freedom of a wide open space. They had been shut for as much as forty-eight hours on end in cells the size of cupboards." Y was not particularly shocked at these conditions, nor did they alter his general attitude towards the Republic. On the whole he regarded his experiences as rather amusing.

At a meeting of the small group of Communist writers in London I told these stories, for a reason which I explained in words such as these: "Of course I understand that you have no reason to believe these particular incidents. But I know enough to know that they are characteristic. Therefore, if you do not believe what I know to be typical, I shall know that you are ignorant of facts which in my opinion you should certainly know. Whether you know them or not, and whether you deny them or not, has become extremely important to me. For if you are ignorant of them, or if you deny them even among yourselves, I shall feel that to belong to a Party whose members have no knowledge of the Party's actions, is a responsibility I cannot share. On the other hand, if you admit them, and if you argue that it is necessary to deny them in public, I shall feel that you are serious, and perhaps I shall accept your point of view."

When I had finished speaking, one writer got up and said: "It is typical of Comrade Spender's bourgeois mentality that he invents stories of this kind." Another then said: "Even if what Comrade Spender says is not altogether invented, it is characteristic that he draws attention to these incidents which are quite unimportant, in order to defend himself from having to face the real issues." A third, who was well-disposed toward me said: "Look here, Stephen, you ought to remember that as your friend Y was himself in prison where he claims that these things happened, he is likely to have an embittered attitude. So you should not attach importance to his evidence."

It was useless to say that Y was not in the least embittered and that this was my reason for choosing his story out of several others which I might have quoted. Nor would it have helped to say that according to the arguments which had just been used we might ignore all the crimes of Fascism as being either irrelevant to the historic achievements of Hitler, or else as resting on the evidence of people who, having themselves been beaten and bullied and tormented, were embittered and prejudiced witnesses. I had discovered that these people did not consider that they were in any way answerable for the actions of the Cause which they supported.

I began to wonder how much Communists know about Communism. I still wonder. Other Communists do not say to them: "We have slave camps in Russia." Quite the contrary, if a fellow Communist even suggested this, he would be accused of occupying himself with unimportant details, if not of being a Fascist. At what point in Mr. Pollitt's career can a fellow member of the Comintern or Cominform have taken him aside and told him anything of Russia which was not propaganda?

The members of the Party know less than outsiders imagine about actual conditions in Communist-dominated countries. However, they do know about certain principles of dictatorship, because these are part of their ideology. Thus when I met M. Rákosi, the Communist Deputy Prime Minister of Hungary in 1947, almost the first remark he made to me was that the British Labor Government was "Fascist." When I asked him what he meant by this, he said: "For two reasons. Firstly, they have not filled the British Army with Socialist generals. Secondly, they have not taken over Scotland Yard."

This attitude has implications which have become more obvious today than they were twelve years ago. They were underlined for me by Beneš in an interview which I had with him in Prague in the winter of 1946. Beneš said that he thought the rulers of Russia probably could not have achieved their revolution without the terrible means which they had used. But, he added with emotion, he thanked God that he had never been called upon to use such means and he hoped that he would not have to.

In writing this essay, I have always been aware that no criticism of the Communists removes the arguments against capitalism. The effect of these years of painful experiences has only been to reveal to me that both sides are forces producing oppression, injustice, destruction of liberties, enormous evils. It is to be said for capitalism that since it has long been established it can afford the luxury of freedom in the arts and in debate amongst political parties; but at the same time capitalism as we see it today in America, the greatest capitalist country, seems to offer no alternative to war, exploitation and destruction of the world's resources. Communism, if it could achieve internationalism and the socialization of the means of production, might establish a world which would not be a mass of automatic economic contradictions.

However, even on the assumption that world revolution could be achieved and a Communist political and economic system be established throughout the world, the culture and well-being of the new classless society would depend on one further assumption: that the Dictatorship of the Proletariat would "wither away."

Marx and the Communist writers assume always that this will be so. They do not need to be precise about how the withering will happen. Their thought is that the destruction of capitalism is accomplished according to laws which are the mechanical working out of contradictions within the capitalist system itself; that the seizure of power by the proletariat, although partly the result of human volition, also follows the same mechanical development. Thus, when the fatality of this action has achieved itself, the mechanistic necessity for the whole process of decay of capitalism and rise of the proletariat will fall away. The withering of the dictatorship will follow automatically from a situation where the workers have no more enemies.

If this were true, the objections to Communism would be objections to temporary inconveniences. Very inconvenient, it is true, for the victims of revolutionary action and propaganda, but still a price worth paying for an international world where all nations lived in harmony one with another.

But if it be not certain that that dictatorship will wither away, then criticism of the Communists and their methods today becomes criticism of the dictatorship of tomorrow and the day after tomorrow and the day after that.

Now one of the lessons of the last thirty years has certainly been that a dictatorship established in the modern world, with all the modern resources of secret police, propaganda, terror, etc. is extremely difficult to remove. Stalin, Hitler, Mussolini and Franco have none of them been seriously threatened by revolt within their own countries. Those who have fallen have only done so as the result of the complete ruin of their nations, brought on them by other countries. It seems reasonable to think then that a world dictatorship would be the most immovable dictatorship of all. Nor, in the light of Russian experience, can one believe that Communism or any other party would produce dictators, bureaucrats and police who were willing to "wither away."

Thus, to study the characteristics of the commissars and dictators of today is to learn something of the laws and the nature of the Communist State which may gain power tomorrow; and which, if it gains power, will not abandon it.

Amongst the Communist intellectuals during the 1930's I noticed behavior which in Eastern Europe has today become institutionalized in the Syndicates of Writers which dictate to novelists and poets what they should think and feel. The main preoccupation of the groups of writers who met to discuss the perennial problem of Art and Society was that literature should demonstrate Marxist theories of the superiority of the proletariat and the necessity of revolution. This intellectual view of society inevitably extended far beyond any individual experience. Experience could only be drawn on in order to illustrate an aspect of a foregone conclusion, arrived at independently of the experience.

However sincere the Marxism of the writers, the domination of a theory in their minds which has preceded every experience, had certain inevitable results. Since what was most important was to be a theoretical Marxist, it followed that the best Marxists, who were often the worst writers, had an advantage over those writers who with humility looked to their experiences for their art. It meant that the theoreticians automatically became literary critics, analyzing the whole of literature, past and present, according to the ideological views of the writer. Thus, I have listened to a Communist poet explaining to a Hampstead Literary Society on the occasion of a Keats anniversary that, although Keats was no Marxist, we could at least claim that in being the son of an ostler, and ill with consumption which the State did not attend to, he had the merit of being a victim of capitalism. And to the same writer pointing out that Joyce's *Finnegan's Wake* illustrates the disintegration of thought and language of the bourgeois individualist world. It was he also, by the way, who, when Virginia Woolf took her own life in 1941, wrote in a manner of congratulating her on having chosen the path of historic necessity, and indicating that other bourgeois writers could be expected to follow her example.

I listened with disgust to the dogmatic crowing of inferior talents. There was something degrading about the assumption that a political theory of society could place him who held it in a position where he could reject the insights of genius, unless these proved to be, after all, applications of a political theory to aesthetic material.

I felt scarcely less revulsion for that extensive Marxist literary criticism which interprets literature as myths consciously or unconsciously invented by writers to serve the interests of some historically ascendant class. To my mind, although poets such as Dante and Shakespeare are certainly in a sense both men of their time and political thinkers, there is a transcendent aspect of their experience which takes them beyond human social interests altogether. Society may follow them into luminous revelations about the universal nature of life which are quite outside and beyond the preoccupations of any particular historic epoch, and in that sense society may be elevated by them; but their illuminations are not just the projected wishful thinkings of their society.

To me the beliefs of poets are sacred revelations, illustrations of a reality about the nature of life, which I may not share, but which I cannot and do not wish to explain away as "social phenomena." If art teaches us anything, it is that man is not entirely imprisoned within his society. From art, society may even learn to some extent to escape from its own prison.

Not to believe that in some sense art is the communication of experience unique to the individual artist is to judge art simply as an expression of social needs. This means that, since poets and artists are not the best judges of the ideology which is an expression of the development of society, political theorists are in a position to dictate to them what society needs from their art. This, I found, was the attitude of the Communists.

I remember very well during the 1930's a meeting held by the organizers of the Group Theater to discuss a verse play of mine, *Trial of a Judge*, which had been performed. A smartly dressed young Communist woman got up and protested against the play. She and her fellow Communists, she said, were deeply disappointed. They had expected this play to outline a situation in which the Fascists were capitalists, the liberals were feeble and the Communists were right—which they knew very well. But instead of this, it showed a tendency to sympathize with the liberal point of view. Moreover, in the last act there was even an element of mysticism. Now, she said, it is not liberalism or mysticism which we want from our writers but militant Communism. And so on.

Her point of view was exactly that of Harry Pollitt, who, whenever I met him, would say: "Why don't you write songs for the workers, as Byron, Shelley and Wordsworth did?" An unanswerable question—unless I wish to get the English

Romantic poets into some kind of posthumous disgrace. It may seem that the young girl and Harry Pollitt are crude examples; Stalin would be a still cruder but more effective one. Sometimes a great deal of crudeness is expressed with a certain subtlety. For example, in Czechoslovakia in 1947, the Russian Professor of Russian at one of the great Universities, himself a Communist (and a man of intelligence and charm), defended the attack by the Soviet Union of Writers on Pasternak, Zoschenko and others, on the grounds that Russia did not need good writers. "Of course, these are our best writers," he said, "but we cannot afford to have good writers. Our best poets write poems which depress the people by expressing a suicidal sense of the purposelessness of life. But we want people to work as they have never done before, so we cannot permit writers to say that they are unhappy."

But in the midst of this folly, let me not lose sight of the main issue. Perhaps violence, concentration camps, the perversion of the sciences and the arts are justified if these methods result eventually in making the classless society. This is the argument which I have always had in mind, an argument of such weight that if it were true it would make objections to a Communism which could really create a just international society, trivial.

My conclusion is, though, that the Communist Parties of the world, as they are organized today, could not make a better world. They might even make a far worse one. The reason why I think this is that too much power is concentrated in the hands of too few people. These few people are so protected from criticism of their conduct on any except Party lines, that neither they themselves, nor anyone else is protected from their worst human qualities: savagery, vindictiveness, envy, greed and lust for power.

Because I do not believe that the central organizations of the Communists are capable of making a classless society, or indeed of doing anything except establish the rule of a peculiarly vindictive and jealous bureaucracy, I do not feel that I should surrender my own judgment to theirs, however powerful and effective theirs may be, however ineffective my own.

The Communists represent a degree of centralization on a scale never known until now. The political Party—which is the only political party—is itself centralized, and dependent on the directives of a few men. All other functions of the State are centralized also on to the political direction.

The effect of centering art on to politics would, in the long run, mean the complete destruction of art, and it would eventually mean great misfortune for many people, even if it were impossible to endanger the police-protected, central authority. In Russia, the arts are in fact already effectively destroyed, as the Communists themselves sometimes rather surprisingly admit. (Ilya Ehrenburg explained to me in Paris in 1945 that the Russians would not take part in an exhibition of international painting because they had no good painters. He went on to say that the novel of today was American and that Russia excelled only in music. But a Hungarian Communist said to me in 1946 that the Russians had destroyed literature and painting in Russia, and were now proceeding to destroy music.)

Now the artist is simply the most highly developed individual consciousness in a society. He does not have an official generalized view of human needs and activities, but he does have a profound insight into the feelings and experiences, the state of happiness and unhappiness of individuals. To say that the artist is an individualist is not to say that he creates only out of himself only for himself. It is to say that he creates out of a level of his own experiences, which has profound connections with the experiences of many people on a level where they are not just expressions of social needs.

Literature and art are therefore a *témoignage*, a witnessing of the human condition within the particular circumstances of time and place. To make individual experience submit to the generalization of official information and observation, is to cut humanity off from a main means of becoming

conscious of itself as a community of individuals existing together within many separate personal lives. It is difficult
to believe that a central authority of the State which denies
writers and artists the freedom to express their intuitions if
these are contrary to the politics of the State has the vitality
and moral force to give people happy lives. All it has is a
machinery and an organization to take the place of living. To
destroy the freedom of art is really a kind of madness, like
destroying the freedom of the individual to have ears to hear
sounds to which his mind is sensitive, and to replace them
with microphones which are only tuned in to hear what the
State directives wish him to hear, which are the sounds relayed
by the State amplifiers. Yet the destruction of this freedom is
justified by a slogan: that freedom is the recognition of necessity. The political freedom of necessity is the necessity of the
State version of the needs of generalized, collectivized man.
The freedom of art speaks for the individuality of each human
being. Although art is not the same as politics, art is political
in that it is forever widening our conception of human freedom, and this widening process alters our conception of life
from generation to generation, and ultimately has an effect on
the political aims of society.

An unfriendly critic might well say that this essay is more
effective as a criticism of myself than of Communism. I hope
he would say this, because I have intended to criticize myself
in relation to Communism, rather than to embark on the hopeless task of criticizing Communism. Communism is the belief
that society can be altered by turning men into machines for
altering society. If one is dissatisfied with society in its present
form—as I am—one cannot criticize this view, one can only
relate oneself to it, using it as a means of criticizing and testing oneself and one's beliefs. That is what I have tried to do
here.

Looking back, I can see that my self-criticism begins with
my first interview with Pollitt, when he spoke of the necessity

of hating capitalism. In fact, I felt no such hatred in my heart.

I was driven on by a sense of social and personal guilt which made me feel firstly that I must take sides, secondly that I could purge myself of an abnormal individuality by cooperating with the Workers' Movement.

It is clear to me now that I did not need to join the Communists, because I had already taken sides. My side was whoever believed in social justice, freedom, and telling the truth about the methods which it was necessary to use in order to attain these ends. If politicians cannot make an honest and open side, then the intellectuals must choose to support the least dishonest politicians, at once helping them and criticizing them and exposing their methods of violence and lies.

The conflict of the liberal conscience of men of good will in the 1930's centered on the problem of means and ends. It was argued that in order to gain power you had to use bad means, while indignantly denying that you were doing so. My duty as a writer and an intellectual was to state this dilemma.

To some extent, after my initial mistake, I did state it. Nevertheless, I reproached and criticized myself for that which was not only of value in me, but was duty: this was a sense of social anguish, together with the reality within myself of an intractable personality which would not fit into a social movement.

I allowed myself to be forced into the position of feeling guilty not only about my own indecisions, but about the very virtues of love and pity and a passion for individual freedom which had brought me close to Communism. The Communists told me that these feelings were "bourgeois." The Communist, having joined the Party, has to castrate himself of the reasons which have made him one.

It is evident to me now that my duty is to state what I support without taking sides. Neither side, in the present alignment of the world, represents what I believe to be the only solution of the world's problems. This is: for the peoples and nations who love liberty to lead a movement throughout the world to improve the conditions of the millions of people who care more for bread than for freedom; thus raising them to a level of existence where they can care for freedom. The interests of the very few people in the world who care for the values of freedom must be identified with those of the many who need bread, or freedom will be lost.